CU01510517

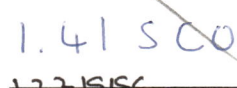

369555

CONTEMPORARY HISTORY IN CONTEXT
Published in association with the Institute of Contemporary British History

General Editor: Peter Catterall, Director, Institute of Contemporary
British History

Titles include:

Oliver Bange
THE EEC CRISIS OF 1963: Kennedy, Macmillan, de Gaulle, and
Adenauer in Conflict

Christopher Brady
UNITED STATES FOREIGN POLICY TOWARDS CAMBODIA,
1977–92

Peter Catterall and Sean McDougall (*editors*)
THE NORTHERN IRELAND QUESTION IN BRITISH POLITICS

Helen Fawcett and Rodney Lowe (*editors*)
WELFARE POLICY IN BRITAIN: The Road from 1945

Harriet Jones and Michael Kandiah (*editors*)
THE MYTH OF CONSENSUS: New Views on British History, 1945–64

Wolfram Kaiser
USING EUROPE, ABUSING THE EUROPEANS: Britain and European
Integration, 1945–63

Spencer Mawby
CONTAINING GERMANY: Britain and the Arming of the Federal
Republic

Jeffrey Pickering
BRITAIN'S WITHDRAWAL FROM EAST OF SUEZ: The Politics of
Retrenchment

L. V. Scott
MACMILLAN, KENNEDY AND THE CUBAN MISSILE CRISIS:
Political, Military and Intelligence Aspects

Paul Sharp
THATCHER'S DIPLOMACY: The Revival of British Foreign Policy

Contemporary History in Context
Series Standing Order ISBN 0–333–71470–9
(*outside North America only*)

You can receive future titles in this series as they are published by placing a standing order.
Please contact your bookseller or, in case of difficulty, write to us at the address below with
your name and address, the title of the series and the ISBN quoted above.

Customer Services Department, Macmillan Distribution Ltd
Houndmills, Basingstoke, Hampshire RG21 6XS, England

Macmillan, Kennedy and the Cuban Missile Crisis

Political, Military and Intelligence Aspects

L. V. Scott
Senior Lecturer
Department of International Politics
University of Wales, Aberystwyth

First published in Great Britain 1999 by
MACMILLAN PRESS LTD
Houndmills, Basingstoke, Hampshire RG21 6XS and London
Companies and representatives throughout the world

A catalogue record for this book is available from the British Library.

ISBN 0–333–75260–0

 First published in the United States of America 1999 by
ST. MARTIN'S PRESS, INC.,
Scholarly and Reference Division,
175 Fifth Avenue, New York, N.Y. 10010

ISBN 0–312–21915–6

Library of Congress Cataloging-in-Publication Data
Scott, L. V. (Leonard Victor), 1957–
Macmillan, Kennedy, and the Cuban Missile Crisis : political,
military, and intelligence aspects / L.V. Scott.
p.   cm. — (Contemporary history in context series)
Includes bibliographical references and index.
ISBN 0–312–21915–6 (cloth)
1. Cuban Missile Crisis, 1962.   2. Kennedy, John F. (John
Fitzgerald), 1917–1963.   3. Macmillan, Harold, 1894–   .   4. Cuban
Missile Crisis, 1962—Foreign public opinion, British.   5. United
States—Foreign relations—Great Britain.   6. Great Britain—Foreign
relations—United States.   I. Title.   II. Series.
E841.S36   1999
973.922—dc21   98–42415
                                                                    CIP

This book is printed on paper suitable for recycling and made from fully managed and sustained forest sources.

10   9   8   7   6   5   4   3   2   1
08   07   06   05   04   03   02   01   00   99

Printed and bound in Great Britain by
Antony Rowe Ltd, Chippenham, Wiltshire

With all my love to
Frances, **James** and **Lucy**

Contents

Preface   viii

General Editor's Preface   xi

List of Abbreviations   xiii

1 Improbable History   1

2 The Cuban Revolution and British–American
   Relations   13

3 Discovery and Blockade: Informing or Consulting?   37

4 Converging Perspectives and Divergent Views   58

5 Westminster and Hyde Park: British Politics and
   the Crisis   77

6 Diplomatic Initiatives and Devious Approaches   94

7 Ormsby-Gore and Penkovsky: British
   Contributions?   113

8 Thor and Vulcan: British Gods of War   131

9 'The Frightful Desire to *Do* Something'   153

Conclusion   179

Appendix: Nuclear Arsenals – The Cuban Missile Crisis   190

Notes   191

Bibliography   236

Index   242

Preface

Writing in the early nineties, a leading scholar of the Cuban missile crisis observed that the events of 1962 had made a profound impact on those alive at the time. I was five years old in October 1962 and have no recollection whatsoever of the events described in this book. In the United States schoolchildren received instruction on surviving nuclear bombs from a cartoon character named Bert the Turtle, whose strategy for dealing with thermo-nuclear attack was to 'Duck and Cover'. Together with my contemporaries at Waterloo Road School, Blackpool, I received no such advice from cartoon amphibians or indeed any of the teachers. Notwithstanding the truly excellent education I received at junior school, had nuclear war engulfed Blackpool in October 1962, I would have been wholly unprepared.

The genesis of this study lies not in memory, but in my later concern – academic and political – with nuclear weapons and British defence policy. Against a background of teaching on Cold War history, one specific moment focused my interests and energies. In 1991 Peter Hennessy delivered a lecture at Aberystwyth on the Special Relationship which *inter alia* described the role of Bomber Command's V-bomber squadrons during the Cuban missile crisis. It was this lecture that sparked the research that led both to this book, as well as to a separate study on the Command and Control of British Nuclear Weapons, 1945–64, conducted with my colleague, Stephen Twigge. *Macmillan, Kennedy and the Cuban Missile Crisis* is therefore but one ripple from Peter Hennessy's well-aimed pebble.

During the course of my ensuing research I have been helped by numerous individuals and institutions, and it is my pleasure as well as my duty to record my indebtedness to them. The Department of International Politics at Aberystwyth has provided an academic and professional environment that has sustained and motivated me in my endeavours. With the support of the Department I was able to secure financial and research support from the University of Wales, Aberystwyth, the University of Wales and the Welsh Higher Education Funding Council. The international Nuclear History Program funded the research project on the Command and Control of British Nuclear Weapons, which was also a great benefit to the study of the missile crisis. Through these various bodies I have benefited from a number of researchers: Stephen Blackwell, Huw Evans, Kerry Longhurst, Sue Marlow, and Mark Smith. To all these people and organisations I record my gratitude.

I have also received help and advice from a variety of academics and former diplomats, military officers, politicians and officials: Professor John Baylis, Professor Bart Bernstein, McGeorge Bundy, Air Vice-Marshal Ian Campbell, Chester Cooper, Maurice Frankel, Professor Raymond Garthoff, Air Vice-Marshal Arthur Griffiths, Lord Hailsham, Lord Healey, Sir Nicholas Henderson, Professor Peter Hennessy, Michael Herman, Robert McNamara, Professor Tom Paterson, Group-Captain Kenneth Pugh, Sir Frank Roberts, Professor Scott Sagan, Professor Steve Smith and George Stalker. I am in particular indebted to Group Captain Ian Madelin of the MOD's Air Historical Branch whose expertise corrected various misperceptions.

Several people have made a very significant contribution to this book both in collaborative research efforts and in reading the various manuscripts. My two friends and colleagues, Stephen Twigge and Guto Thomas, have been of enormous help in producing this book, as has my editor, Dr Peter Catterall, whose patience and insight have improved and refined my analysis. I am also grateful to Sunder Katwala of Macmillan for his help at various stages in the production of the book, and to Helen Brocklehurst for compiling the index.

The bulk of the research for this book was undertaken at the Public Record Office, Kew Gardens, and I wish to record my gratitude to the PRO and its staff. I am also grateful to the following: the staff of the Dwight D. Eisenhower Library at Abilene; Stephanie Fawcett and Paul Agnew of the John F. Kennedy Library at Boston; Nia Mai Williams of the Bodlein Library, Oxford, the archivists of the Central Intelligence Agency. I am also grateful to the trustees of the Macmillan papers for permission to quote from Harold Macmillan's diaries.

Finally, it is an academic custom to thank those who have helped, but not to berate those who have hindered. In departing from this convention, I make note of two people who have not only demonstrated not the slightest interest in the events of October 1962, but done everything possible – from depriving the author of his sleep to eating parts of the manuscript – to obstruct and delay this book. Nonetheless, it is to them – James aged four and Lucy aged one, together with their mother, Frances – that I dedicate this book.

Aberystwyth   L.V. Scott

General Editor's Preface

One of the key objects of the **Contemporary History in Context** series is to re-examine the recent past and challenge conventional interpretations. In the case of Britain's role in the Cuban missile crisis the conventional case was already being established during the crisis and was reinforced by the Opposition in the parliamentary debates which followed. Britain was portrayed as merely an onlooker, barely consulted whilst American brinkmanship took the world to the edge of nuclear war. Macmillan had painted himself as an international statesman in the 1959 election with considerable success. Cuba was used by Labour to portray this image and the idea of the 'special relationship' as threadbare. In that sense it served as a stick with which to beat a government which was already in difficulties. But it was a line which Macmillan saw as 'rather dangerous'. He therefore noted in his diary the need to let the truth be known 'through judicious leaks'.

The problem is, of course, what was the truth? Macmillan's view, in the same entry, was 'I think we played our part perfectly. We were "in on" and took full part in (and almost responsibility for) every American move. Our complete calm helped to keep the Europeans calm.' The British were certainly in on the action more than some contemporary comment made out. As Len Scott shows, British officials were informed of the missiles well in advance of the Americans going public on the affair. Indeed, the Americans could hardly have failed to consult not just the British but the other European allies given the ramifications of the crisis. Cuba was by no means the only issue. One key sensitivity was whether there was a linkage to Berlin, and how the handling of the crisis might affect the situation there, a matter in which the European allies had a direct interest.

The actual detail of how the Administration intended to handle Cuba was more of a domestic matter. These issues were nevertheless discussed at considerable length with the

British, not least in the lengthy telephone conversations between Kennedy and Macmillan. Whether British comments had more than a confirmatory effect is open to doubt. But then, once the crisis had actually started, whatever their previous differences over policy towards Cuba, there was little serious division of opinion between the British and Americans over the appropriate course of action. Macmillan could not fault Kennedy's handling of the crisis. The part Macmillan felt he himself played so well was thus a fairly circumscribed one. In a cold war crisis there was little scope for other than a supporting role, in every sense of the word. The British may have taken, and continued to take, a more sanguine view of Castro than the Americans. Such differences, however, paled into insignificance when more important matters, not least Berlin, might be at stake. Macmillan's role was therefore largely, as he himself recognised, to do nothing but act as the President's sounding board and support the calling of the Russian bluff.

It was an unheroic role at which Macmillan chaffed, not least for obvious political reasons. But it was not the role contemporary wisdom portrayed. Len Scott's account, the first full study of British policymaking during the Cuban crisis using recently released documents, illustrates a far more involved, if not necessarily more influential role was being played by the British than has often been thought.

PETER CATTERALL

List of Abbreviations

BMEWS	Ballistic Missile Early Warning System
CIA	Central Intelligence Agency
CINCLANT	Commander in Chief, Atlantic Command
CND	Campaign for Nuclear Disarmament
COCOM	Co-ordinating Committee on Export Controls
DEFCON	Defence Condition
ExComm	Executive Committee of the National Security Council
GRU	Chief Intelligence Directorate of the Soviet General Staff
HMG	Her Majesty's Government
ICBM	InterContinental Ballistic Missile
IRBM	Intermediate Range Ballistic Missile
JIB	Joint Intelligence Bureau
JIC	Joint Intelligence Committee
KGB	Soviet Committee of State Security
MCC	Marylebone Cricket Club
MI5	British Security Service
MOD	Ministry of Defence
MRBM	Medium Range Ballistic Missile
NAC	North Atlantic Council
NATO	North Atlantic Treaty Organisation
NEC	National Executive Committee
NIE	National Intelligence Estimate
NSC	National Security Council
OAS	Organisation of American States
PAL	Permissive Action Links
POL	Petroleum, Oil, Lubricants
QRA	Quick Reaction Alert
RAF	Royal Air Force
SIS	Secret Intelligence Service
SAC	Strategic Air Command
SLBM	Submarine Launched Ballistic Missile
SSBN	Nuclear-powered Ballistic Missile Submarine
TUC	Trade Union Congress
USAF	United States Air Force

1 Improbable History

On Sunday 28 October 1962 the British Defence Secretary, Peter Thorneycroft, arrived in Whitehall. 'It was very quiet, rather a lovely morning', he recalled, and as he walked into the Ministry of Defence, he thought: 'My God I wonder whether this really is it.'[1] The previous evening, his American counterpart, Robert McNamara, recounts that, 'as I left the White House and walked through the garden to my car to return to the Pentagon on that beautiful fall evening, I feared I might never live to see another Saturday night.'[2] Other British Cabinet ministers worried that war was imminent. Lord Hailsham, whose wife had just given birth, considered whether to baptise the child himself.[3] In Washington, on the morning of Sunday 28 October, the KGB reported to Moscow that the President of the United States had gone to church.[4] With the world on the brink of nuclear war, Khrushchev and his Presidium colleagues debated whether Kennedy was making peace with his creator before making war with the Soviet Union.

Bertrand Russell, the Cambridge philosopher, and doyen of radical anti-nuclear protesters, later wrote:

> It seemed probable that, at any minute, war between America and Russia would break out and would involve, in all likelihood, the extinction of the human race. If you had private affections, if you had children or grandchildren for whom you had hoped a happy future, if you had friends whom you loved, you could expect their death in the coming week. Within this brief period of time, there would cease to be any to enjoy the poetry of Shakespeare, the music of Bach or Mozart, the genius of Plato or Newton. All the slow building up of civilisation in art and science would be at an end.[5]

In October 1962 the world went to the brink of Armageddon. The United States' Strategic Air Command (SAC) moved to the alert state of DEFCON-2, an unprecedented and unrepeated state of readiness, corresponding to preparedness

1

for nuclear war. One in eight of SAC's B-52 strategic bombers remained in the air, circling to their 'fail safe' positions, waiting for the 'go-codes', while US InterContinental Ballistic Missiles (ICBMs) and Submarine Launched Ballistic Missiles (SLBMs) on Polaris submarines were made combat ready, capable of attacking targets in the Soviet Union within twenty to forty minutes. There is now also reason to believe, contrary to the received wisdom, that Soviet bombers and missiles were at a heightened state of readiness and that at one point Soviet ICBMs were made combat ready, with warheads mated to missiles. In Britain, the Royal Air Force's (RAF) and Thor Intermediate Range Ballistic Missiles (IRBMs) assumed a heightened state of readiness. American nuclear forces in Britain, and elsewhere, also prepared for war.

In the Caribbean, by the weekend of 27–8 October, American preparations for an invasion of Cuba were well advanced, ready for an attack the following week. Had President Kennedy decided to invade Cuba, most American and British decision-makers feared a Soviet response in Europe. War in Europe, or the use of nuclear weapons in the Caribbean, risked escalation to global nuclear war. Precise estimates of the devastation or casualties in such a war are impossible. Yet, had the Cuban missile crisis led to full-scale nuclear conflict, hundreds of millions of people would have perished. On 23 October, when the American evangelist, Billy Graham, preached in Buenos Aires about 'The End of the World', the prospect seemed very real.[6]

Yet, as the crisis reached its climax, ordinary life in Britain continued much the same. As SAC bomber and missile crews were preparing for nuclear war, Spurs beat Orient to go top of the First Division, while in Perth, MCC were losing to Western Australia (with Fred Titmus becoming the first English batsman to score a century under the threat of nuclear war). Although there were public demonstrations against President Kennedy's (and Premier Khrushchev's) actions, the week of Britain's greatest peril passed with little disruption to everyday life. In contrast to the United States, there were no reports of panic buying of food or the building of nuclear fall-out shelters. Nor was there any large-scale population movement out of towns and cities. Possibly the most notable 'evacuation' was when two prominent anti-nuclear campaigners, Pat Arrowsmith and Wendy Butlin, fled to the west coast of Ireland, only to return on Saturday 27 October to join the political protest against American action.[7] As a barometer of normality, the Royal Family went about their everyday duties, with the Queen taking an active interest in the crisis.[8]

On Wall Street shares fell. Macmillan was concerned about the financial consequences for Britain and met with the Chancellor of the Exchequer, Reginald Maudling, on 22 October: 'His advice was sensible. He would see the Governor of Bank of England. There would be heavy buying of gold and a general fall of all stocks and shares – but no panic.'[9] In fact, the following day the pound remained stable,[10] and by the end of the week, *The Times* reported that city markets were 'shaken, nervous and tender but with actual net price changes far less than might at first have been expected'.[11]

Not surprisingly, there was widespread concern at events in the Caribbean. A study of British popular attitudes toward the prospect of world war, notes 'a stronger sense of repressed tension', and quotes the recollections of an insurance salesman:

> I have over 700 families on my books, and the thing that struck me most about the Cuban affair was the fact that when the crisis was at its height, nobody dared mention it. My policy-holders, normally talkative, looked worried out of their lives, but paid their premiums like automatons, and studiously avoided any mention of the thing that was obviously uppermost in their minds.[12]

This 'repressed tension' clearly took different forms. The editor of the *New Statesman*, Kingsley Martin, wrote:

> At best we have to expect one of the prolonged crises to which the British public has become almost indifferent. Characteristically the caretaker remarked to me this morning that two wars in a lifetime was enough and if there was a third he'd be pleased if it was nuclear and he knew nothing about it.[13]

In similar vein Basil Boothroyd wrote in the humorous magazine, *Punch*:

I don't like the way strangers were exchanging bright
good mornings last week, and jollying the ticket collectors,
and standing back to let each other get on the buses. At
Victoria I saw no fewer than three old ladies having their
bags forcibly taken from them and carried to the barrier . . .
I found the air of camaraderie infectious, I frankly admit,
so who am I to object that my cab-driver, a folded photo-
graph of Mr Kennedy tucked under his window handle,
actually got out and opened the door for me . . . a thing
I don't remember happening for seventeen or eighteen
years.[14]

Others were less phlegmatic than Mr Boothroyd and the
caretaker at the *New Statesman*. For many, the Cuban crisis
was the latest phase of Cold War confrontation, which only
a year earlier had nearly led to fighting between Soviet
and American troops in Berlin. Around the country, anti-
nuclear protesters, church groups and students demonstrated
in support of peace. Forty sixth formers at Midhurst Grammar School went on strike in protest at the degenerating
world situation, marching through the town, and calling
upon other pupils to follow suit.[15] The government received
letters and petitions protesting against western reactions
to the missiles in Cuba from groups as diverse as the Bristol
and Clifton Protestant League, the Scottish Co-operative
Women's Guild and 240 miners from Douglas colliery.[16]

Both the Campaign for Nuclear Disarmament (CND) and
the more radical Committee of 100 attempted to organise
large scale rallies. In the House of Commons, Macmillan
made a short statement on 25 October when Parliament
met to prorogue. Notwithstanding Gaitskell's criticisms of
Kennedy's failure to consult about the blockade, the occasion was marked by a notable degree of bipartisanship.
On the left of the Labour Party, however, 37 MPs quickly
condemned American action, and indeed demanded that
the West should increase its trade with Cuba, while both
the Oxford and Cambridge Unions passed motions protesting against Kennedy's actions.[17]

For ministers, diplomats and other British officials, the
Cuban missile crisis was the latest in a series of confrontations with the Soviets. Ever since Khrushchev's threat in

1958 to sign a separate peace treaty with the German Democratic Republic there remained the prospect of confrontation. While Khrushchev's foreign policy sought accommodation with the West, he also pursued other, less compatible, goals. Khrushchev himself exhibited what one Foreign Office official described as qualities which 'we have always most feared . . . audacity and adventurism'.[18] The same official lamented during the missile crisis: 'We knew where we stood much better with Stalin.'[19] For Harold Macmillan, the week of the crisis was 'the week of most strain I can ever remember in my life'.[20] More disconcertingly (for a man having ultimate responsibility for British nuclear weapons), he claimed that, 'neither Sir Alec Home nor I ever slept at all during the whole seven days'.[21] The five hour time difference meant that Kennedy's evening calls came late at night in London. More reassuringly, the Defence Secretary was not exhausted: 'What is the point of being exhausted about things which you can really do nothing about'[22] – an indication that within the Cabinet the brunt of activity was borne initially by Macmillan and his Foreign Secretary, Lord Home, and then later by a small group of senior Cabinet members comprising Macmillan, his deputy, Rab Butler, Home, and Edward Heath, the Lord Privy Seal.

How close Britain came to destruction, and how near the world was to nuclear oblivion, are matters for speculation and debate. Less than twenty years earlier British cities had been attacked by the German Air Force. Yet the advent of nuclear weapons had wrought fundamental changes in the nature of warfare. Whereas the *Luftwaffe* killed some 60 000 British civilians, a fraction of the nuclear weapons targeted on the United Kingdom in 1962 would have annihilated millions. In 1955, the government was told that ten H-bombs over London and other industrial centres could leave 12 million people dead, four million casualties and 13 million trapped in their homes by fall-out.[23] By 1962 the Soviets had hundreds of nuclear missiles targeted on western Europe, and bombers and submarines capable of attacking military and urban/industrial targets in the United Kingdom. One further change in warfare wrought by nuclear weapons was that the decision-makers, such as Peter Thorneycroft and Robert McNamara, were themselves likely to perish in any major conflict. This was well illustrated in Secretary of State Dean Rusk's quip to his deputy, George Ball, on 23 October: 'We have won a considerable victory. You and I are still alive'.[24]

By 1957, the British government had embraced the idea that defence against nuclear weapons was impossible and that only nuclear deterrence could provide national security. By 1962 the UK was not only the world's third nuclear power, but host to an arsenal of American nuclear weapons and sixty Thor IRBMs operated under dual-key arrangements between the RAF and the United States Air Force (USAF). Had nuclear war occurred in 1962, the United Kingdom would have been both an indispensable front line for the West's nuclear offensive and a priority target for the Soviets. As a nuclear weapons state herself, Britain could have delivered devastating attacks on Soviet and Eastern European territory far surpassing the level of damage inflicted on Nazi Germany by the allied air offensive. From 1939 to 1945, Bomber Command dropped 1 996 036 tons of bombs on Germany;[25] according to one account, Bomber Command could target the equivalent of 230 000 000 tons of high explosive on the USSR in October 1962.[26]

The Cuban missile crisis is the most intensely studied crisis of the Cold War. It remains of great interest to historians, political scientists and students of crisis management. Fascinating and often fierce debate has been generated among academics, and indeed former officials, about a range of issues. The 'lessons of the crisis' have been a matter of contention, as well as a legacy for policy-makers in the nuclear age. Recent American historiography has produced a wealth of new material that has reinvigorated old debates and stimulated new ones.[27] This recent historiography has had very significant implications for those studying the crisis in search of broader lessons.[28] Most intriguingly, important studies have now begun to emerge based on access to Soviet archives.[29] Until recently, however, little work was done on British and other European aspects.[30]

AIM OF STUDY

The aim of this book is threefold. First, to provide a detailed archival-based account of the crisis, from the British (mainly British government) perspective. While there is a voluminous, largely American, literature on the missile crisis, the British side of the story has received little attention. This is a curious omission, for several reasons. In 1962 Britain was the third nuclear weapons state and it is known that the alert condition of British nuclear forces was raised during the crisis. Yet American studies of the role of nuclear weapons in the crisis have paid little or no attention to Bomber Command.[31] Second, there is *prima facie* evidence that British officials played significant roles. Most notably, the British Ambassador to Washington, Sir David Ormsby-Gore, is credited with several interventions in American decision-making. Third, Kennedy administration contacts with the British government provide sources of information about American attitudes, in particular concerning President Kennedy's thinking. What Kennedy said to Macmillan over the telephone, and to Ormsby-Gore in Washington, are of interest in gauging the President's attitude as the crisis unfolded.[32] British documents have also cast light on other issues and controversies generated in the American literature.

Underpinning this aim is the belief that the events of 1962 should be set in a broader political context than Soviet–American crisis management. When the world learned of the missiles on 22 October 1962, Harold Macmillan noted in his diary that it was the 'first day of the World Crisis'.[33] American analyses of the crisis, have often taken the discovery of the missiles in Cuba as their starting point, suggesting that the Soviets caused the crisis by destabilising the *status quo*. Recent scholarship has re-focused attention on why Khrushchev deployed the missiles. This has placed greater emphasis on Soviet concern with defending the Cuban revolution, and Khrushchev's irritation at the deployment of Jupiter IRBMs in Turkey. Moreover, recent revelations make clear the importance of NATO nuclear forces in Kennedy's efforts to resolve the crisis.[34]

The Soviet deployment of nuclear missiles in Cuba occurred during a turbulent and dangerous phase of world politics. Events in the Caribbean and the situation in Europe, most importantly Berlin, are an integral part of the story. While it may be questioned how far Khrushchev's action in the Caribbean was driven by his goals in Berlin, it is clear that, from the outset of the crisis, leaders and officials in Washington and London feared that American action in the Caribbean would provoke Soviet action against West Berlin. The European dimension also provides a rather different perspective on the nature of the crisis. Many Americans were frightened, not just because Kennedy and Khrushchev were 'eyeball to eyeball', but because they felt threatened in a way they had not been before. Europeans had learned to live with Soviet nuclear weapons and the historically unprecedented conglomerations of military power deployed upon, and adjacent to, their territories. The European experience of Soviet theatre nuclear forces, in itself, puts into perspective the reaction of American political and military leaders who took the world to the brink of extinction because they were unable to live with the kind of threat to which Europeans had become accustomed.

Second, the book reassesses the significance of the missile crisis for understanding the 'special relationship' between Britain and the United States. Shortly after the missile crisis, in December 1962, Dean Acheson famously declared that 'Great Britain has lost an empire and not yet found a role'.[35] David Nunnerley has argued that the crisis 'told much of the relationship between allies in the nuclear age, and in particular the limitations on the ability of lesser powers to influence the course of events in a super-power confrontation'.[36] In his view, 'Britain seemed a small and rather insignificant island during the Cuban confrontation',[37] echoing Peter Thorneycroft's comment that, 'in common with the rest of the world, we were all bystanders.'[38] The Defence Secretary believed that the only person who had a role was Macmillan.[39] In contrast, McGeorge Bundy, who was intimately involved in liaison between the two governments, did not think that Macmillan's 'advice on the Cuban missile crisis was very important'.[40] David Ormsby-Gore later reflected that, 'I can't honestly think of anything said from London that changed US action – it was chiefly reassurance to JFK.'[41] While noting the close personal relations between

Kennedy and Macmillan (and between Kennedy and Ormsby-Gore), most writers have downplayed the importance of British views, and emphasised that while the British government was informed, it was not consulted.[42]

British–American relations during the crisis are here reassessed in the light of recent evidence and scholarship. The broad conclusion is that the pattern of UK–US relations is more complex and more ambiguous than usually depicted, reflecting the fact that the 'special relationship' is best conceived as a mixture of personal and institutional relationships. The book casts light on diplomatic and military dimensions, and possibly the most intimate aspect of the 'special relationship' – that between the respective intelligence communities. At the personal level the most significant relationships are those between Kennedy and Macmillan and between Kennedy and Ormsby-Gore. The role of the British ambassador in particular raises various intriguing issues.

Such matters are of interest in assessing the political and diplomatic relations between the USA and UK. Yet, notwithstanding the importance of the missile crisis in British–American diplomacy, the Cuban missile crisis was a crisis about nuclear weapons. Britain was a nuclear weapons state inextricably involved in American nuclear operations and preparations. The idea that Britain might exercise influence in American counsels of war had been both an article of faith for proponents of an independent British deterrent and (one) justification for British nuclear policy. How far the events of October 1962 could be construed as an acid test of this most specific and crucial aspect of the 'special relationship' is examined. The story of the missile crisis is, in itself, an important episode in British nuclear history, and one further aim is to contribute to the growing literature in this field.[43]

The idea that Britain was not consulted is assessed. On the crucial question of whether Kennedy should use force against Cuba, the British Prime Minister was clearly asked for his views by the President. This leads to the third aim: to examine and appraise Macmillan's handling of the crisis and his balancing of calculations about the 'special relationship' against his fears of escalation to war in Europe. The development of Macmillan's views during the crisis, his advice to Kennedy and his attitude to British and NATO military preparations inform an assessment of Macmillan's actions (and inaction).

A secondary aim of the study is to examine British domestic aspects of the Cuban missile crisis. Potentially, a crisis of this nature had important consequences for debates about nuclear weapons and Britain's relationship with the US. In the late 1950s, British society had witnessed growing opposition to nuclear weapons, including American nuclear bases on UK territory. The growth of CND after 1958 and its development as a mass protest movement prompted fierce conflict within the Labour Party. Within Britain, there was increasingly polarised debate over national security policy of a kind never before witnessed in a nuclear weapons state. The Cuban missile crisis has been regarded as a watershed in the fortunes of the anti-nuclear cause in Britain, and the re-emergence of a national consensus on national security. As Richard Taylor argues:

> Despite the protestations of CND's leaders to the effect that the Cuban crisis had exacerbated the cold war, brought nuclear war nearer, and thus made the unilateralist case even more persuasive and urgent, there was no doubt that the prevailing mood, of both the country *and the Movement* was one of relief that nuclear war had been avoided, and a lessening of tension and urgency on the nuclear issue. As far as the Movement was concerned the Cuban missile crisis thus marked a crucial downturn in activism. The spark had gone: activists breathed a sigh of relief, and devoted rather more time to ordinary life and rather less to campaign activities.[44]

The decline of CND had important implications for the Labour Party and therefore for British politics as a whole. While it can be argued that Hugh Gaitskell and his supporters had already turned the tide against the unilateralists, and while centrifugal forces within the anti-nuclear movement were apparent by 1962, there are, nevertheless, grounds for seeing the Cuban crisis as decisive. Whether diminishing concern with nuclear weapons was the correct lesson to draw from the crisis is another matter.

For Britain, and for the Macmillan government, the Cuban missile crisis came during a period of change and choice for British foreign policy. The latter part of 1962 marked an important point of departure in Britain's foreign policy. After the debacle of Suez, Macmillan strove to re-establish the 'special relationship' with Washington, while pursuing entry into the European Economic Community (EEC), together with a reappraisal of Britain's colonial role, particularly in Africa. Domestically, Macmillan was under growing pressure to revitalise what was seen as an increasingly moribund party. As Gaitskell moved Labour away from the electorally damaging posture of unilateralism and united it around opposition to membership of the EEC the Conservatives were in trouble. In July 1962 Macmillan had purged his government by sacking a third of the Cabinet. Increasingly his foreign policy, and in particular the relationship with Kennedy, assumed a greater significance in the political fortunes of the government. When Skybolt was cancelled in December the ensuing crisis threatened the survival of the government. How far Kennedy's offer of Polaris at Nassau reflected his personal and political relations with Macmillan and how far these were affected by what happened in October 1962 are of great interest to students of the 'special relationship' and British nuclear weapons policy.

ORGANISATION

The structure of the book is designed to co-ordinate the chronological with the thematic. Chapter Two examines the Cuban–American confrontation and the problems this created for the Macmillan government. Chapter Three studies how the discovery of the missiles, and the Kennedy administration's decision to impose a 'quarantine' around Cuba, were communicated to the British government and examines the implications of this for the 'special relationship'. The terms blockade and quarantine are used interchangeably in the study, depending on context – this is discussed further in Chapter Four, where British doubts about the blockade are examined. Chapter Five analyses the domestic political context and in particular the reactions of the Labour and anti-nuclear movements. Chapter Six looks at the diplomatic context of any prospective British initiative, and how the government responded to approaches from Soviet officials. The contribution made by two individuals is examined in Chapter Seven: Sir David Ormsby-Gore, HM Ambassador to Washington, and Oleg Penkovsky, a western spy in the Soviet defence establishment run in a joint operation by the British Secret Intelligence Service (SIS) and the US Central Intelligence Agency (CIA). Military co-operation, and the activities of RAF Bomber Command during the crisis, are examined in Chapter Eight. Chapter Nine examines the climax of the crisis, including the initiative devised (though not pursued) by the British government to assist a settlement. The final chapter provides a conclusion and overview.

It is generally (though not universally) accepted that October 1962 was the closest the world has been to nuclear war. Diplomatically, it was both the climax of Khrushchev's adventurist foreign policy, and an important turning point in East–West affairs. Macmillan indeed described it as 'one of the great turning points in history'.[45] What lessons can be learned for western and British defence and foreign policy, particularly with regard to nuclear weapons, are questions that retain an interest and significance long after the events and indeed after the Cold War itself. Understanding what happened presents challenges and opportunities for historians and other scholars. Writing in 1963 the British Ambassador to Havana, Bill Marchant, confessed that 'even with the full benefit of hind-sight I find it difficult in reviewing the local scene over these last twelve months, to piece together a probable and coherent sequence of events which can be seen to have led up to that most improbable piece of history, the story of the Cuban missile crisis'.[46] Over thirty years later, with the benefit of much hindsight and decades of scholarship, the task of the historian may be easier in some respects, more difficult in others, but the improbability of the events is no less diminished.

2 The Cuban Revolution and British–American Relations

> I sympathise with the rebellion – not with the rebels . . .
> It may be that as the pages of history are turned brighter
> futures and better times will come to Cuba. It may be
> that future years will see the island as it would be now,
> had England never lost it – a Cuba free and prosperous
> under just laws and a patriotic administration, throwing
> open her ports to the commerce of the world, sending
> her ponies to Hurlingham and her cricketers to Lord's,
> exchanging the cigars of Havana for the cottons of
> Lancashire, and the sugars of Matanzas for the cutlery
> of Sheffield. At least let us hope so.[1]

Cuba's cricketers never made it to Lord's. The hopes of
the young Winston Churchill in 1898 reflected a previous
British involvement in Cuba's history, and an acceptance
of the pre-eminent American role in Cuban affairs that
characterised British policy in the nineteenth century and
thereafter. This chapter briefly traces the history of Cuban–
American affairs, and examines the impact of Castro's revolution on British–American relations.

American involvement in Cuba dated back to the nineteenth century. In 1823, President Monroe famously declared
that any attempt by European powers to 'extend their system to any portion of this hemisphere' would be considered
'dangerous to our peace and safety'.[2] By the turn of the
century, what many Americans saw as anti-imperialist, and
indeed humanitarian, impulses underpinned American intervention in Cuba. The Spanish had responded to Cuban
insurgency in 1895 with brutal oppression. The United States
intervened in 1898 after the cruiser *Maine* was sunk with
heavy loss of life. The war of 1898 brought to an end 400
years of Spanish colonial rule in Cuba. It did not lead to

13

Cuban self-determination. Instead, under Theodore Roosevelt, US policy in Latin America transformed the Monroe doctrine from a deterrent to European imperialism into a policy of American intervention and the promotion of American interests. The Platt Amendment of 1901 made clear that Cuban sovereignty was limited and subordinate to American interests. In 1903 a treaty ceded the naval base at Guantanamo Bay to the United States. American troops intervened directly in Cuba on three occasions in the following years.

In 1934, Theodore Roosevelt's approach gave way to Franklin Roosevelt's 'Good Neighbor Policy' and an explicit renunciation of the Platt Amendment. Notwithstanding changes in American political attitudes, however, American economic control (and exploitation) of the Cuban economy grew. By the 1950s, Americans owned 40 per cent of the Cuban sugar industry, 80 per cent of utilities and 90 per cent of the mining industry.[3] The United States received some two-thirds of Cuban exports and supplied about three-quarters of its imports. Havana became a haven for gambling and prostitution, much of it organised by the American Mafia.

The 1959 Cuban revolution challenged American hegemony in 'its own backyard'. The charismatic Fidel Castro emerged as a revolutionary icon of global significance. The character and ideology of Fidel Castro swiftly assumed a central importance to the future direction of the Cuban revolution. The issues of when, why, and in what ways Castro became a communist or Marxist remains a matter of great significance in understanding the Cuban revolution and its international consequences. In 1963 (by when he had openly declared himself a Marxist–Leninist), the erstwhile British ambassador to Havana, Bill Marchant, described him as:

> a natural 'do-gooder' and he fancies himself as such. I feel sure he has Walter Mitty-like dreams of himself in shining armour, mounted on a white horse leading the poor and oppressed of Latin America to freedom and prosperity . . . a genuine passion for the poor and under-privileged is definitely built into his make up and the warmth of affection he professes for the Cuban peasant is almost certainly genuine . . . It may well have been his

romantic student woolly 'do-goodism' that first involved Castro in his early relations with communists. I am sure the appeal was not an intellectual one . . . I cannot ever see him as a good routine, line-toeing communist. His strength lies in his individuality. Shave off his beard, put him into a collar and tie and business suit and I am not sure at all that he could hold his job down at all.[4]

Marchant felt that it was 'impossible to say exactly how much he really believes in what he is saying . . . but like every good emotional actor he gives the impression of passionate conviction'.[5] Castro displayed a lawyer's capacity to mislead and distort, though Marchant doubted whether he was 'any more dishonest than most politicians, probably less so than the run of Latin America'; notwithstanding his ability to 'think clearly and quickly', Marchant opined, he 'would I think have got a good Second rather than a First Class at Oxbridge'.[6]

What class of degree General Batista, the corrupt Cuban despot, might have obtained, is not recorded. The collapse of his regime, and Castro's seizure of power in January 1959, however, had enormous implications for Cuban–American relations and indeed world affairs. Whether the deterioration in Cuban–American relations after the revolution was inevitable, and how far it reflected errors of judgement by the American and Cuban governments, remains a matter of debate. Certainly the Eisenhower and Kennedy administrations believed, as did the US Congress, that the United States was entitled to intervene in the affairs of its Caribbean neighbour. In part, this reflected American geo-strategic assumptions about Latin America dating back to the Monroe doctrine. The principal American motivation in the 1950s, however, was hostility to communism, and the United States acted overtly and covertly to prevent revolutionary contagion in Latin America and preserve American political and economic interests.

The Cuban revolution presented a fundamental challenge to American hegemony and the assertion of the Monroe doctrine. This challenge was political, economic and strategic in nature. American economic interests influenced congressional and administration reaction. Yet more important was hostility to communism in the United States, which American political leaders articulated and aggravated. The Cuban communists, the Popular Socialist Party (PSP), however, had played no direct role in the Cuban revolution and indeed previously had actively collaborated with Batista. Two of Castro's closest lieutenants, Raul Castro and Che Guevara, it has recently been revealed, were secret members of the PSP.[7] Yet, most significantly, the Soviet government had no contact with, or indeed little knowledge of, Fidel Castro. Initially, many Soviet experts described the Cuban revolution as petit bourgeois in nature, and the prevailing opinion in Moscow was that Castro would not move beyond 'bourgeois–democratic' reforms.[8] Castro made clear on his visit to the United States, in April 1959, that he was not a communist and he was opposed to communism. Whatever the complexities of Castro's relationship with socialism and with the Soviets, fear of communism in America's 'backyard', nevertheless, magnified and distorted the Cuban revolution in American eyes. Growing numbers of Cuban émigrés fleeing Castro's Cuba acquired a growing symbolic and political significance in the US, and assisted the view that communism had taken hold in Latin America.

Critics of American antagonism toward Castro argued that this fear became a self-fulfilling prophecy: economic, political and military pressure drove Castro into the hands of Moscow. This view was widely shared in Britain. If Americans were afraid that Soviets would build missiles bases in Cuba, *The Guardian* argued in April 1961, 'surely it would be wiser' to do everything possible 'to wean Cuba away from the Russians.'[9] Whether the United States could have co-existed with the Cuban revolution, and who was responsible for the collapse of relations between Washington and Havana after 1959, remain contentious issues. This deterioration became increasingly apparent as 1959 progressed. When Castro met Nixon on his visit to the US, the Vice President found him an impressive figure in key respects, though naive and ill-informed about communism.[10] The manner in which former officers of the Batista regime were dealt with, however, aroused considerable criticism in the United States, and in turn provoked Cuban denunciations of their critics. In Britain there was greater understanding for the new regime. The Labour leader Hugh Gaitskell, for example, was 'decidedly sympathetic' toward Castro, 'excusing the early executions which his Washington enemies were using to discredit him'.[11] Others on the left were increasingly supportive of Castro's revolution and hostile to American attempts to subvert it.

As Winston Churchill had noted in 1898, Britain had once played an important role in Cuban affairs. British investments in the railways and the tobacco industry had been extensive, and in the 1920s and 1930s Britain was Cuba's second best customer. By the 1959 revolution Britain's economic interests in Cuba were limited, though by no means insignificant in the eyes of either Havana or London.[12] Before the revolution supplies of military equipment to the regime were an issue of political controversy in Westminster. In October 1958 the Macmillan government, in the face of Labour opposition, agreed to sell 17 *Sea Fury* fighter aircraft, with supplies of air to ground missiles, to the Batista regime. Castro announced a boycott of British goods and drafted 'Law No. 4 of the Sierra Maestra, on the English aggression against the people of Cuba', intended to confiscate the property of British companies in retaliation.[13] Ironically, the Macmillan government was prepared to supply arms to the Batista regime at a time when the Eisenhower administration had imposed an arms embargo on the dictatorship.[14] Potentially most significant, British shipping was important in Cuba's trade, and in particular British tankers transported oil to Cuba.

In power, Castro exhibited little animosity toward the British, at one point telling the British Ambassador, Alfred Fordham, that 'your Conservatives are more revolutionary than we; they call themselves Conservatives in order to avoid being mistaken for Communists'.[15] Castro delayed imposition of Law Number 4 as he hoped to normalise British–Cuban relations.[16] His motives were economic and military – later in the year he attempted to procure British Hawker jets to replace the more obsolete *Sea Furies*. The Macmillan government was sympathetic. 'It would seem unfortunate', the Foreign Secretary, Selwyn Lloyd, told US Secretary of State Herter, 'to treat more harshly a left wing government struggling, however misguidedly, to carry through an idealistic programme after we have been willing to do business with Batista'.[17] The dispute over the sale of the *Hunters* highlighted British–American differences over the situation in Cuba. The British doubted American claims that Castro's downfall was only a matter of time.[18] There was also disagreement over the risk that Castro would turn to the Soviets if denied help elsewhere. Lloyd informed Herter that: 'if we in the Western world continue to give the impression that we are implacably imposed to the present regime in Cuba and that we will do nothing to help the Cubans so long as Castro is there, we may drive them more and more into the arms of the Communists politically and economically'.[19] Not everyone in the Eisenhower administration saw this as a problem. The Director of the CIA, Allen Dulles, confided to the British Ambassador, Sir Harold Caccia, his personal belief that the sale of the *Hunters* would encourage Castro to seek help from the Soviets.[20] Such Soviet arms shipments would then help unify the opposition, much as it had done in Guatemala in 1954 (when the CIA intervened to help overthrow the leftist government).

In the face of American pressure the government decided against the *Hunter* deal, and indeed from August 1960 no British arms were licensed for export to Cuba.[21] Although the Cuban government gave the impression that the sale of the *Hunters* was 'the touchstone of the British attitude towards Cuba',[22] when London refused to sell the aircraft Cuban leaders 'seemed at some pains to put most of the blame on to the United States'.[23] Earlier in the year, a strike at the Shell oil refinery might have provoked the expropriation of British property. Instead, in February 1959 Castro lifted the boycott on British goods, while obtaining generous concessions from Shell, partly British-owned, in forgoing expropriation at that time. In January 1960 the British Ambassador reported that during the first year 'our relations with the Revolutionary Government were on the whole surprisingly tranquil', with British exports to Cuba growing to a record £15 million, the first British trade surplus with Cuba.[24] Notwithstanding these quite cordial relations, Castro chose to nationalise Shell in the summer of 1960 when it, and the two American oil companies (Esso and Texaco), refused to process Soviet crude oil.

Whatever Castro's early tactical concessions to the British, the strategic objectives of the Cuban revolution soon brought problems with the Americans. Economic ownership was vital to agrarian reform, which was pivotal to the revolution. The extent of American domination of Cuban agriculture, however, meant that any public ownership of the means of production inevitably invited conflict with the United States. The involvement of communists in government, and resignations of non-Communists, exacerbated Washington's fears. From October 1959 relations between Havana and Moscow were seen to gain momentum. Establishing cause and effect in the deterioration of relations between Havana and Washington is a matter for debate. The subsequent pattern of events, including clandestine relations between Moscow and Havana, is now more clearly established.[25]

When Castro first came to power, many informed Americans, including the likes of Dean Acheson, believed that he would not turn to communism.[26] Although some State Department officials continued to hope a *modus vivendi* with Castro was possible, a clear consensus emerged in Washington during 1959 that the Cuban revolution was a growing threat to American interests and security. British views of Castro were more sanguine. There was concern at the spread of revolution to Commonwealth countries in the region and those where Britain still had an imperial role. Notwithstanding Cuban support for revolution abroad, Castro was a figurehead and inspiration for the poor and oppressed of Latin America. Yet British officials and ministers held a very different view of Communism in the Third World, and how it should be dealt with, than their American counterparts. They also had a different view of the effectiveness of sanctions against Cuba. From Havana the British Ambassador warned in early 1960 that 'American intervention or economic reprisal could be disastrous for Cuba, but it would also provide an invaluable weapon for the communists.'[27] On the other hand, there was recognition of the impact of communism in Cuba on American attitudes. As the Foreign Secretary, Lord Home, explained to one of his Cabinet colleagues: 'The existence of a Communist regime in the Caribbean must be a matter of deep concern to us, but to the Americans it is a calamity.'[28] The differences in British and American attitudes towards communism in Cuba were nevertheless symptomatic of broader disagreements over the challenges of communism and nationalism in the Third World.

Macmillan himself strongly doubted the effectiveness and prudence of economic sanctions. Yet he also wanted to support his ally. In his memoirs he recalled that after initial American attempts at a 'co-operative' approach to Castro were rebuffed:

> Eisenhower could now only rely on economic pressure, in which he urged us to join, to rally the Cuban people against their new oppressors. While accepting the President's analysis, I expressed doubts as to whether economic hardship would encourage opposition to Castro, especially if it could be blamed on the Americans and mitigated by Russian help. Nor could I agree to operate any blockade, whether of tankers or other ships. In peace time, we had no legal power to prevent tankers taking Russian oil to Cuba.[29]

BAY OF PIGS

The suggestion that economic pressure was the only option available to Eisenhower was disingenuous. In March 1960 Eisenhower had authorised the CIA to devise a programme of covert action against the Castro regime.[30] In July 1960 Eisenhower had written to Macmillan explaining developments in Cuba and setting out his own thinking. 'The critical element now', the President explained, was 'the degree to which Cuba had been handed over to the Soviet Union as an instrument with which to undermine our position in Latin America and the world'.[31] As there seemed to be no chance of changing Castro's attitude, 'we must rely, frankly, on creating conditions in which democratically minded and Western orientated Cubans can assert themselves and regain control of the Island's policies and destinies'.[32]

Macmillan's immediate reply to Eisenhower expressed robust support, though it was reticent on British involvement in economic sanctions. 'Castro is really the very devil. He is your Nasser, and of course with Cuba sitting right on your doorstep, the strategic implications are even more important than the economic. I fully understand your apprehension', he wrote.[33] Macmillan knew, however, that it would require legislation to stop British tankers carrying oil to Cuba. He nevertheless approved the principle of overthrowing the Cuban leader: 'I feel sure Castro has to be got rid of, but it is a tricky operation for you to contrive, and I only hope you will succeed'.[34] Conscious of the need for deniability, the following week he sent a more cautious telegram to Eisenhower, stating that 'Further more everything I hear of the state of feeling in other Latin American countries confirms the importance of avoiding any action which might create the impression that the United States was actively intervening in Cuba.'[35]

In private Senator Kennedy suggested that the United States should have embraced Castro when he visited America in 1959.[36] In the 1960 Presidential election campaign he nevertheless used Cuba to attack Nixon from the right. By the time Kennedy took office in January 1961 preparations were well advanced for the attempted overthrow of Castro by CIA-supported émigrés. The subsequent invasion at the Bay of Pigs proved a personal and political disaster for the new President.

In Britain, there was widespread condemnation of US involvement in the Bay of Pigs affair. Kennedy may well have consulted Macmillan about the operation, including the likely Soviet response.[37] Subsequently, in the view of his biographer, Macmillan 'showed himself 100 per cent loyal in support of a colleague in adversity'.[38] British public responses were rather different. *The Guardian* argued that 'invasion by proxy' was 'morally indistinguishable from open aggression' and 'exactly the same manoeuvre which was used by Hitler in Austria and by Stalin in Czechoslovakia'.[39] Moreover, Kennedy had 'strengthened the appeal of communism in Latin America, Africa, and Asia' and made the watchwords of 'democracy sound like the camouflage of imperialism.'[40] *The Financial Times* described the 'barely credible ineptness' of the operation.[41]

The British Left, and indeed European democratic

socialists in general, supported the principles of Kennedy's *Alliance for Progress*, announced in January, and its goals of economic progress and social justice in Latin America. As Arthur Schlesinger reported to the President on his return from Europe:

> The first reactions to Cuba were, of course, acute shock and disillusion. For some months nearly everybody in Western Europe, and especially perhaps the democratic left, had been making heavy emotional and political investments in the new American administration. Everything about this administration – the intelligence and vision of the President, the dynamism of his leadership, the scope and generosity of his policies, the freshness of his approach to the cold war – had excited tremendous anticipation and elation . . . Kennedy was considered the last best hope of the west against communism and for peace. Now, in a single stroke, all this seemed wiped away.[42]

The Bay of Pigs 'was a great blow' Hugh Gaitskell told Schlesinger.[43] Within the Labour movement the debate over nuclear weapons was raging fiercely, and Kennedy's action weakened Gaitskell's efforts to change party attitudes on defence and foreign affairs. He told Schlesinger: 'The right wing of the Labour Party has been basing a good deal of its argument on the claim that things had changed in America. Cuba has made great trouble for us. We shall now have to move to the left for a bit to maintain our position within the party.'[44] In public, Gaitskell deplored Kennedy's failure to 'stop the disastrous and futile escapade' at the Bay of Pigs, and warned, emphatically, that further attacks on the island would have very dangerous world-wide consequences.[45] On the other hand, he now publicly described Castro as 'an avowed dictator who has exiled, imprisoned or executed most of those who made the Revolution with him'.[46]

While the government refused to be drawn on Kennedy's support for the rebels, American involvement raised parallels with Britain's behaviour at Suez six years earlier. Various chords were struck on both left and right. Denis Healey, the Shadow Foreign Secretary, warned the Kennedy administration: 'that many friends it has won throughout the world by its vigorous policies in many fields would be deeply dismayed if it turned out that the United States Administration were smudging this image by the illegitimate use of violence to solve political problems all too reminiscent of the precedent set by Her Majesty's Government at Suez'.[47] Privately, and echoing Gaitskell, Healey complained bitterly to Schlesinger, 'I've staked my whole political career on the ability of the Americans to act sensibly.'[48]

Memories of Suez were by no means confined to the left. Air Chief Marshal Sir John Slessor told the English-Speaking Union in 1963: 'We are not all unqualified admirers of the C.I.A. We took a pretty low view of the Bay of Pigs affair; that did fan the latent resentment of those (and there were many) who – perhaps understandably – had been extremely angry with America over their handling of the Suez affair.'[49] One consequence of the Bay of Pigs in Britain was to tarnish the reputation and credibility of the CIA. Scepticism at the revelations of the missiles in 1962 was only allayed by publication of the photographic evidence. Denis Healey, for example, was dismissive of initial claims about the missiles because of the events of April 1961.[50]

The Bay of Pigs fuelled Kennedy's fixation with Cuba. Moreover, the broader implications for East–West relations were a matter of deep concern to the President, his advisers and allies. One fear was that Khrushchev would be emboldened by Kennedy's failure and press his advantage in Berlin. The Vienna Summit between the two leaders in June 1961 failed to defuse the problem of Berlin and reinforced mutual misperceptions of the two leaders.[51] Khrushchev's ultimatum at the summit, and the ensuing crisis over Berlin later that year, presented dramatic challenges to western leaders, and in the opinion of some officials created a more dangerous situation than in October 1962.

BRITAIN, NATO AND SANCTIONS AGAINST CUBA

Meanwhile, in the Caribbean, American pressure against Cuba soon ranged across the spectrum of diplomatic, economic and paramilitary activity. In November 1961, President

Kennedy authorised *Operation Mongoose* 'to help Cuba over-throw the Communist regime'.[52] In January 1962, the United States persuaded members of the Organisation of American States (OAS) to suspend Cuba from membership. The CIA actively conspired, including with figures from the American Mafia, to assassinate the Cuban leader.[53] Military contingency plans for an invasion of Cuba were drawn up and rehearsed.

Within the British government there was growing concern at American policy and attempts to increase economic press-ure on the Castro regime. British attitudes reflected both principle and interest. As Harold Macmillan told Dean Rusk, 40 per cent of the UK's gross national product was ac-counted for by overseas trade.[54] Balance of payments crises were emerging as a major concern for British governments. Moreover, as a leading maritime nation, Britain had a long-established interest in preserving international trade and freedom of the seas. British and American attitudes toward trade with 'the Sino–Soviet bloc' were also at variance. Within Whitehall, the Coordinating Committee on Export Controls (COCOM), the principal means of controlling strategic exports to the Sino–Soviet bloc, was regarded as 'a non-sense',[55] while the Prime Minister believed that it rested 'on *no* reasoning, merely on Congressional lobbying'.[56]

Pressure from Washington on its allies over Cuba was mounting. In February 1962 Kennedy embargoed all US trade with Cuba, save critical medical supplies. In the summer he asked NATO for controls on transhipment to Cuba on US embargoed goods, the addition of Cuba to the COCOM list and inclusion of Cuba in the system of reporting to NATO credits granted to the Soviet bloc. In June 1962, in preliminary discussion in the NATO Political Committee, the British persuaded their allies against common economic measures that could become public knowledge and against the inclusion of Cuba in the COCOM list. All the other NATO countries, however, agreed to the inclusion of Cuba in the NATO system for credit reporting. Within the Cabi-net, there was disagreement over how far the government should move. The Foreign Secretary, Lord Home, advo-cated some accommodation with the Americans, arguing with the President of the Board of Trade, Frederick Erroll, that: 'As you know, the Americans feel very strongly in-

deed about Cuba. In the interests of Anglo-American relations we do not wish to seem less sympathetic to them
than other NATO countries, in view of the pledge given
by the Prime Minister to President Eisenhower to help the
United States over Cuba.'[57] NATO had already accepted,
with British agreement, that Cuba was economically and
politically integrated with the Communist bloc, and as the
Foreign Secretary argued, 'we cannot take a contrary view
now without exposing ourselves to charges of hypocrisy or,
at best, inconsistency'.[58] This did not mean treating the
Cubans as fully paid up members of the bloc, which the
Americans themselves had recognised when they accepted
that visible measures would be counterproductive. Home
wanted to subscribe to reporting credits, and to a Danish
proposal to keep exports to Cuba under review to ascer-
tain whether 'strategic materials' were involved.

The President of the Board of Trade, however, was against
further restrictions:

> it seems entirely consistent with the line we have taken
> hitherto for us to continue to oppose any economic
> measures which would amount to recognition that Cuba
> is a member of the bloc. If we give way on the proposal
> to report credits we should then be open to a charge of
> inconsistency in resisting the American's other proposals
> if they later revert to them. Thus even if we are alone in
> this, I think we must stand firm on this matter of credit
> reporting.[59]

Erroll also objected to the Danish proposal on the review
of strategic goods as it would revive American demands to
add Cuba to COCOM and 'would clearly imply our reporting at the end of the period (presumably to NATO or
even to COCOM) what goods had been sent. This would
be little different from adding Cuba to the COCOM list'.[60]
Macmillan agreed with Erroll.[61]

Home deferred to these objections. Within the NATO
Political Committee, however, the British attitude caused
widespread astonishment and 'distress' to the American
representative.[62] The Foreign Secretary noted that 'our
attitude profoundly shocked the Americans and was received
with bewilderment and dismay by our other allies . . . our

performance at the Paris meeting will cause much bitterness in Washington'.[63] While opposed to the extension of
COCOM, the Foreign Secretary was concerned lest British
opposition to credit reporting 'lead to a major row' with
the Americans, 'in which we could not expect the support
of any of our European partners, to most of whom our
attitude is incomprehensible'.[64] The President of the Board
of Trade, however, felt that 'If we give way now . . . we
shall be pushed into an even more restrictive policy.'[65]

When the US Secretary of State, Dean Rusk, visited London
on 24 June the British attitude was made clear to him by
the Prime Minister and the Foreign Secretary. Home

> said that he very much doubted, and his doubts were
> shared by the Cabinet, whether economic sanctions ever
> had much effect. They had failed with Mossadeq and
> Nasser and there was great reluctance to contemplate
> them in the case of Cuba. He realised that Cuba was a
> very sensitive spot for the United States. We had readily
> agreed not to supply arms but the request, which was
> now before the NATO Council, that we should report
> any credits that we gave to Cuba and agree to discuss
> any significant trade in strategic items, presented con-
> siderable difficulties. He admitted that we were in min-
> ority of one in the NATO Council in hesitating to accept
> these proposals and he hoped that we should find some
> way out.[66]

Macmillan went further, stating that he

> strongly disagreed with the whole idea of COCOM. If
> you refused to sell things to Communist or other countries,
> they soon learned how to make the items themselves.
> The whole idea was ridiculous in itself and particularly
> so to a country like the United Kingdom, 40 per cent of
> whose gross national product was accounted for by over-
> seas trade. The comparable figure for the United States
> was 6 per cent.[67]

Nevertheless, Macmillan now 'saw no objection to merely
reporting'.[68]

The following day Rusk and his officials met Home at
the Foreign Office. The Foreign Secretary emphasised that

the Cabinet were still not happy with the NATO resolution. Rusk made clear that at the Punta del Este conference, the Americans had sought to isolate Cuba which had become a base 'for the export of arms and subversive influences into neighbouring States in Latin America'.[69] In addition, 'for domestic political reasons it was important for the United States Government to be able to demonstrate that this was a problem which the United States shared with its allies'; action of this kind was necessary to defuse Congressional pressure for 'a more militant policy'.[70] Unable to persuade Erroll of the need for greater flexibility, Home took the matter to Cabinet, where on 26 June, and with Macmillan now behind him, the 'balance of opinion' favoured the Foreign Office view.[71] On 18 July, the NATO Council duly agreed to reporting on credits to Cuba.[72]

Behind growing economic and political disagreement over Cuba there was also military and intelligence co-operation between Britain and the United States. In May 1961, the Pentagon considered that Cuban military efforts against the Guantanamo naval base could make the naval air station untenable for flight operations. Accordingly, they looked to the airfield on Mayaguana Island in the British colony of the Bahamas, which was already in use by the USAF as a long-range proving ground. Ambassador Bruce was asked to approach the British government for permission to pre-stock supplies at the airfield which was to be used in an emergency.[73] It appears that the British government took the decision in early October when the Joint Chiefs of Staff told the Commander in Chief, Atlantic (CINCLANT) that the British Government had agreed to the prepositioning of supplies and equipment at Mayaguana subject to the conditions that 'nothing is to be put in writing', and that, 'facilities are not to be put to active use without prior agreement of [the] British Government'.[74]

One irritant in the situation was the activities of Cuban émigré groups, many of them funded by the CIA. In particular, *Alpha 66* waged a series of attacks on targets in Cuba and against ships trading with Havana. On 10 September 1962 they attacked two cargo ships, one of which was British, just north of Cuba.[75] There was concern within the Foreign Office at these incidents: 'We do not believe that this particular group of militant exiles enjoys any support from the Americans but it is likely that they make some use of American territory'.[76] The Royal Navy was required to maintain patrols off the Bahamas to prevent Cuban exiles using outlying islands as bases,[77] and to protect British shipping. In October two British frigates, based in Bermuda and British Guyana, were tasked with the protection of British ships from *Alpha 66*.[78] There have also been claims of direct CIA involvement in the sabotage of British exports. According to the *New York Times* the CIA contaminated the sugar transported on board the SS *Streatham Hill*, a British freighter under Soviet lease, with a 'harmless but unpalatable substance' when it put into San Juan for repairs.[79] As this action took place on American territory and involved the use of chemical agents the President was reportedly furious at the CIA, ordering that the sugar should not be allowed to leave. It has also been suggested that the CIA sabotaged the supply of Leyland trucks to Cuba.[80]

More significantly for British–American relations, the British Embassy in Havana provided information on Cuban developments. When, in January 1961, the Eisenhower administration broke off diplomatic relations with Havana, the British did not follow suit. There were some 40 000 Jamaicans and British West Indians in Cuba for whom the British government had accepted diplomatic responsibility and who, with several hundred white British nationals, were the largest unassimilated foreign community in Cuba. The British embassy in Havana became, the Foreign Office believed, 'the State department's major source of information about internal developments in Cuba'.[81] The Pentagon and the American intelligence community also appreciated the information they received.[82] Intelligence co-operation over Cuba developed during the summer. Although the British were not formally told of the US aerial reconnaissance programme,[83] the Pentagon did agree to provide them with a copy of the August US National Intelligence Estimate (NIE) on Cuba.[84]

Nonetheless, for many Americans continuing British trade with Havana was a growing irritant. During the summer of 1962 Soviet military aid to Cuba increased dramatically. American pressure mounted on its NATO allies. In September, President Kennedy was reported to have told con-gressional leaders that British, German, Norwegian and Greek ships were involved in the supply of arms to Havana.[85] The British again resisted pressure for Cuba to be added to COCOM, though within the Foreign Office it was accepted that, as British arms were no longer sold to Cuba, British ships should not carry them.[86] However, the government still did not have legal powers to prevent British ships, under their own or other flags, from trading with Cuba. From Washington, Ormsby-Gore argued that there were: 'strong arguments against any interference with the right of our ships to carry what they like where they like. In informing the [NATO] Council of our action you may wish to point out that, whatever its practical effect, it has not been without cost to us in terms of principle'.[87] The govern-ment was aware that they 'had no power to control the employment of British ships in the Cuba trade or else-where'.[88] The Minister of Transport wrote to the Chairman of the General Council of British Shipping asking British ship owners to refrain from shipping arms and military equipment to Cuba. Foreign Office officials felt that it 'would be surprising if they did not co-operate'.[89] Nevertheless, this was seen as 'little more than a "window dressing" operation', as it was believed that 'military supplies are carried to Cuba in Communist ships while other cargoes are diverted to Western ships'.[90]

Within NATO the Americans again pressed for Cuba to be added to the COCOM list, and there was pressure at the NATO Council in September for active measures against the violation of the Monroe doctrine. Toward the end of September the Foreign Secretary travelled to Washington and met President Kennedy. He reported to Macmillan: 'On Cuba the President said he simply couldn't understand why we could not help America by joining an embargo on Trade. Luckily there was not time to go far into the matter, but I gave the reason why we could not take the action he wanted. He admitted there might be two views as to whether or not embargo was wise but why could we not do this for America and for a NATO ally who was hard pressed.'[91]

Home recognised the domestic circumstances facing Kennedy ('the Republicans are gunning for him in a big

way') but felt that 'he really fears that Russia will provoke
an intervention by the US in order to wipe out Berlin'.[92]
Macmillan's cable to Home demonstrates the depth of feeling
within the government and the rift between Washington
and London on the issue: 'I hope we shall not agree to
COCOM or anything approaching it. There is no reason
for us to help the Americans on Cuba.'[93] Home reported
the 'intense feelings' in Washington over Cuban trade to
the Cabinet on 9 October, and it was agreed to give consideration to making arms exports to Cuba illegal.[94]

   With NATO unwilling to agree effective sanctions against
Cuba, the Americans now threatened unilateral action. The
principal European maritime countries trading with Cuba
(Norway, Denmark, Sweden, West Germany, Italy, Greece
and the UK) were told on 2 October that Washington intended a range of measures: American ports would be closed
to 'all ships of any country if any ship bearing the flag of
that country hereafter carries arms to Cuba'; no US government cargo would be carried in a foreign ship whose owners participated in Bloc-Cuban trade; no US ships would
trade with Cuba; and American ports would be closed 'to
any ship that on the same continuous voyage was used or
is being used on Bloc-Cuban trade'.[95] Closing American
ports to ships involved in the supply of arms to Cuba was
in British eyes 'unprecedented in time of peace but, if applied
to British shipping entirely contrary to the convention of
1815'.[96] Closing ports to ships engaged in trade with the
Bloc was also contrary to this convention. The embassy
mentioned the 1815 Convention to the State Department,
but avoided using it as point of argument as aside from
legal qualifications, 'there is no doubt that from a pre-
sentational and public relations point of view our stand on
this would be ridiculed'.[97] In the event, the promulgation
of the measures was postponed when the crisis erupted.[98]

   The public mood in America strongly supported Kennedy's
actions. American dock workers of the International Longshoremen's Association announced on 10 October that they
would boycott any ship trading with Cuba or the Soviet
Union and any of the same ownership trading with Cuba.[99]
There was particular American irritation at the chartering
of British tankers to transport oil from the Black Sea ports

to Cuba. Between the beginning of July and the end of September, 31 British ships had called at Cuban ports, thirteen of which were tankers carrying oil from the Black Sea.[100] On 20 October, Ormsby-Gore warned the Foreign Office of the domestic pressure on the President. In September Kennedy had signed the joint Congressional resolution giving authority for the use of force to prevent the extension of the Marxist–Leninist regime by force or threat of force, though 'with some reluctance', according to Ormsby-Gore.[101] The ambassador reported that 'criticism of Her Majesty's Government is exceedingly strong and few voices have been raised in our defence'.[102]

After explaining that a Gallup poll showed 63 per cent of Americans were against military action to overthrow Castro, Ormsby-Gore observed that 'What is new is the bitterness towards American's allies and their unhelpfulness. But it is conceivable that pressure on the President to take more drastic action against Cuba might reach disturbing proportions if the Republicans do well at the November elections and if evidence of Soviet shipments shows that offensive weapons are being supplied.'[103] Moreover, he warned that although there was 'a large element of electioneering in the present fuss there is genuine and rising concern, especially in military circles, which the President will have to take into account'.[104]

Some British officials queried the government line. Ambassador Marchant in Havana questioned continuing opposition to an economic embargo. Given the avowed American intent to bring Castro down, Kennedy would have no alternative short of the morally objectionable and militarily hazardous option of invasion, which would be 'the very worst of all possible solutions and one that we should make considerable sacrifices to avoid', Marchant argued.[105] He therefore advocated turning Cuba into a 'failed satellite' by denying vital spare parts for motor cars and trucks, additives for cracking plants, irrigation pumps, and electrical equipment and also urged 'a really serious propaganda exercise'.[106] With 'so much single minded, purposeful effort from the Soviet side going into the Cuban venture only those who still believe in miracles can imagine that it will fall down of its own accord', he warned.[107]

The Minister of State at the Foreign Office, Joseph Godber, argued, however, that while Britain was 'deeply and irrevocably opposed to Communism' and its embrace in Cuba:

> However much we may deplore this development it has never been Britain's policy to seek by force to change the internal political direction of any country. Communism may have been imposed on the Cubans, but it has been imposed by the Cubans themselves however much they may now be assisted by Soviet Russia. Nor do we believe that economic sanctions or blockade are right in such a case. Whatever the ethics of their use, and this is questionable, there is no likelihood that they would be successful in bringing down the present regime. What would happen is that we should be merely forcing Castro to depend more and more completely on the Soviet Union, and we make it easier for him to consolidate his own position at home by building up hatred against the West.[108]

These high-minded sentiments neglected episodes of British intervention in other countries. They nevertheless illustrate how British views were increasingly at variance from mainstream American opinion on Cuba and how Castro was to be dealt with.

The supply of Soviet arms to Cuba increased pressure on Kennedy to take action. This was fuelled by claims that Soviet nuclear missiles were being installed in Cuba. On 4 and 13 September Kennedy issued statements warning of the grave consequences of such action. On 7 September he also sought Congressional authorisation to call up 150 000 reservists. The American military had conducted major manoeuvres in the Caribbean in the spring, summer and autumn of 1962, and leaked plans for an amphibious exercise, Phibriglex-62, to be held in mid-October, which involved liberating the island of Vieques, off Puerto Rico, from a fictional dictator by the name of Ortsac (Castro spelt backwards).[109] If the pressure in the period 1961–2 was designed to intimidate, however, its effects was to further cement relations between Havana and Moscow. Soviet arms shipments increased, and in the spring of 1962 Khrushchev had the idea of deploying nuclear missiles in Cuba capable of reaching American territory. If these weapons were intended to deter Washington their immediate effect was to provoke a possible attack.[110]

Active debate remains about Khrushchev's motives in deploying the missiles, and these are discussed in later chapters. Whether or not a principal aim was to deter an American invasion, the Soviets sought to deploy the missiles in secret and to use various diplomatic channels to deceive President Kennedy. Georgi Bolshakov, a Washington TASS correspondent and Soviet military intelligence (GRU) officer, had served as a diplomatic back-channel between Khrushchev and Kennedy from May 1961.[111] Ormsby-Gore learned of Bolshakov's role, and informed the Permanent Secretary at the Foreign Office, Sir Harold Caccia, on 22 January 1962.[112] Similar assurances that no offensive weapons would be installed in Cuba were given by the Soviet Ambassador, Anatoli Dobrynin, who was not told about the missiles beforehand,[113] and from the Soviet Foreign Minister, Andrei Gromyko, on 18 October, who was involved in Soviet decision-making and who assured Kennedy that there were no offensive weapons in Cuba.[114] It is now known that the first medium-range missiles arrived in mid-September, followed over the next few weeks by their warheads and a panoply of tactical nuclear weapons.[115]

Ascertaining whether there were 'offensive' missiles in Cuba became a priority for the American intelligence community. Reports from agents, refugees and foreign nationals, including the French and Dutch intelligence services, provided some indications, but the overwhelming majority of these related to Surface to Air Missiles (SAMs). Both the French and the Dutch intelligence services alerted the Americans to the presence of offensive missiles in August and September respectively.[116] The French warning was clearly an error, as the MRBMs did not arrive until September, although the French were surprised when Kennedy publicly denied the presence of offensive forces on 30 August.[117] Subsequently, information from the French was of value in identifying the site at San Cristobal, in western Cuba.[118] By the beginning of October, CIA sources had identified the SS-4 installation; photographic evidence of the bases was eventually provided by a USAF U-2 mission, flown on 14 October.[119]

It has also been suggested that the British Ambassador learned of the missiles, but 'fearing that his communication system with London was too vulnerable to tapping, rightly refused to pass on the information'.[120] However, in his report to the Foreign Secretary in November, Ambassador Marchant made clear that while Soviet military deployments and ground to air missile sites were identified

> What we did not see anything of until too late was the vital equipment and the larger missiles which were almost certainly moved only by night. In fact we saw no rockets of any kind in or around Havana until the 25th of October when a convoy of several ground to air missiles appeared in the city itself in broad daylight and larger ones, presumably ground to ground missiles, after dark.[121]

Henry Brandon, Chief US correspondent of *The Sunday Times*, recalled that during a visit to Cuba, 'about the 11th October', he was told by a Cuban official that 'we can now hit Florida'.[122] Brandon discussed the conversation with the Ambassador. Although such information was useful to the CIA it was of limited value – the CIA office responsible for collating reports from agents, émigrés and refugees was swamped, mostly by reports mistaking the large Soviet surface to air missiles for ground to ground missiles. As Ambassador Marchant explained later to the Foreign Secretary, for the past two years 'we have lived in an atmosphere of the wildest rumours ninety per cent of them totally without foundation and many of them specifically about gigantic nuclear missiles'.[123] The CIA had, indeed, received some 3 500 reports from émigrés or agents concerning possible missile deployments, of which only eight were retrospectively deemed to be 'reasonably valid indicators' of the deployment.[124] As Marchant commented: 'Intelligence agencies must therefore be excused if they tended to discount the hundreds of recent rocket stories from their usually unreliable sources'.[125] Brandon himself arrived in Washington on 20 October, and was quickly 'scooped' by President Kennedy.[126]

IRRITANT IN THE SPECIAL RELATIONSHIP

Various studies have depicted a very warm personal and political relationship between Kennedy and Macmillan.[127] Trade with Cuba was, nevertheless, one of several irritants in British–American relations. There were other disagreements about Laos, and, in particular, over the supply of Hawk missiles to the Israeli government. Macmillan believed that the Americans had deceived him over the Israeli affair, and told Home on 1st October that we 'must always have this mind in discussing other subjects with them'.[128] Economic sanctions against Castro's Cuba is nevertheless an interesting issue in British–American relations. Even though the 'special relationship' was crucial to Macmillan, and although Kennedy made clear that, whatever the merits of the case, he needed British support, the Prime Minister was unmoved. The British government was prepared to protect British interests even when this meant being in a minority within NATO. Macmillan was defending a principle as well as showing 'the world we are not so easily pushed around by the United States'.[129] He was also protecting British trade and shipping interests, and it remains open to doubt whether he could have carried the Cabinet (or the Conservative Party) on a policy which abandoned both principle and interest to curry favour in Washington. Moreover, although on specific issues Macmillan was prepared to go against the rest of NATO, British attitudes generally accorded with those other Europeans wishing to trade with Cuba. Alistair Hennessy and George Lambie argue that over time these European attitudes to trade were, indeed, vital to the survival of the Cuban revolution.[130]

With the discovery of Soviet missile bases, Cuba assumed a global significance. NATO had discussed the Cuban situation in September, and the issue of active measures to isolate Castro's regime was a major issue of contention within the alliance. The British were the principal obstacle to concerted, if limited, NATO action, though other maritime trading nations shared Whitehall's concerns. Kennedy did have reasons not to inform or consult his allies when the Soviet missiles were discovered, but it is difficult to escape the conclusion that the attitude of the NATO allies was a factor in Kennedy's decision not to consult on how to respond to the discovery of the missiles. British policy toward economic sanctions against Cuba therefore demonstrated that an independent British policy carried a price in Washington. With the discovery of Soviet nuclear missiles in Cuba, miscalculation by Kennedy, or indeed by Khrushchev, carried the risk that a far higher price might have to be paid by Britain, as indeed by the rest of humanity.

3 Discovery and Blockade: Informing or Consulting?

On Sunday 14 October 1962, a USAF U-2 photographed the construction of Soviet Medium Range Ballistic Missile (MRBM) bases in Cuba.[1] By the following evening, key officials around Washington were alerted, and on the morning of Tuesday 16 October the President was told. In the ensuing five days Kennedy and his advisers debated how to respond. America's allies were not consulted during this period. Dean Rusk told the first meeting of (what became) the Executive Committee of the National Security Council (ExComm): 'there is no such thing ... as unilateral action by the United States' – the US had forty two allies and any American response, Rusk warned, 'will greatly increase the risks of direct action' elsewhere.[2] Rusk therefore advocated consultation with NATO.[3] Other counsels prevailed, though Kennedy remained concerned at the possibility of losing the support of his NATO allies. Yet, although Kennedy accepted that the British would need to be informed sometime before the other allies, he decided not to seek Macmillan's advice, at one point dismissing the idea of consulting the British about military action – 'They'll just object.'[4]

According to his brother, it was on the afternoon of Saturday 20 October that President Kennedy finally decided to impose a naval blockade or 'quarantine' around Cuba.[5] It was only after this decision that key NATO leaders were told of the situation. Kennedy's unwillingness to confide in his allies provoked much criticism in Britain, among the press and from the Opposition. In Parliament the leader of the Labour Party, Hugh Gaitskell, declared that if the government had not been consulted it was 'a very unsatisfactory state of affairs that one member of an alliance can take unilateral action even though this may clearly involve the gravest danger to other members of the alliance'.[6]

Air Chief Marshal Slessor told the English-Speaking Union the following spring:

I find it difficult to convince myself that it would not
have been possible and desirable for the President to
get on the telephone to the Prime Minister – say on the
Wednesday before, the 17th, when the photographic evidence was irrefutable and it was clear that some action
was inevitable. It may be argued that if anyone were told,
all the NATO Allies would have to be told. I'm not sure
there would have been any harm in that; but I do think
we were in a special position in that we had SAC and
Polaris submarine bases in our country, and our own
strategic nuclear force closely integrated with SAC. Here
again it is a question of treating us as an Ally and not a
satellite.[7]

Kennedy's unwillingness to consult Macmillan before taking his decision has been viewed as of great significance in
assessments of the value and meaning of the 'special relationship'.[8] This chapter reappraises British–American
relations in the light of recent archival disclosures and revises
previous interpretations. It also focuses on the role of the
British Ambassador, Sir David Ormsby-Gore, and the subsequent pattern of communication between the American
and British governments, which cast light on aspects of
the 'special relationship'.

The idea that the United States should consult NATO
allies on its response to the discovery of Soviet nuclear
missile in Cuba presupposes that this was not simply an
American problem in America's backyard. Consultation
between the British and American governments also needs
to be set in historical and political context. Whatever right
the British felt they had to be consulted in 1962, only six
years earlier the British and French governments had conspired to deceive Washington about military action outside
the NATO area of operations. Second, as has been seen,
Cuba was an irritant in relations between Britain and the
US, and European trade with Cuba was seen by Americans
to undermine American economic warfare against Cuba. If
Macmillan could tell his Foreign Secretary that there was
'no reason for us to help the Americans on Cuba',[9] there
were many Americans who believed the British had for-
feited any right to be consulted over Cuba.

Nevertheless, in Britain there was a strong expectation that Britain should be consulted, and students of the 'special relationship' have concluded, for reasons adumbrated by Air Chief Marshal Slessor, that the absence of such consultation demonstrated Britain's subordinate position. Moreover, and most crucially, that area where British and American officials most clearly feared a direct Soviet response was Berlin. There is evidence that Kennedy's handling of the Bay of Pigs operation had been guided by his concern about a Soviet response against Berlin.[10] The link between the two had been expressed by the President at the end of September to Foreign Secretary Home, when he made clear his fear that the Soviets wished to provoke an American intervention against Cuba 'in order to wipe out Berlin'.[11] The idea that Khrushchev was attempting to provoke a US attack on Cuba to create the opportunity for seizing Berlin was one explanation proffered for the deployment of the missiles, and which, as Dean Rusk observed, invited parallels with Soviet action in Hungary at the time of the British/French attack on Suez.[12] Kennedy himself made this parallel in his meeting with the Joint Chiefs of Staff on 19 October.[13] Notwithstanding such arguments in favour of consultation, Kennedy informed Macmillan on 22 October: 'I have found it absolutely essential, in the interests of security and speed, to make my first decision on my own responsibility.'[14]

It is now clear, however, that the British government learned of the discovery of the missiles through intelligence channels as early as Friday 19 October. Indeed one recent account has claimed that Macmillan learned in this way on Wednesday 17 October.[15] That the British were informed earlier than has been supposed provides a different picture of events, and raises questions about consultation and communication between the British and American governments during the crisis. It does not, however, change the fact that Kennedy took the decision to impose the quarantine without consultation, and then informed Macmillan and other NATO allies thereafter (though before taking action).

By coincidence, senior members of the British intelligence community were in Washington for a conference on intelligence methodology at CIA headquarters.[16] The British representatives included the Director of the JIB, Sir Kenneth Strong, the Chairman of the Joint Intelligence Committee (JIC), Sir Hugh Stephenson, the Cabinet Secretary-designate, Sir Burke Trend, and Thomas Brimelow from the Washington embassy.[17] The British officials were formally briefed by the CIA on Friday 19 October.[18] According to the CIA's Deputy Director for Intelligence, Ray Cline:

> I misled them all week into thinking my preoccupation with business was about Berlin, not Cuba, and only got permission from President Kennedy to brief Strong and Trend orally before their departure on Friday, 19 October. My exercise in deception was totally successful because these British friends took several occasions during the week to argue with me that the Russians would never put missiles in Cuba because of the risk to their interests in Europe.[19]

Previous accounts have suggested that the British officials deduced that a crisis about Cuba was imminent from the actions of American officials in Washington.[20] American disclosure rather than British intuition now explains how London received some early warning that a crisis was imminent.

ORMSBY-GORE'S INITIAL ROLE

Who knew what in Washington, and how, and when, this information was transmitted to London is important in evaluating broader issues of British–American consultation. Several accounts suggest that the delegates at the conference discussed the issue with Ormsby-Gore on the Friday. Elie Abel states that on the morning of Friday 19 October Ormsby-Gore called in Strong and Stephenson, who had sensed that a crisis of some sort was brewing: 'they sat around the circular table in the Ambassador's office and speculated together'.[21] Ormsby-Gore himself later recalled that 'by Friday it was quite clear that something of a major crisis was developing. And I – with my advisers – guessed what it was, and we sent off a warning telegram to London.'[22] How far Strong and Stephenson confided in Ormsby-Gore is not clear, although John McCone told the President that Strong had reported to his ambassador and directly to his government.[23] Ormsby-Gore's subsequent report to Lord Home states that 'it was partly fortuitous that we ourselves were able to guess what was afoot before the end of the week'.[24] According to Macmillan, Ormsby-Gore alerted London on Friday to expect an impending crisis 'probably about missiles in Cuba'.[25]

However, it was not until the afternoon of Saturday 20 October that Ormsby-Gore cabled Sir Harold Caccia, warning that:

> You should know that within the administration there is also increased concern following recent Intelligence estimates of the build-up of Soviet arms. The anxiety is occasioned not only by the quantitative increase in the number of weapons and military personnel, but also by reports which suggest that the types of arms introduced may not be entirely defensive . . . There has been much activity in the State Department, CIA and the Defence Departments in the past few days which suggests that contingency plans are being put into a state of readiness, and assessments of the situation are being brought up to date urgently at the President's request.[26]

The reference to weapons that might 'not be entirely defensive' looks in hindsight to involve missiles, though it should be noted that Ilyushin-28 bombers with the range to reach Florida, and which could be configured to carry nuclear weapons, had been identified by the CIA earlier in October.[27]

On Saturday evening, 20 October 1962, the President telephoned Ormsby-Gore and invited him for lunch the following day.[28] At this meeting the British government first learned of how the Americans intended to respond. Kennedy had asked Ormsby-Gore to come unseen to the White House where he met with the President, alone, just before lunch.[29] Ormsby-Gore (eventually) provided Macmillan with two reports on this meeting, which provide insights into his relationship with the President. 'We were quite alone and he told me that no one else outside the United States

Government was being informed of what was going on',
Ormsby-Gore explained.[30] The President told him that a
major photo reconnaissance effort by U-2 aircraft had shown
that medium range offensive missiles had arrived in Cuba.
One type on fixed sites had an estimated range of 2 000
miles. The other was mobile with an estimated range of
1 500 miles. The President thought that there were perhaps thirty to forty missiles already on the island and that
more were on their way. These missiles were assumed to
be armed with nuclear warheads. Kennedy emphasised the
very serious problem posed for his government: he had
made publicly clear that, 'if Cuba became an offensive military
base of significant capacity for the Soviet Union, then the
United States would do whatever must be done to protect
its own security and that of its Allies'; this clear warning of
where the United States would draw the line now meant
that the administration had to decide what action to take.[31]

The President explained that his government had concluded they had two alternatives:

(i) They could order an all-out air strike first thing Monday
morning to take out all the known missile sites and the
missiles themselves insofar as they had been able to pin-
point their present whereabouts. The Military authorities estimated that such a strike would eliminate at least
fifty per cent of the Cuban missile potential but it would
inevitably cause a large number of casualties to Russians
as well as Cubans. The strike would be followed by the
imposition of a blockade of Cuba.

(ii) They could impose almost immediately a blockade
without first carrying out an air strike. They would stop
and search all ships suspected of carrying goods which
would help to build up the military potential of Cuba.
This would mean leaving the Cubans with their present
offensive capacity, such as it was, but would demonstrate
America's determination not to allow the build up to
proceed any further.[32]

Ormsby-Gore was then asked to choose between the options, without, of course, having consulted London. The
choice excluded a purely diplomatic response and/or a private
approach to Khrushchev (which Macmillan subsequently

thought worth considering). Had Kennedy simply asked Ormsby-Gore for his views on how to respond he might well have been given a very different answer. The framing of the question meant that Ormsby-Gore could be seen, as Schlesinger recorded, to express 'strong support for the quarantine'.[33] The suggestion that Ormsby-Gore was presented with the 'various alternatives', namely 'air strike, blockade or going to the United Nations', and opted for the blockade is therefore misleading.[34] Ormsby-Gore's report to Macmillan, makes clear the views he expressed:

> The President then asked me for my views as to which of these two courses I felt was the correct one. I said that I saw very serious drawbacks in the first course of action he had outlined to me. Very few people outside the United States would consider the provocation offered by the Cubans serious enough to merit an American attack. I thought that in the circumstances America would be damaged politically, and in any case I could not believe that the missiles so far landed constituted any significant military threat to the United States. Even with these weapons in existence on Cuba the United States could presumably overwhelm the island in a very short time if they decided at some future date that this had to be done. I thought that we ought also to bear in mind possible repercussions on the Berlin situation. American action of this kind might well provide a smoke-screen behind which the Russians might move against Berlin under favourable conditions. Therefore, of the two alternatives he had put to me I would certainly favour the second, although this would have far-reaching political implications including the probability of a major Russian reaction perhaps in the Berlin context.[35]

The President explained that he and his colleagues had also decided on the blockade. At this point he alluded to other options, including a full-scale invasion, for which 'they might never have a better opportunity'; they could also 'do nothing at all and go on as before, but he thought that this was not only politically impossible but was in any case too dangerous'.[36]

Khrushchev's actions were, Kennedy believed, 'a direct

challenge by the Soviets to the United States'; if the President did nothing his friends and allies would conclude that he was afraid to move and Khrushchev would assume 'that the Americans, for all their tough words, would be prepared to sit supine and inactive whatever he, Khrushchev, did'.[37] Kennedy's initial reaction to the discovery had been bellicose.[38] Rather more reflectively, he confided to Ormsby-Gore that:

> he could not help admiring the Soviet strategy. They offered this deliberate and provocative challenge to the United States in the knowledge that if the Americans reacted violently to it, the Russians would be given an ideal opportunity to move against West Berlin. If, on the other hand, he did nothing, the Latin Americans and the United States' other Allies would feel that the Americans had no real will to resist the encroachments of Communism and would hedge their bets accordingly.[39]

The idea of an American invasion of Cuba drew a forthright response from the British Ambassador who counselled against military action:

> In answer to this, I said that I was sure that an invasion at this time would be most unwise. I had seen no evidence that the conditions in Cuba were such that the Americans could expect any widespread popular support for their action and history indicated that an invasion without internal popular support usually led to endless trouble. The idea of a puppet regime kept in power by American marines was not a happy prospect. In any case, this could provide the Soviets with the opportunity to take over West Berlin at a moment when United States political stock would be at a very low ebb and the Americans could be blamed for triggering off this exchange of pawns in the most reckless manner. Nevertheless, I could well understand the political dangers and the internal difficulties of doing nothing but I supposed that the blockade itself would give us many headaches and we would have to prepare for vigorous Russian reactions to it.[40]

Ormsby-Gore also inquired about the legality of the blockade. Kennedy explained it would be instituted under the terms of the Rio treaty and that a meeting of the OAS would be called urgently and they would expect to get a two-thirds majority in favour of the course of action they were taking. I said that I feared that the invocation of the Rio treaty would not help us very much as I presumed the United Kingdom had no legal obligations under its terms. Our traditional attitude with regard to the freedom of the seas would put us in an awkward position. Here the President commented that he understood that most of the British shipping taking part in the Cuban trade was not operated by the more respected companies. He also made it clear that shipments of POL [Petroleum, Oil, Lubricants] would be denied to Cuba. Such shipments would be regarded as assistance to the military potential of Cuba and in any case, in view of the action they were taking, there seemed to be little point in adopting half measures. Certainly the denial of POL to Cuba would have the most disastrous effects on the Cuban economy.[41]

Kennedy's comments on POL are rather curious, as there was now general agreement within his government to defer inclusion of POL in the quarantine. The embargo of POL was vigorously opposed in London (see Chapter Four) and in the event Kennedy chose not to include it at this stage.

MACMILLAN'S INITIAL REACTION

At 7 pm, Sunday 21 October, Ormsby-Gore cabled Macmillan to expect 'an extremely important message on Cuba', by teletype, which would arrive at Admiralty House (10 Downing Street was being refurbished at the time) at 10 pm London time; the President had 'stressed that not only are the contents of the message confidential in the highest degree but that the fact that you are receiving a message at this time should on no account become known'.[42] This message was to give Macmillan 'advance notice of a most serious situation and of [Kennedy's] plan to meet it'.[43] Photographic intelligence had established beyond doubt that the Soviets were engaged in a major build-up of medium-range missiles in Cuba. Six sites had so far been identified, 'and two of them may be in operational readiness'; it was 'clear that a massive secret operation has been proceeding in spite of the repeated assurances we have received from the Soviet Union on this point'.[44] Kennedy then explained that, 'after careful reflection', his government had 'decided to prevent any further build-up by sea and to demand the removal of this nuclear threat to our hemisphere'.[45] While this decision had already been taken in Washington, Kennedy promised consultation in the future:

> This extraordinarily dangerous and aggressive Soviet step obviously creates a crisis of the most serious sort, in which we shall have to act most closely together. I have found it absolutely essential, in the interests of security and speed, to make my first decision on my own responsibility, but from now on I expect that we can and should be in the closest touch, and I know that together with our friends we will resolutely meet this challenge. I recognise fully that Khrushchev's main intention may be to increase his chances at Berlin, and we shall be ready to take a full role there as well as in the Caribbean. What is essential at this moment of highest test is that Khrushchev should discover that if he is counting on weakness or irresolution, he has miscalculated.[46]

How much Macmillan knew beforehand about the missiles is unclear. Whether the impression, subsequently generated by Ormsby-Gore and others, that he had been prepared for the news is accurate, Macmillan's reaction to Kennedy's message does not suggest a sense of urgency: while 'it was difficult at so dangerous a moment to reconcile myself to inaction', he decided, 'not even to warn the Foreign Secretary; it would be better to wait until the Ambassador came'.[47] Macmillan's Private Secretary minuted that after reading Ormsby-Gore's telegram advising that it was 'essential' that Macmillan be at Admiralty House to receive Kennedy's message in person, 'the PM decided to stay at Chequers and not come up to London until after lunch on Monday, 22 October. Subsequently, after reading the President's personal message the PM said he would come up to meet the American Ambassador at noon on Monday.'[48] Perhaps reflecting his own rather languid style, Macmillan's behaviour may well also reinforce the impression that he was already aware of the impending crisis.

Ormsby-Gore did not immediately brief Macmillan on his conversation with Kennedy, and a detailed report was not sent until the evening of Monday 22 October. There was a further delay before it reached the Prime Minister late in the evening.[49] This meant that Macmillan did not have Ormsby-Gore's report when he received the American Ambassador at noon on Monday, nor before he and the Foreign Secretary composed a formal reply to the President. Even then, Ormsby-Gore chose not to impart to Macmillan some of Kennedy's more private and highly significant views, including those concerning the Jupiter missiles in Turkey. 'I had previously hesitated to report these remarks because in some instances they were so frank that I doubt very much whether he would repeat them to any member of his administration except his brother Bobby', Ormsby-Gore eventually reported on Tuesday 23 October.[50] It was not until the Ambassador received Macmillan's frank expression of doubts (see below) about Kennedy's course of action that he imparted these views to the Prime Minister.

Macmillan's concern at Kennedy's chosen course of action was communicated to Ormsby-Gore, for his personal use, in a telegram on 22 October.[51] The Prime Minister also wanted to know whether Kennedy intended to seize Cuba. Ormsby-Gore replied that it was clear during their talk on Sunday morning, 'that the President does not expect or intend that the present course of action should lead on to an American seizure of Cuba'; moreover, having passed up this chance, 'he could see no likelihood of their ever being offered an equally good excuse for an invasion.'[52] Ormsby-Gore felt that while this indicated Kennedy's mood, there was nevertheless the risk of an unintended clash over the Guantanamo naval base or between United States and Cuban ships.

Macmillan also wondered whether Kennedy intended some kind of international conference. Ormsby-Gore explained that, while Kennedy had not referred to this, 'he certainly hopes that the crisis will be resolved through negotiation and discussion.'[53] More significantly, Ormsby-Gore reported that:

> I had some indication of the scope of his thinking when he said with great seriousness that the existence of nuclear arms made a secure and rational world impossible. We must somehow find a means to get rid of nuclear weapons. He also said that intermediate range missile bases in Turkey and elsewhere had become more or less worthless. He was not doubtful whether they had been a good plan in the first place. Whether political developments would enable him to do a deal on the reciprocal closing of bases it was hard to tell at the moment, but certainly from a military point of view he could see no objection.[54]

Ormsby-Gore's conclusion was that the President hoped and expected that, 'the crisis will be resolved through East–West discussions and he realises that these discussions will include, as well as Cuba, Berlin, foreign bases, disarmament, etc.'[55] This had potentially enormous implications for British and European diplomacy and security, and it is a matter of interest that the Ambassador did not immediately report these statements to Macmillan, reflecting the importance which Ormsby-Gore attached to their sensitivity and confidentiality.

In addition to messages, Kennedy despatched various emissaries to America's NATO allies. Dean Acheson, accompanied by the CIA's Sherman Kent, Chairman of the Board of National Estimates, went to Paris to brief President de Gaulle, the French government and the North Atlantic Council (NAC); Ambassador Dowling flew to West Germany to brief Chancellor Adenauer; Chet Cooper assisted Ambassador Bruce with the British. En route to their various capitals Acheson and his colleagues landed at Greenham Common air base, to be met by David Bruce, armed with a service revolver and a bottle of scotch.[56]

Bruce and Cooper called upon Macmillan at Admiralty House the following noon.[57] An advance draft of the President's speech had not, however, reached London and did not arrive until much later in the afternoon. Macmillan was anxious to read this before communicating with the President.[58] Bruce did deliver a further message from the

President in which, *inter alia*, he told Macmillan that he wanted him to be the first allied leader to be informed of events, 'in order that we should have the opportunity, should you wish it, to discuss the situation between ourselves by means of our private channel of communication.'[59] According to Cooper:

> The Prime Minister was alone except for his Private Secretary [de Zulueta]. It was evident that the Prime Minister had some advance general knowledge of the developing situation in Cuba (as indeed he should have since we had briefed various members of the British intelligence community several days before in Washington). However, Mr Macmillan obviously had no idea of the extent or precise nature of Soviet offensive capabilities in Cuba. His first reaction, which he addressed more to himself than to the Ambassador, was to the effect that the British people, who had been living in the shadow of annihilation for the past many years, had somehow been able to live more or less normal lives and he felt that the Americans, now confronted with a similar situation would, after the initial shock, make a similar adjustment. 'Life goes on somehow'.[60]

Dino Brugioni's interpretation of this response is that Macmillan 'immediately began to downgrade the Cuban missile threat. Sarcastically, he observed that the British had learned to live under the shadow of Russian missiles and that the Americans might have to make a similar adjustment.'[61] However, as Sherman Kent explains: 'the Prime Minister was obviously aware that this might be misinterpreted, and went to considerable length to explain to the Ambassador that this was more a philosophical commentary on human nature than any indication on his part that he was not sympathetic with the US position or shocked at the news'.[62] Brugioni asserts that: 'Macmillan, seemingly blissfully ignorant of the President's feelings, was not at all sympathetic to the American position as stated by Ambassador Bruce.'[63] Bruce's report of the meeting cabled to Washington made clear that Macmillan 'accepted [the] validity [of the] evidence [of the] existence [of] offensive capabilities and considered [the] situation grave'.[64] The

Ambassador was later, however, reported to have 'left the Prime Minister angry, depressed and uneasy'.[65] According to Cooper's memorandum:

> After my recitation of the present Soviet offensive strength in Cuba, Mr Macmillan said that, if the President were convinced that a meaningful offensive capability were present, 'That was good enough for him'. He did not spend more than a few seconds on the photographs. Although the Prime Minister did not develop this theme in my presence in detail, he did indicate that he felt that a blockade would be difficult to enforce and that the US would have problems in getting solid UN support. He also ruminated about whether it would not have been better to have confronted Khrushchev privately with our evidence and given him a private ultimatum . . . Lord Home then joined the Prime Minister and the Ambassador for a discussion of policy matters and I was excused.[66]

Macmillan's doubts about the wisdom and necessity of Kennedy's chosen course of action, expressed in the presence of the American Ambassador, were not immediately communicated to Washington by Bruce. Brugioni states that Lord Home was concerned that Macmillan's 'oblique demeanour' would be misunderstood by his American visitors and 'tried to mitigate Macmillan's adamant position'.[67] Bruce did report that Macmillan and Home had speculated about Soviet reactions, and that both believed Khrushchev might retaliate with an embargo against American access to Berlin or with some form of harassment against 'foreign, especially Turkish bases'.[68] They also suspected that Khrushchev might suggest a meeting with the President and drag the matter out.

Macmillan's doubts about Kennedy's actions were communicated directly to Ormsby-Gore:

> Since it seemed impossible to stop his action I did not make the effort, although in the course of the day I was in a mind to do so. I feel sure that a long period of blockade, and possibly Russian reaction in the Caribbean or elsewhere, will lead us nowhere. Therefore he must decide whether he wants a *coup de main*, which will at least put one card in his hands, or face a conference

where Berlin, nuclear disarmament and many other issues will have to be discussed . . . You will, realize, for your personal information only, that I could not allow a situation in Europe or in the world to develop which looks like escalating into war without trying some action by calling a conference on my own, or something of the kind, to stop it.[69]

How far Macmillan seriously considered challenging Kennedy's decision to impose the blockade is a matter for speculation. Lord Hailsham later described Macmillan's message as rather foolish.[70]

Macmillan's response to Kennedy was 'not altogether easy to draft'.[71] He wanted to demonstrate support for the Americans, but there were issues of international law as well as European and British public opinion to consider. Europeans had lived under the Soviet 'nuclear shadow' for many years. Moreover, he was concerned that Khrushchev's real purpose was in Berlin. At the same time it was also 'important that our reply should show no hesitation or weakness'.[72]

When he drafted the reply, Macmillan did not have Ormsby-Gore's initial report of his meeting with the President (which arrived around 10:30 pm, shortly before Kennedy made the first of his telephone calls[73]). The text of the President's speech arrived about 5 pm, and Macmillan and Home composed the reply with the help of their advisers. Macmillan felt at the time that 'it was a pretty good document',[74] balancing British concerns about the legality of the blockade, likely Soviet reactions in Europe and the need to support the United States. The message read that:

> Ambassador Bruce called to see me this morning and gave me evidence of the Soviet build-up in Cuba. I quite understand how fiercely American public opinion will react when it knows these facts. I have this moment received through our teleprinter the text of your proposed declaration tonight. Let me say at once that we shall of course give you all the support we can in the Security Council.[75]

Ormsby-Gore had made clear to Kennedy that British concern with the freedom of the seas might be a problem.

Macmillan, while alluding to potential legal difficulties was, nevertheless, clear in his support for Kennedy:

> I hope that you can provide us immediately with the best legal case that can be made in support of the broad moral position so that our representative can weigh in effectively. Of course the international lawyers will take the point that a blockade which involves the searching of ships of all countries is difficult to defend in peacetime. Indeed quite a lot of controversy has gone on in the past about its use in wartime. However, we must rest not so much on precedent as on the unprecedented condition of the modern world in a nuclear age.[76]

Doubts about the legality of American action immediately emerged in the press, and indeed within the Cabinet (see below). The Lord Chancellor was to endorse the Foreign Office view that the quarantine did not conform with international law.

Macmillan's main concern, however, was how Khrushchev would respond, and in particular, what action the Soviets would take in Europe:

> What I think we must now consider is Khrushchev's likely reaction. He may reply either in words or in kind or both. If he contents himself with the first he may demand the removal of all American bases in Europe. If he decides to act he may do so either in the Caribbean or elsewhere. If he reacts in the Caribbean his obvious method would be to escort his ships and force you into the position of attacking them. This fire-first dilemma has always worried us and we have always hoped to impale the Russians on this horn. No doubt you have thought of this but I would be glad to know how you feel it can be handled. Alternatively, he may bring some pressure on the weaker parts of the free world defence system. This may be in South-East Asia, in Iran, possibly in Turkey, but more likely in Berlin. If he reacts outside the Caribbean – as I fear he may – it will be tempting for him to answer one blockade by declaring another. We must therefore be ready. Any retaliatory action on Berlin as envisaged in the various contingency plans will lead us either

to an escalation to world war or to the holding of a conference. What seems to be essential is that you and I
should think over and decide in what direction we want
to steer things within the Alliance and elsewhere. We
should take counsel as soon as we have the Russian
reaction.[77]

In addition to professions of support, Macmillan also felt
it necessary to draw Kennedy's attention to the political
needs of the Alliance:

> While you know how deeply I sympathise with your diffi-
> culty and how much we will do to help in every way, it
> would only be right to tell you that there are two
> aspects which give me concern. Many of us in Europe
> have lived so long in close proximity to the enemy's nuclear
> weapons of the most devastating kind that we have got
> accustomed to it. So European opinion will need atten-
> tion. The second, which is more worrying, is that if
> Khrushchev comes to a conference he will of course try
> to trade his Cuba position against his ambitions in Berlin
> and elsewhere. This we must avoid at all costs, as it will
> endanger the unity of the Alliance.[78]

Thus despite doubts about Kennedy's action, Macmillan
expressed British support and counselled against a trade
that would sacrifice European security. It was only the
following day that Ormsby-Gore reported that, privately,
Kennedy saw no military value in the Turkish Jupiters and
envisaged a negotiated settlement involving a broader agenda
that the Caribbean. By the end of the week Macmillan was
engaged in devising an initiative designed to facilitate such
a settlement. Macmillan's initial and considered reaction
was supportive of Kennedy, despite much criticism in Britain
of American action. His response compares with that of de
Gaulle, who was also sceptical about the effectiveness of a
blockade but gave his general support to the Americans.[79]
Like Macmillan he was dismissive of the UN, and also
expected a Soviet response against Berlin.

British public reactions were much less supportive. On
the right, although the *Daily Express* expressed strong support for the President, the *Daily Mail* declared, to the

annoyance of the American Ambassador, that the 'world cannot help fearing that in thus advancing to the brink of war, President Kennedy may have been led more by popular emotion than by calm statesmanship . . . The perilous trend of events now set in motion must be halted before it is too late.'[80] *The Guardian* argued that 'a limited military action will be hard to justify. In the end the United States may find it has done its cause, its friends, and its own true interests little good.'[81] Left-wing Labour MPs were outraged: 37 of them signed an Early Day Motion demanding that the West should increase its trade with Cuba and that 'Britain should resist all proposals for an economic or shipping boycott.'[82]

Doubt about the prudence of Kennedy's action lessened as Khrushchev backed away from a naval confrontation, and then appeared to retreat altogether. Macmillan, however, was phlegmatic over press reaction, telling Ormsby-Gore on Tuesday that 'the Press is not too bad but of course they are a little sceptical about the facts of the Soviet build-up in Cuba'.[83] Concern about American failure to consult with the British before deciding upon a blockade was not dissipated so easily.

Macmillan himself appears to have shared the irritation at Kennedy's failure to consult, though in his published account he recorded that American dealings with NATO in the crisis were 'more than correctness demanded'.[84] In public Macmillan insisted that 'the American government not only preserved diplomatic propriety but maintained the closest possible co-operation with their allies' at this time.[85] According to Cooper's account of his meeting with Hugh Gaitskell and George Brown on 23 October, however, 'Gaitskell said that he had [just] been with [Macmillan] . . . and that the Prime Minister expressed annoyance about the lack of advance knowledge of US actions.'[86]

Cooper was aggrieved at this and pointed out to Gaitskell 'in fairly strong terms' that there

> were two aspects to the question of advanced knowledge: one was the developing situation in Cuba and the other was US intentions with respect to Cuba. In connection with the former, I told Gaitskell that we had occasion to discuss Cuba with several important people in the Brit-

ish intelligence community who happened to be in Washington during the week of 15 October, and that several of them had been given a formal briefing on Friday, 19 October. We could only assume that they notified their government of the developing situation in Cuba. With respect to US intentions, I noted that we had hoped to get an advanced copy of the President's statement to the Prime Minister 12 hours before the broadcast, but that this was not possible, because the President himself had not decided on the precise language of his statement until fairly late in the day . . . This was unfortunate, but in the nature of the circumstances, was all that could have been done.[87]

Macmillan's carefully drafted reply did not excite enthusiasm in Washington. It reached the President before his National Security Council meeting at 3 pm, where Dean Rusk observed that, 'for a first reaction to information of our proposed blockade it was not bad', adding that, 'it was comforting to learn that the British Prime Minister had not thought of anything we hadn't thought of'.[88] Kennedy was less happy: 'The President commented that the Prime Minister's message contained the best argument for taking no action. What we now need are strong arguments to explain why we have to act as we are acting'.[89] Kennedy nevertheless read out Macmillan's message, with its expressions of both support and warning, to the Congressional leadership at an ill-tempered meeting, shortly before his historic appearance on American television.[90] In his reply to Macmillan, Kennedy was at pains to rebut the suggestions that his actions were driven by domestic political calculation.[91] 'I assure you most solemnly', Kennedy wrote, 'that this is not simply a matter of aroused public opinion or of private passion against Cuba'.[92] Instead, it was 'so deep a breach in the conventions of the international stalemate that if unchallenged it would deeply shake confidence in the United States, especially in the light of my repeated warnings'.[93] Failure to react would invite still more dangerous moves, Kennedy argued. Accepting that European opinion needed careful attention, he reminded Macmillan that the United States too had been 'living under a missile threat,

we too have been doing that for some time'; while promising to be in the closest touch over Berlin, Kennedy had
little reassurance to offer, however, over the fire-first problem
from which he could see 'no sure escape'.[94] He nevertheless assured Macmillan that his naval commanders were
instructed to use the minimum of force.

In conclusion, it is now clear that relations between the
British and American governments during the first phase
of the crisis were different to how they appeared. British
officials in Washington were told about the missiles earlier
than has been believed, though it is still unclear how, and
when, Macmillan was briefed. The distinction between being
informed and being consulted is generally accepted. Ormsby-
Gore later made clear to the Foreign Secretary that, 'although
care was taken to gain support for the President's decision,
the decision was his alone. It cannot be said that other
governments were consulted with any intention of their advice
being taken into account'.[95] This distinction is, nevertheless, rather less clear cut than appears. Sir Evelyn Shuckburgh
argued in November 1962 that HMG 'were consulted in
the sense that we were given time to express an opinion
on the action which the President had decided he must
take'.[96] The government had thought this decision right,
so it had not raised any objection. 'If we thought it wrong
we should have said so', Sir Evelyn concluded. Given the
additional time afforded by the Washington contacts, the
British could have expressed their views at a more timely
point in US decision-making. Yet Whitehall did not act
with great urgency, and Macmillan adopted a 'wait and
see' approach. In any case British officials were not briefed
until the Friday and the President took his decision on
the Saturday. Whether pre-emptive British intervention would
have influenced Kennedy at this stage is open to serious
doubt. Nevertheless, it might be argued that there was at
least a form of consultation. Yet it was, in any case, one
thing for Kennedy to consult his allies – it was another, as
Ormsby-Gore made clear, to be guided by their opinions.
As the world moved toward the most serious nuclear confrontation of the Cold War, Kennedy's promise to Macmillan
that they would be in the closest contact now offered an
acid test of the 'special relationship'.

While Macmillan was irritated at the lack of consultation, and sceptical at Kennedy's chosen course of action, his attitude has some echoes of his behaviour over Suez, when 'militarist' impulses gave way to 'defeatist' political calculations.[97] In his memoir Macmillan states that indeed, 'in my first draft, I had thought of advising him to seize Cuba and have done with it; at any rate to avoid drifting into the situation which we had done at Suez.'[98] In addition, as he noted in his diary, 'I was alarmed lest Kennedy 'miss the bus' – he may never get rid of Cuban rockets except by trading them for Turkish, Italian or other bases. Thus Khrushchev will have won his point.'[99]

Moreover, in his first telephone conversation with Kennedy, on 22 October, the tenor of his advice was clear: 'what worries me, I'll be quite frank with you, [is] having a sort of dragging-on position. If you occupy Cuba, that's one thing. In my long experience we've always found that our weakness has been when we've not acted with sufficient strength.'[100] What worried Macmillan, so he told Kennedy, was the prospect of negotiating with Khrushchev, with 'all the cards . . . in this man's hands . . . And if we do have to talk to him, and meet him, in the last resort the more cards in our hands the better, in my view. You may say that's rather tough, and perhaps more cynical, but I think the more cards in our hands the better . . .'[101] As de Zulueta emphasised to Ormsby-Gore, Macmillan's 'personal feeling is somewhat in favour of a rather more decisive action than the Americans have in fact so far taken'[102] (a statement which might have surprised anyone reading his earlier message to Kennedy). As the week progressed, Macmillan's toughness abated. By Thursday, he advised against military action. This change in mind may well be explained by recognition of the risks of escalation, which Kennedy himself shared. Another explanation is that Macmillan learned from Ormsby-Gore of Kennedy's intentions, and adjusted his advice accordingly. If so, Ormsby-Gore's role was crucial to how the government handled the crisis and its relations with Washington.

4 Converging Perspectives and Divergent Views

Whenever and however the British government was told about the Soviet missiles, the decision to impose a naval quarantine around Cuba was taken by the American President and then communicated to his NATO allies. The issue of whether Britain was being consulted or merely informed assumed an immediate political significance in Britain. Kennedy's decision to impose the embargo without any consultation provoked strong public reactions. Gaitskell complained in Parliament on 30 October that 'It was a matter of great concern, I think to us all, that the British Government were not consulted before the decisions were taken.'[1] While the Labour leader spoke more in sadness than anger, colleagues on his left drew rather different conclusions. 'We now see that there is no special relationship, and never has been', declared one back bench Labour MP.[2] 'We are told,' wrote Richard Crossman in *The Guardian* on 26 October: 'that Britain's nuclear weapons do give us a place in the councils of the nations. And in particular make sure that the Americans will listen to us more than to any other ally. Well, after last Monday night, that little myth is exploded.'[3] In the *New Statesman*, Anthony Howard argued that the 'British government could hardly have its dependent status more brutally spelled out to it than it has this week'.[4]

For Macmillan, any irritation at Kennedy's behaviour quickly gave way to much more serious concern about what would happen next. Over the following week the President kept his promise to maintain the closest touch with the Prime Minister, and in addition to Ormsby-Gore's access to Kennedy and his senior advisers the President and the Prime Minister spoke regularly over the telephone. The existence of these discussions was kept secret and Macmillan became irritated that public ignorance of them created a wrong impression of his role, feeling 'that it is rather a bore, and has some dangers. The British people must not feel themselves slighted.'[5]

At what stage Britain had a right to be consulted over the imposition of the quarantine raises interesting issues, including the still contested question of Khrushchev's objectives and whether missiles in Cuba were part of a political strategy for resolving the problem of Berlin. Consultation was not simply a matter of diplomatic etiquette, nor of Britain's status in the 'special relationship'. It was potentially crucial for Britain's security. If Khrushchev responded against Berlin (or Turkey) American action in the Caribbean would have triggered armed confrontation in Europe. The British role in West Berlin, and the alignment of Kennedy's and Macmillan's approaches there, meant that Whitehall had every reason to be consulted over action that could provoke a Soviet response. The American strategist, Bernard Brodie, was told by a senior Foreign Office official that after Kennedy's speech on 22 October, he and his colleagues 'expected to a man, that the Russians would be in West Berlin the following day'.[6]

For the United States too, there were reasons to consult their closest NATO allies, other than diplomatic largesse. In Washington during the crisis, the Ambassadorial group on Berlin was used as the forum for briefing the British, French and West Germans on developments in Cuba. Within the group, American officials felt that, 'it would be advisable, as far as possible to tie the British, French, and Germans into the action we are taking in Cuba by letting them know in advance what we intended to do', although it was also recognised that there was a risk that prior notification might provoke public opposition from Macmillan.[7]

Moreover, the reactions of the allies prove critical to the outcome. Kennedy was deeply concerned to remain in control of events, conscious of how actions and reactions could lead down what Sherman Kent called the 'unintentioned stairway to general conflict'; yet, as Kent noted, even if events stopped a long way short of the cataclysm, 'there was still room for a thundering crisis, the outcome of which would depend in significant measure upon the way in which our allies would respond – whether they would support us or back away'.[8]

There were also treaty obligations. In the event of

aggression launched from Cuban territory against the United States, Article 6 of the NATO treaty meant that an attack on America would be treated as an attack on all the members of the alliance. Moreover, Article 4 of the treaty stated 'the Parties will consult together whenever, in the opinion of any of them, the territorial integrity, political independence or security of any of the Parties is threatened.'[9]

The United States had also undertaken in April and May 1962 to consult its NATO allies, if time permitted, concerning the use of nuclear weapons anywhere in the world.[10] These undertakings were separate from the specific and long-standing British–American agreement on the use of American nuclear forces from British territory, which President Kennedy reaffirmed in February 1961. In his televised address of 22 October Kennedy had stated that it would be 'the policy of this nation to regard any nuclear missile launched from Cuba against any nation in the Western Hemisphere as an attack by the Soviet Union on the United States, requiring a full retaliatory response upon the Soviet Union.'[11] Although this was not itself incompatible with a commitment to consult on using nuclear weapons, it did have major implications for NATO strategy. The Kennedy administration was currently engaged in moving American and NATO strategy away from 'Massive Retaliation' to a more flexible and credible posture, that was not based on an all-out nuclear attack against limited Soviet aggression.[12] The President's televised statement, made without any consultation with allies, appeared to discard the central assumptions of the new approach.

If the United States government believed that the Cuban deployment was designed to secure Khrushchev's goals in Berlin, or if Khrushchev could be expected to react to the Cuban blockade there, then the British, as indeed other NATO allies, had good reason to be consulted. What is very clear is that American officials, not least Kennedy himself, were convinced that Khrushchev would respond to the quarantine of Cuba against Berlin, Kennedy had already told Ormsby-Gore that he anticipated a Soviet response in Berlin, and when Dean Acheson briefed the North Atlantic Council on 22 October 1962 he warned: 'Some retaliatory action against Berlin seemed inevitable.'[13] Perhaps most significantly, Dean Rusk told the British, German and French Ambassadors that the American government believed that Khrushchev had intended to come to the United Nations in November with the missiles in place and with demands for major concessions over Berlin.[14] Moreover, the Secretary of State: 'wished to emphasise that this assessment of Russian strategy indicated why Cuba could not be regarded as just a problem for the Western hemisphere. It involved us all, and this was one reason why the United States had decided on a policy of minimum force.'[15] While the argument that 'more violent methods' could imperil western interests elsewhere might reassure Europeans, Rusk's statement begged the obvious question of why, if Cuba was an alliance problem, had the United States acted unilaterally.

KHRUSHCHEV'S MOTIVES

The issue of why Khrushchev deployed the missiles in Cuba has preoccupied American scholars. The consensus among American analysts of the crisis was that the principal reason for the deployment was to redress the imbalance in strategic nuclear forces.[16] Key American decision-makers believed that this was the principal reason for Khrushchev's actions, and discounted the idea that defending Cuba was the primary Soviet concern. Disagreement remains about Khrushchev's decision and the relative significance of different factors in Soviet policy-making. This disagreement extends to Soviet analysts and officials, though as Lebow and Stein observe, 'almost every Soviet official who claims any knowledge of the missile deployment insists that one of the important objectives was to protect Fidel Castro and his revolution'.[17] Khrushchev himself stated that the defence of Cuba was the principal motivation, though he also noted other factors in the decision, notably 'the "balance of power" and the desire to give the Americans "a little of their own medicine"'.[18] The study of Lebow and Stein provides support for Khrushchev's account, but also attaches greater significance to the role of the Jupiter missiles in Turkey and to the Soviet domestic political context in Khrushchev's decision.[19]

What is clear from British and American records is that Berlin was seen by British and American officials, including both heads of government, as a crucial factor in Soviet calculations. A considered Whitehall analysis of why Khrushchev deployed the missiles did not appear until after the crisis was resolved.[20] The Foreign Office disseminated a tentative assessment of Soviet motives on 2 November.[21] The Joint Intelligence Committee did provide an appreciation of the validity of the photographic evidence, which was circulated to the Cabinet on 26 October.[22] The JIC was:

> in agreement with the US authorities that a Soviet MRBM capability is being built up in Cuba which could, in our assessment, be up to 1100 nm range. Based on the evidence available we are not in a position to assess whether the capability extends (as the US authorities believe) to the IRBM, i.e. 2 200 nm.
>
> Provided nuclear warheads are available, missile units in Cuba could be allocated certain strategic targets on the American Continent at present allocated to other Soviet forces. If all known sites are completed, we estimate that the overall Soviet initial launch capability against the US will have increased significantly by the end of 1962.[23]

This preliminary analysis was based solely on photographic evidence, and without more basic data, 'a firm UK assessment was difficult'.[24] There is nothing to indicate that British officials were aware of, or could discern, anything which their American counterparts could not. In particular, the JIC noted that: 'Neither we nor the US authorities have any evidence on which to judge whether nuclear warheads have or have not reached Cuba'.[25]

The British intelligence community did not fully endorse US appreciations. On IRBMs, the JIC stated that 'on the basis of the evidence available we cannot positively identify the sites as being associated with the 2 200 nm missile'.[26] Similarly, although accepting that there were MRBMs, and while not disagreeing with the US assessment, the JIC felt that there was 'the possibility that these sites are for the 650 nm missile [SS-3 NATO-designation]' rather than the 1100 nm SS-4 (NATO-designation).[27]

In Cabinet on 23 October the Foreign Secretary told his colleagues that it was difficult to assess Khrushchev's policy:

> President Kennedy has suggested that it might be either desperation or ambition and both were possible. Soviet setbacks in agriculture and the failure of their economy to meet earlier hopes of overtaking the West might be leading Mr Khrushchev into a military gamble... But he himself thought it unlikely that Mr. Khrushchev wanted to start a war. It was more probable that he was seeking to improve his bargaining position, particularly in relation to Berlin, and that he wanted the United States Government to appreciate from their own experience the Soviet reaction to the presence of United States' missile bases in Europe close to Russia and their determination to secure their removal.[28]

Home's assessment in Cabinet appears to have excluded both the defence of Cuba and the redress of the missile gap as explanations for Khrushchev's action. The considered views of the JIC are not yet available, though the Foreign Office's submission to the JIC on 26 October can be read, as the Foreign Office Northern Department's analysis was given to the US embassy:

> It must be assumed that [the] Soviets calculated that [the] US would sooner or later become aware of [the] extent of [the] missile sites (they cannot be camouflaged) and that some vigorous response would have to be forthcoming from Washington. But [the] value of [the] missile sites was presumably so great that the Soviets felt justified in taking [the] risk; moreover they may have banked on installation being erected very quickly. In an air of generally peaceful east–west relations with themselves doing everything to play down an imminent Berlin crisis, they may have hoped that [the] US, finding themselves faced with a fait accompli, and recognizing a Soviet commitment even if in general terms to defend Cuba and protect shipping to it, would in [the] end accept [the] situation with nothing more than loud noises and appeals to [the] UN etc. at which incidentally [the] whole [issue of] foreign bases could be raised.[29]

The Northern Department's preliminary conclusion concerning Khrushchev's objectives was that:

> We think it unlikely that [the] Soviets really believed that installation of [the] missile sites was necessary solely for the defense of Cuba and would be accepted as such. It seems much more likely that [the] Soviets decided to install [the] missile complex because once it became fully operational at [the] end of this year, it would have given them [a] significant increase in their nuclear strike capacity against [the] US and – an important aspect – a capacity inside the US warning network. It would have represented an extremely tempting short cut towards reducing [the] imbalance in strategic striking power between [the] Soviets and US without [the] Soviets having to wait years to achieve this. Hitherto [the] amount of damage [the] Soviets could inflict on US territory in [the] event of war would be less than [the] US could inflict on Soviet territory – an imbalance made worse by [the] US decision to produce 800 Minuteman missiles, and one which could not quickly be redressed by increased Soviet missile production.[30]

The argument that the deployment was, in part, a response to the US ICBM build-up, was emphasised in the Foreign Office assessment in November.[31] Nevertheless, the analysis implied that the missiles in Cuba would significantly alter the strategic balance and indeed ministers were later advised that it was an 'attempt to alter, on a massive scale, the delicate balance of power on which the peace of the world rests'.[32] In the White House on 16 October, McGeorge Bundy had asked whether the Soviet deployment changed the strategic balance. McNamara replied, 'Mac, I asked the Chiefs that this afternoon, in effect. And they said "substantially". My own personal view, is not at all.'[33] Ormsby-Gore clearly agreed with McNamara, telling Kennedy that the MRBMs were not a significant military threat.[34] Whitehall, however, shared the view of the US Joint Chiefs.

One reason for this was that the Foreign Office attached importance to the circumvention of Ballistic Missile Early Warning System (BMEWS) coverage. In the event, the Americans were able to provide some early warning of missile attack from Cuba by adapting satellite tracking and other radar stations.[35] The unsatisfactory nature of these ad hoc arrangements was demonstrated when the US North American Air Defense Command was falsely alerted to a ballistic missile launch from Cuba early on 28 October.[36] In October 1962 construction of the BMEWS system was not finished. The Fylingdales station in Yorkshire was not due for completion until 1963, and it seems that the Jodrell Bank telescope, then the only British means of detecting a ballistic missile by radar, 'remained in a position to be activated by the declaration of "state of military vigilance."'[37]

The implications of missiles in Cuba for the strategic balance were potentially crucial for European security. McGeorge Bundy minuted Kennedy on 22 October:

> Mr President: The one thing I left out of the message to the Prime Minister is that if the Soviet nuclear build-up in Cuba continues, it would be a threat to the whole strategic balance of power, because really large numbers of missiles from this launch could create a first-strike temptation. Any such shift in the balance would be just as damaging to our allies as to us. The missiles that are there now do not create this hazard but a further build-up would. This is probably the most important single justification of our action from the point of view of the west as a whole.[38]

Dean Acheson spoke in similar vein to the North Atlantic Council on 22 October when he said that 'the action taken by the Soviet Union in Cuba was an important step towards readjusting the nuclear balance between the Soviet Union and the United States and therefore constituted a threat to NATO as a whole'.[39] American vulnerability to Soviet attack remained a central and unsolveable problem for NATO, permeating western debates about a credible NATO strategy over the ensuing decades.

Policy-makers on both sides of the Atlantic clearly saw the links between the situation in the Caribbean and position in Europe. The key concern was Berlin. The Northern Department's assessment stated that:

> if Khrushchev was to bring things to a head fairly soon over Berlin something must be done urgently to rectify

> [the] imbalance if [the] Soviets would be negotiating
> politically in an inferior military position. Khrushchev
> may well have calculated that once [the] Cuban missile
> complex [was] completed he could frighten [the] Americans
> off taking determined action in Berlin by pointing to
> their own vulnerability to attack from his Cuban base
> and thus obtain heavy leverage in negotiations on Berlin
> which he has been planning for the end of [the] year.[40]

The analysis was essentially consistent with that of the State
Department, and the CIA. The (retrospective) judgement
of the CIA was that while Khrushchev 'believed the creation of Soviet missiles bases in Cuba would greatly enhance
the USSR's ability to deter another US-sponsored attempt
to destroy the Castro regime', the

> basic motivation underlying Khrushchev's bold gamble
> in deploying strategic missiles in Cuba was the compel-
> ling need of a dramatic breakthrough which would
> strengthen the USSR's position on a whole range of
> questions in the contest with the US. The Cuban venture
> had the direct and immediate purpose of strengthening
> Khrushchev's position for a major diplomatic showdown
> on the Berlin and German questions which he planned
> to launch before the end of the year.[41]

There had been some divergence between the Foreign Office
and the State Department over Khrushchev's attitude towards
Berlin, as Dean Rusk told the French, German and British
Ambassadors on 24 October.[42] The State Department's 'more
alarmist assessment' focused on Soviet insistence that western troops must leave Berlin.[43] The Americans believed that
during the summer Khrushchev had decided that negotiations would not achieve Soviet objectives. Yet there were
indications of Khrushchev's strong personal commitment
to his objectives in Berlin. Together with other factors, such
as the situation in East Germany and the state of Sino–
Soviet relations, the Americans believed that the Soviets
had concluded a showdown on Berlin was inevitable. However, 'there were also indications that the Soviet Government and Khrushchev personally had become doubtful as
to whether they could win in a showdown and that alter-

natives might be either ignominious retreat or nuclear war'.[44] The Soviets had publicly and privately made clear that they wanted a Berlin settlement in a relatively short time, though not until after the US Congressional elections. The American government therefore, 'tended to believe Soviet action was probably geared to a showdown on Berlin, intended to be timed with Khrushchev's arrival in US [in late November] and completion of installation of these missiles in Cuba'.[45]

The Foreign Office's 'tentative' estimate of Soviet actions, on 2 November, concurred:

> the Soviet Government saw the need for some action which could quickly provide some addition to their capability to strike at the United States, in order to provide greater backing for their pressures on the West on a wide range of issues, and in particular to enable them to apply adequate leverage upon the Americans for a settlement of the Berlin question on terms which would enable Khrushchev to claim that he had carried out his promises. The installation of missiles in Cuba was meant to provide the Soviet solution to this problem.[46]

Sir Frank Roberts, UK Ambassador to Moscow, was unconvinced that Berlin was the specific objective of Khrushchev's manoeuvre. For Khrushchev there was a link between Berlin and Cuba:

> It certainly exists, because in Khrushchev's calculations there must be some connexion between Berlin and virtually every act of policy. The question of questions, he is inclined to say, is disarmament; but the more immediate problem is Berlin; a solution of which would significantly contribute to disarmament.
>
> From this starting point and recalling Khrushchev's well-known proclivity for setting out on courses of action without correctly foreseeing where they could lead him, coupled with his undoubted talent for making the best of the resulting situation, I cannot help feeling that the purpose of installing the missiles in Cuba was general rather than precise i.e. to strengthen the Soviet power position in the world *a toutes fins utiles*. In [this] context

disarmament (more especially in the sense of dismantling bases) and Berlin would naturally loom large.[47]

'The essential purpose, as I judge it', Roberts explained on 8 November

> was strikingly to increase the Soviet Union's military strength relative to that of the United States, and thereby to improve the Soviet Union's bargaining power. I do not believe that this objective related primarily to a particular issue (i.e. Berlin) at a particular time (i.e. this month) but that it was intended to apply to all issues and for the foreseeable future.[48]

The Soviets did not raise the issue of Berlin during the Cuban missile crisis,[49] and when it was suggested to Khrushchev that American pressure on Cuba should be met with Soviet pressure against Berlin, he angrily dismissed the idea.[50] This in itself does not prove that Berlin was not an original objective.

Whether Berlin was Khrushchev's principal objective when he embarked upon his Caribbean adventure it was very much in the minds of Kennedy and Macmillan as they contemplated the evolving crisis. In his reply to Kennedy, Macmillan had emphasised the risks to the alliance and the probability that Khrushchev would respond to the blockade with action in Europe. Later, on the evening of Monday 22 October, he discussed the matter directly with the President. Then, and on subsequent nights, the two leaders spoke directly on the telephone. For the Prime Minister these conversations 'were a great comfort . . . since I felt all the time intimately informed of each changing aspect of these terrible days'.[51] Macmillan's direct communications with Kennedy during the crisis were unprecedented, and no other allied leader was afforded such an opportunity.

The first considered British public response to the crisis was the Foreign Secretary's televised speech to the International Chamber of Commerce on the evening of 23 October. Lord Home also dealt with the situation in the Himalayas, where China had used military force against India over their territorial dispute. On Cuba, it was made clear that the British government condemned Soviet behaviour and supported the United States:

By putting medium-range and intermediate range ballistic missiles into Cuba, Russia is deliberately placing her own power in a position to do three things – to threaten the United States, to threaten the Caribbean, and beyond those two to threaten South America. We must recognize that this is plainly an act of power . . . We shall support the United States in the Security Council so as to try to bring the new danger in this new area under control.[52]

The general expression of support for the US in the Security Council satisfied the Americans, but disguised British misgivings about the legality (and prudence) of American action. The legal question presented problems for the management of British–American relations.[53] As noted, American economic warfare against Cuba had been a major irritant. Now the government's legal advisers believed that American blockade did not conform to international law. This issue was interwoven with the domestically difficult issue of American interference with British ships. The government therefore sought to persuade British ship owners to co-operate with the US navy, while reserving their legal rights.

LEGALITY OF THE BLOCKADE

Ormsby-Gore had warned Kennedy on 21 October that the legal issue would cause problems for the British. The US government justified the quarantine under articles 6 and 8 of the 1947 Inter-American Treaty of Reciprocal Assistance (Rio Treaty), whereby action could be sanctioned by a two thirds majority of the OAS, in the face of a 'fact or situation which might endanger the peace of America'.[54] As Ormsby-Gore had reminded the President, Britain had not signed the Rio Treaty. Neither, of course, had the USSR, and the idea that countries could be bound by treaties which they had not signed was highly problematic. Nevertheless, the US Attorney General, Robert Kennedy, told the National Security Council on 22 October that in his opinion the 'blockade action would be illegal if it were not supported by the OAS' – a view not shared by Secretary Rusk.[55] President

Kennedy agreed with his brother, telling Congressional leaders that OAS endorsement was necessary, although, the quarantine could still be made legal by an American declaration of war.[56] Nevertheless, the announcement of the quarantine preceded the vote of the OAS, on 23 October. Although the American legal position was based on support of the OAS, it was made clear to the British, French and West German Ambassadors by Paul Nitze on 22 October that the Americans would 'go ahead if necessary even if this support was not forthcoming'.[57]

At the request of the Cabinet, the American legal position was considered by the Lord Chancellor, Lord Dilhorne.[58] After consulting the Solicitor-General, Sir Peter Rawlinson, the Attorney-General, Sir John Hobson, and Sir Francis Vallat, the Legal Adviser to the Foreign Office, he reported their judgement on the legality of the blockade, which was circulated to Cabinet on 25 October.[59] The paper endorsed the Foreign Office view. Dilhorne explained that:

> In our view the imposition of the 'quarantine' cannot be justified as 'pacific blockade' under international law. In fact, the United States' conduct is not in conformity with international law.
>
> We think that the most favourable line of argument that can be advanced in support of the United States is that the conduct of Cuba and the Soviet Union constitutes a threat to the United States of such imminence as to necessitate the taking of immediate steps to render that threat nugatory. But we doubt that this can be established as the United States' action appears to be designed to prevent the threat becoming imminent.
>
> If the threat could be regarded as immediate, the right of self-defence would entitle them under international law to destroy the missile sites and they would be equally entitled to stop war-heads reaching those sites. The issue depends on the immediacy of the threat being sufficient to justify the United States in acting before having recourse to the Security Council.[60]

Dilhorne and his colleagues were well aware of the political realities facing the government and he advised that, when confronted in Parliament, the best line 'would be to state the accepted principles of international law as to the right of self-defence, but to refuse to express any opinion as to their applicability in circumstances which are not yet fully known'.[61] He nevertheless recommended that HMG should make clear to the US government their views on the illegality of the situation, and endorse a demand by the General Council of British Shipping that the legal rights of British ships be preserved. While in the present circumstances the government should co-operate 'and not stand on our rights, we [should] not concede that they have any legal right to search or detain British ships on the High Seas'.[62]

Dilhorne's paper provoked a spirited exchange with Lord Hailsham, the Lord President, a constitutional lawyer, and subsequently the Lord Chancellor himself. While accepting that 'the right of blockade cannot be exercised in peace under any canon of international law so far accepted', Hailsham questioned whether the Americans should be told in such blunt terms, arguing that:

> On purely legal grounds international law is not an exact science; my father used to say with some justification that it was almost entirely invented by text book writers. But at any rate it develops with rather more fluidity than municipal systems. In particular classical international law implies a distinct difference between peace and war (in the latter of which cases blockade is a normal right on which we have always insisted). I doubt whether this theory, based on the sailing ship and the canon, can be strictly applied any longer to the age of the nuclear warhead and the rocket trained on 'friendly' territory and ready to go off at a moment's notice. Article 51 of the Charter preserves the right of self-defence, and since this includes war, cannot the greater include the less? In other words are we not in danger of making asses of ourselves?[63]

Reflecting recently, Hailsham argued that: 'Article 51 of the U.N. Charter, expressly reserves the right of self-defence. Since the Russian actions were obviously aggressive and threatened the very existence of the USA, Kennedy was clearly entitled to take the counter measures which he did.'[64] The view that Article 51 of the UN Charter provided sufficient legal justification for Kennedy's action was taken at the time by Dean Acheson, and the US Attorney General's deputy, Nicholas Katzenbach.[65]

Foreign Office doubts about the blockade extended to scepticism at the use of the term 'quarantine', which the Americans had adopted to distinguish their activities from a blockade, which was recognised as an act of war. The British Ambassador to the UN, Sir Patrick Dean, was instructed by the Foreign Office to suggest more precise language in drafting the UN Security Resolution, as the 'use of a word such as "quarantine" may lay the resolution open to unnecessary criticism and ridicule.'[66] The term quarantine was first proposed within the State Department 'for historical and psychological reasons', in part associated with Franklin Roosevelt's call for a quarantine of the aggressors before the Second World War. Dean Rusk himself initially considered the distinction between 'quarantine' and blockade might be seen as a semantic 'gimmick', but was persuaded of the case for 'a defensive quarantine'.[67] In considering the possible extension of the quarantine to POL, Macmillan used the term 'siege' in Cabinet on the Tuesday. More substantively, the Foreign Office was keen to have the Security Council Resolution amended to provide authority for the continuation of American measures, so as to provide a more tenable legal position.[68] Whatever the legal niceties, the Soviets would, of course, have vetoed any such resolution in the Security Council.

On 22 October Macmillan had responded to Kennedy before receiving the considered views of his legal officers, though he was well aware of the general issues, and clearly felt the need to subordinate respect for international law to political support for Kennedy. Macmillan thus sought to steer around the legal objection, telling the House of Commons on 25 October: 'I do not think that this is the moment to go into the niceties of international law'.[69] The Foreign Secretary was also concerned about the public presentation of the government's views, and minuted the Prime Minister on 27 October:

> Some time before Parliament meets I would like a word about this [the legality of the American blockade]. I don't

much like serving written notice on the United States now but what I am more concerned about is what is said in the House of Lords. I should have thought it would be impossible for the Lord Chancellor to refuse to give an opinion if he is directly challenged to do so. But if he has to give an opinion it may be difficult for him to fudge it. And yet I am very anxious that we should not publicly take sides against the United States by saying that Her Majesty's Government doubt whether the blockade is legally justified.[70]

While the Foreign Office was naturally concerned with the principle of the blockade, the Prime Minister and his colleagues also had to consider the stopping and searching of British ships. In Cabinet the view was expressed that 'there were objections in principle to allowing British ships in peacetime to be searched on the high seas', though the government 'had no objection to the imposition of the blockade since British ships had already been instructed not to carry arms to Cuba'.[71] Macmillan suggested to a sympathetic Ambassador Bruce on 24 October, that if the government was to tell the US authorities where British ships were and what they were carrying, it would only be necessary for them then to identify themselves to any American warships.[72] On 25 October, Ormsby-Gore was instructed to explain that:

British shipowners have shown a sympathetic understanding of the American dilemma but are anxious lest their cooperation in the immediate context of the arms blockade should, by setting a precedent, prejudice their long term interest. Her Majesty's Government view the situation in a similar light. As a leading maritime nation we feel bound to avoid as far as possible any situation in which we can be seen to be condoning a breach of the principle of freedom of navigation or of international law relevant to it. Drastic enforcement of the blockade measures against British shipping would cause acute difficulties for us in Parliament and outside, and would be liable to alienate much of the present public sympathy with support for Her Majesty's Government's stand behind the United States.[73]

Moreover, the Americans were to be told that HMG was 'not satisfied as to the legality of the blockade in international law. However, for the reasons given above we are anxious to play down the legal aspects. We think it reasonable that the Americans for their part should help by applying their interdiction to British ships with the utmost restraint and discrimination.'[74] These views were conveyed to the State Department in a meeting between Lord Hood, Minister from the Washington embassy, and George Ball on 25 October.[75] The issue of whether to present the Americans with a further written statement of British legal objections was decided as the crisis was being resolved. Dilhorne did not wish to see the matter aired in public, but was still concerned, 'lest our tacit acquiescence in interference with British ships on the High Seas on this occasion should come to be regarded as precedent justifying similar action in the future'.[76] Sir Francis Vallat, while recognising that 'from the strictly legal point of view it is desirable that we should have our position on record with the Americans', felt the Washington embassy's conversations with the State Department were sufficient.[77] A formal note to the Americans now would be 'otiose'.[78] Macmillan was keen for the matter to be dropped.[79]

The Foreign Office categorised four types of British ships that could become involved in the blockade: those entering the Caribbean from any port, but not destined for Cuba; those destined for Cuba which had not loaded at a Communist port; tankers destined for Cuba from Communist ports; and dry cargo ships destined for Cuba from Communist ports.[80] The Foreign Office hoped that the Americans would agree to confine their action against the first three categories to identification. As to the fourth category:

> it is now more improbable than ever that any British Master would knowingly attempt to carry to Cuba any of the items in the proclamation on interdiction . . . or indeed arms of any description. We realise however that the Russians may try to evade the blockade by using British ships for the carriage of e.g. electronic equipment disguised as innocent cargo. Masters are being asked to exercise the utmost vigilance to guard against this but

we recognise that the blockade forces may on occasion consider it prudent to search a ship in this category. We trust however that the extent to which searches are instituted will be proportionate to the risk involved, which in our estimation is slight.[81]

The government expected that ship owners would instruct Masters to comply with blockade directives, 'while reserving their legal rights where circumstances warrant this'; the Foreign Office was nevertheless clear that, 'Her Majesty's Government must also formally reserve the right to extend such diplomatic and legal protection to British shipping as may be permissible in accordance with international law.'[82]

Ship owners agreed to provide the Ministry of Transport with lists of shipping in the area, which were given to the Shipping Attaché in Washington to reduce risks of delay and inconvenience to ships. George Ball informed Lord Hood that the US Navy had been told that, 'in the case of friendly shipping, they were not expected to do more than a spot check', though tankers carrying freight might need to be inspected.[83] These arrangements did not create problems during the crisis. In the event, only one ship, a Soviet-chartered, Lebanese-registered vessel with a Greek crew, the *Marucla*, was stopped and searched. A British tanker, the *Suiaco*, bound for Jamaica, was allowed through the quarantine line without inspection.[84]

While the Macmillan government subordinated legal contention to political imperative, Macmillan and his colleagues were more adamant on the extension of the blockade beyond cargoes associated with 'offensive' military forces. In Cabinet, Macmillan said that the 'possible extension of the blockade was the point which had caused most difficulty as it was clearly the most dangerous, since it envisaged the interception of aircraft and the reduction of Cuba by siege.'[85] Privately Macmillan believed that such action was 'patently "illegal"'.[86] Ormsby-Gore had made clear to Kennedy on 21 October that Britain was opposed to the inclusion of POL, and on 23 October he was instructed to oppose the suggestion that tankers be covered: 'Oil cannot surely be regarded as an offensive military weapon in terms of President Kennedy's statement or of Mr Acheson's statement [to the NATO Council]. Interdiction of oil supplies to Cuba would strike at the moral basis of the American action and convert a purely military blockade into an economic blockade.'[87] Ormsby-Gore raised the issue at an Ambassadorial group meeting on 23 October, emphasising that it would mean 'putting the squeeze' on the Cuban people rather than being directed against the missiles'.[88] In the event, as Ormsby-Gore reported to Macmillan later that day, Kennedy had decided that, 'for the time being', the Americans would not try and stop the importation of POL.[89] Macmillan remained conscious that the possible extension of the blockade could nevertheless create difficulties. He minuted Home on 26 October, noting that the extension of the blockade would mean trouble. 'We should be studying the possibility *now*.'[90] As the situation deteriorated, extending the blockade emerged as the principal alternative to military action, and was thus supported within ExComm by those anxious to avoid military confrontation. Whether Kennedy would have opted for the state of 'siege' or taken military action remains a major and contested issue. Extending the blockade did resurface in the British–American context in November when Kennedy told Macmillan he was considering it to help force the withdrawal of the Soviet Ilyushin-28 bombers. This is discussed in Chapter Nine.

Thus divergent British and American views over the blockade were managed to avoid the impression of disunity. The Foreign Office sought to accommodate legal principle with political necessity. From the outset, Macmillan subordinated international law to the exigencies of the crisis. His primary concern was how the Soviets would respond to the blockade. Kennedy and his advisers seem to have had little doubt that Khrushchev would react in Europe. This in itself is important in any broader assessment of the 'special relationship'. Having failed to consult Macmillan over the blockade decision, however, the President's recognition of possible global consequences led him into unprecedented discussions with the British Prime Minister. Macmillan was anxious to play a role in any international summit. As the blockade now came into effect, everyone waited to see whether diplomacy or force would settle the issue, and with what consequences.

5 Westminster and Hyde Park: British Politics and the Crisis

During the Cold War British political attitudes to national and European security passed through alternating phases of consensus and conflict. By the early 1960s defence and foreign policy were the focus of intense political debate both between government and opposition and also within the Labour Party. In particular, a bipartisan approach to British and NATO nuclear weapons had collapsed, with Labour and the Liberal Party adopting anti-nuclear policies. With the creation of the CND in 1958 opposition to nuclear weapons led to a mass movement, then unprecedented in twentieth century British politics. This chapter examines the domestic reaction to the missile crisis, and in particular the responses of the Labour, and anti-nuclear, movements. It also briefly explores the domestic political consequences of the crisis for the public debate about British national security.

Toward the end of the 1950s there were fierce arguments within the Labour Party over whether Britain should renounce nuclear weapons regardless of the actions of other states or pursue disarmament in the context of negotiated and reciprocal action.[1] Gaitskell shared his party's opposition to an independent British deterrent, but strongly opposed what was termed 'unilateral nuclear disarmament'.[2] This was nevertheless adopted by Labour Party conference in 1960, provoking a determined and successful effort, heralded by Gaitskell's famous conference speech, to reverse the decision. By 1962 'the unilateralists' were defeated, though Labour was clearly committed against an independent deterrent. There was also strong opposition within the party to both the Thor and Polaris bases. In other respects, however, Labour's thinking on NATO nuclear strategy, influenced by figures such as Denis Healey, resonated with that

77

of the Kennedy administration. In February 1962 Gaitskell met Kennedy at the White House, and found him 'highly intelligent, well-informed, vital, direct, no small talk, no postures, rational, above all rational'.[3] According to one of his biographers, in their discussions on nuclear weapons, the views of Kennedy and Gaitskell were 'nearly identical'.[4]

The Conservatives faced different problems. In part, this reflected the legacy of remaining in office for over a decade and manifested itself in what, in October 1961, Quintin Hailsham described as a feeling of 'fecklessness and disunity' within the party.[5] Foreign policy had been a source of conflict for the Conservatives, most demonstrably over Suez in 1956 and within the party, as elsewhere, Suez was very much the ghost at the feast during the missile crisis. Macmillan's foreign policy was ambitious, and for his critics, consumed a disproportionate amount of his energy. The Prime Minister pursued fundamental changes in British foreign policy, seeking not only membership of the European Economic Community, but also to manage and accelerate decolonisation in Africa.

At the heart of Macmillan's foreign policy was the 'special relationship' with the United States. Macmillan cultivated both Eisenhower and Kennedy, and in particular sought to re-establish relations in the nuclear field that would serve British as well as mutual interests. While the term 'interdependence' was used to characterise British–American relations, the nuclear (and intelligence) relationships were more complex and extensive, and their full story is still only emerging.[6] Whatever Macmillan's success with these objectives, by 1962 the internal problems of the Conservative Party and the increasing credibility of the Opposition posed a growing threat to his government. In July, in a dramatic and draconian attempt to reverse his fortunes and those of his government, Macmillan sacked a third of the Cabinet in what became known as the 'Night of the Long Knives'.[7]

How far domestic political factors influenced the external policies pursued by Macmillan and Gaitskell is difficult to discern. Both parties contained those characterised as 'anti-American', though Gaitskell, at least, could ignore the more virulent 'fellow travellers' within the party. Whereas 'anti-Americanism' was visible on the left of the Labour Party, the 'strength of anti-American feeling in the Conservative party', so Anthony Howard observed, was 'always . . . a skilfully kept secret'.[8] Hostility to the United States, much of it the legacy of Suez, was nevertheless of limited importance to how the Conservative leadership behaved during the crisis. Macmillan was aware of Conservative sensitivities on, for example, the searching of British ships by the US navy, but this owed as much to visceral notions of maritime pride, as anti-Americanism. Overall the Cuban crisis afforded the opportunity of bipartisanship, though this did not preclude criticism of the Kennedy administration on the Opposition benches. As seen in Chapter Two, Labour was strongly critical of Kennedy's actions over the Bay of Pigs. On the other hand, Gaitskell, Healey and other senior figures within the party also had an affinity with the administration's criticisms of NATO strategy and indeed much else in his political outlook. For many progressive Conservatives also, Kennedy was the embodiment of the values and dynamism which they looked for in British society.

Nevertheless, there was vigorous public opposition to Kennedy's response to the missiles, most of it organised by CND and proponents of direct action in the Committee of 100.[9] The scale and significance of these demonstrations was limited. A more general level of disquiet, however, emerged about the possible consequences of American action against Cuba, and at the failure of the Kennedy administration to consult the British government. It is evident that political and press opinion changed during the week of the crisis. As the State Department Bureau of Intelligence and Research reported on 28 October, the British press was almost unanimously opposed to the expected US economic measures against Cuba before President Kennedy's speech, and despite the change in the situation resulting from the evidence of Soviet missiles, only the right wing *Daily Express* at first unreservedly supported the US blockade.[10] Second day editorials were 'somewhat more sympathetic but still displayed reserve regarding American action . . . A swing to editorial understanding and sympathy for the US move appears to be continuing, as the implications of the Soviet gambit sink in.'[11] By then the American embassy believed that a majority of the British people accepted and supported US action. An opinion poll, published in the *Daily Mail* on 25 October, showed that 58 per cent thought that US actions were justified, and 66 per cent thought that Britain should support the US, while only 30 per cent were opposed.[12] This rather sanguine description of British attitudes disguises the doubts of senior policy-makers and opposition leaders about Kennedy's handling of the crisis, and in particular his failure to consult before embarking upon action which was objectionable in principle and potentially hazardous. Nevertheless, there was general, and moreover, growing, support for the American position as the week progressed.

News of events in Washington and the Caribbean had begun to percolate to London over the weekend. The Director of the CIA, John McCone, told the US National Security Council on the afternoon of Monday 22 October that the London *Evening Standard* had printed 'a great deal of information about the existence of Soviet strategic missiles in Cuba'.[13] Hugh Gaitskell was told of the missiles on 22 October, at a dinner given in honour of General Lauris Norstad, the Supreme Allied Commander Europe (SACEUR). Macmillan recounts that he took the Labour leader to the Cabinet room 'and showed him all the documents, and the President's speech. He did *not* take a very robust attitude. He thought his party "would not like it". I doubt if they would like any decision – firm decision – on any subject.'[14] The Leader of the Opposition was therefore informed before the Prime Minister consulted the Cabinet.

For the Cabinet, and for the British people, the Cuban missile crisis began on the morning of Tuesday 23 October. Macmillan briefed his colleagues on the messages from Kennedy, and his initial exchanges with the President, in a meeting lasting some three hours. The Cabinet

agreed that in any immediate comment on the situation Ministers should take the line that the Government were deeply concerned at the provocation presented by Soviet action in Cuba, that they had been kept fully informed of developments by the United States authorities, that they would give full support to the United States in the forthcoming debate in the Security Council and the United Kingdom representative was being instructed accordingly; and that they had no objection to the imposition of the blockade since British ships had already been instructed not to carry arms to Cuba.[15]

Macmillan described his Cabinet colleagues as 'rather shaken but satisfied'.[16] Nevertheless, the blockade caused difficulties for, as noted, the Foreign Office believed that the quarantine was illegal, and as Ormsby-Gore had already made clear to the President, Britain's traditional attitude toward the freedom of the seas would place the government in 'an awkward position'.[17] Writing in the *New Statesman*, Anthony Howard described the possible search of British ships by the American navy as 'a fuse wire that could well set off a dangerous explosion among the traditionalists in the Conservative Party'.[18]

LABOUR PARTY

The attitude of the Opposition leadership was informed by private briefings from both the British and American governments. At 5 pm on Tuesday 23 October Gaitskell, his deputy, George Brown, and the Shadow Foreign Secretary, Harold Wilson, met Macmillan and Home. Macmillan noted in his diary: 'They hadn't much to say. Brown was more robust than G[aitskell]. Fortunately, they all distrust each other profoundly' (shortly after the crisis, Wilson indeed challenged Brown for the deputy leadership of the party).[19] The official record of the meeting, however, shows that Gaitskell made clear both Labour's general support for the government, and his doubts on the blockade. The Labour leader said: 'that there was not much between the two Parties on this question. There would be no wave of anti-Americanism sweeping through the Labour Party. At the same time it had to be recognised that there were certain weaknesses in the American position, in particular on the blockade.'[20]

Macmillan himself was aware of the legal and political problems of a blockade, though he did not share these doubts with the Leader of the Opposition. Gaitskell was particularly concerned about consultation between the two governments and floated the suggestion, raised earlier at the Shadow Cabinet, that Macmillan might go to Washington. He later made the suggestion public. There were echoes of Attlee's famous and dramatic trip to Washington in 1950 when the Labour Prime Minister was seen to voice British concerns about the use of American atomic weapons in the Korean War. Macmillan indicated to Gaitskell and his colleagues that he would consider the idea, and indeed later in the week he made the suggestion to Kennedy.[21] The Foreign Secretary, however, was less convinced. Home told the Labour leaders that so long as the crisis revolved around Cuba, the American public would view a visit from the British Prime Minister with the gravest suspicion, feeling he was pressing Kennedy to pursue a course of 'appeasement'.[22] He repeated this argument to Cabinet on Thursday.[23]

Shortly after meeting the Prime Minister, Gaitskell and Brown went to the home of the CIA Station Chief, Archie Roosevelt, where they were briefed by Chet Cooper and David Bruce, together with two other embassy officers.[24] They were not accompanied by Harold Wilson. According to Sherman Kent: 'Cooper told the story and showed the photographs. Gaitskell, who up until the time had feared that the President was confusing the issue of the Soviet buildup by making it appear that surface-to-air missiles were offensive weapons, confessed his earlier apprehensions and acknowledged the they were ill-founded. He was visibly shaken by the evidence of the long-range missiles.'[25] However, according to Cooper, Gaitskell 'made much of the analogy between Cuba and Turkey and brushed aside most of the standard arguments about the difference between the two'.[26] Indeed, he 'pointed out that the United States had bases in England and bases in Turkey . . . and that if we got the missiles out of Turkey, perhaps the Russians would get their missiles out of Cuba'.[27] In the House of Commons on Thursday 25 October he publicly linked the two by stating that if the United States attacked Cuba because of the existence of nuclear bases, 'it would be very difficult to see how the Russians would not be able to justify a similar attack on Turkey.'[28] The CIA made more impact on the Labour leader with the military case. Gaitskell 'seemed much impressed with the fact that the Cuban missiles were outside the BMEWS system. He felt that this did, in fact, represent a change in the *status quo* and in the "balance of terror" question'.[29]

Roosevelt later recalled that the 'opposition was no problem'.[30] According to Kent, George Brown (who Roosevelt described as a friend[31]):

> was concerned as to whether the United States had employed more or fewer Jupiter missiles in Turkey than the Soviets were putting into Cuba and as to the Soviets' capability for early warning of the firing of these missiles. Cooper said he would try to get enlightenment for Brown on both matters. Brown's point, and one to which Gaitskell assented, was that if the United States did indeed have fewer missiles in Turkey than the Soviets have in Cuba and if the Soviets did have an early warning capability, the argument about the equivalence of the Turks and Cuban bases would be weakened.[32]

Brown's support for the American position is evident. Other senior colleagues were less sympathetic, both privately and publicly. Harold Wilson said on television on 23 October that it would have been preferable if the United States had taken the whole Cuba problem to the United Nations first.[33] Others on the left of the party, including on the National Executive Committee (NEC), could be expected to be hostile toward American action. Strong criticism was not confined to the left, however, as Bruce reported to Washington:

> [The] Embassy was reliably informed [on October 25] Denis Healey told [the] Imperial Defense College audience here [that] evidence of Soviet missile bases and long-range weapons was 'faked'. He was 'rabid' in denouncing [the] 'folly' of US actions in Cuba and found not one single extenuating circumstance to justify it. Actually Healey's attitude on US handling [of the] Cuban situation goes back [a] long way. He told [embassy officials] months ago [that the] US would have to accept [the] facts of life and

learn to live with them. He appears to have lost control of himself in judging elements in [the] present situation. While responsible British opinion has reacted cooly and, on the whole, understandingly to [the] US course in Cuba, others, including [a] small minority of Communists, CND supporters, Pacifists, and disturbed centrists, have violently dissented.[34]

On 24 October the Labour Party NEC released a statement covering both the Chinese attack on India and the Cuban situation. This argued that: 'If long-range missiles have been set up in Cuba, then this presents a serious, new, potential threat to the security of the United States and the other countries of the Western hemisphere. It is also in clear breach of the assurances given by the Soviet Union.'[35] The party called for an impartial UN commission to determine whether long-range missile bases were being installed in Cuba, which was seen within the State Department as an implicit refusal to accept American proof of long-range missile bases. George Brown, however, told US diplomats that he had asked Gaitskell three times to remove conditional language and overcautious attributions. Gaitskell refused not because he, or other senior party leaders, doubted the evidence, but 'because such language was, in his opinion, logically tied to the suggested examination of the evidence 'on [the] spot by [an] impartial commission set up by [the] UN'.[36] Brown himself was completely convinced of the evidence and regarded Gaitskell's reasoning as typical of 'donnish scruples'; the Deputy Leader believed that the US must stand firm and not give a 'bloody inch' – above all it should 'in no circumstances consider dicker[ing] with [the] USSR on Turkish bases'.[37]

The Trades Union Congress (TUC), in contrast, was in no doubt about the existence of the missiles, and who was responsible for provoking the crisis: 'The General Council of the Trades Union Congress are profoundly disturbed to learn that long-range missile bases have been established on the island of Cuba, presenting an additional and serious threat to security and peace. This action of the Soviet Government is in direct conflict with Soviet professions of a desire for peaceful co-existence.'[38] The TUC, however, was 'equally disturbed' at the decision of the United States Government, taken without consultation with its allies or reference to the United Nations, to impose a blockade. In keeping with the Labour Party, the TUC hoped that the United Nations should be used to bring about a diplomatic settlement of the issue.

George Brown's robust assertions about the Turkish Jupiters are of interest. Despite Gaitskell's view that bases in Turkey were comparable, expressed in private to American officials, the NEC statement made no reference to European-based missiles, and made clear that existing bases were different to those in Cuba: 'Although bases already exist on territory adjacent to Russia and both the USA and USSR are already subject to the threat of wholesale destruction by one another, any extension of nuclear weapons to other countries is a provocation which is in conflict with the concept of peaceful co-existence and is thus to be condemned.'[39]

The American government was concerned about British opinion. President Kennedy himself asked Macmillan whether he was having trouble with the Opposition.[40] Ambassador Bruce was anxious to correct the impression created by international media coverage of Labour's attitude. The NEC statement had been 'incompletely reported in world press and interpreted by certain observers (Drew Middleton in *The New York Times*, 25 Oct, for one) as implying soft Labor line on authenticity' of the evidence about the missiles.[41] Bruce's reports of Labour views reflected his good working relations with the Opposition, and his even-handed judgement. Illustrative of this relationship, was his lunch with senior TUC officials on Thursday 25 October.[42] He was particularly impressed by the remarks of George Woodcock, the General-Secretary of the TUC, 'when he observed that no matter what happened in the Cuban affair, his policy would finally be dictated by his instincts; those instincts would be to side with the US, right or wrong.'[43] After lunch, Bruce then met fifteen American journalists for an 'animated cocktail party', where he noted 'considerable suspicion about the British, and perhaps animus against them'; the journalists were clearly 'determined to put across the argument that the government and the Opposition would sell Berlin and Turkey down the river if they could'.[44]

Notwithstanding misrepresentations of Labour's stance, the NEC statement was nevertheless critical of Kennedy. First, the blockade was described to be of 'doubtful legality'.[45] The party expressed 'regret that the fateful decision was taken by the US government without prior consultation with her allies and in advance of the meeting of the United Nations Security Council'.[46] In the House of Commons on 25 October Gaitskell avoided the legal issue but strongly repeated the complaint about consultation, while expressing sympathy for the American position.[47]

Concern at the lack of American consultation was of great importance in the debate over the basing of American nuclear weapons in Britain, and an issue to which Labour returned after the crisis. The legality of the blockade raised rather more technical legal issues in which professional expertise was required by the party leadership. Gaitskell was advised by Sir Frank Soskice, the Opposition Spokesman on Legal Affairs. Remarkably, he showed his legal opinion to Lord Dilhorne, the Lord Chancellor, before giving it to Gaitskell. Dilhorne reported to Macmillan that Soskice believed that: 'It would, I therefore think, for the purpose of public statements on the matter be unwise to assume that the [United States'] action must be treated as unlawful even if the quarantine extends not only to Cuban ships but to Russian and United Kingdom ships and the ships of other countries as well.'[48] Dilhorne, believing that the blockade was illegal, therefore told Macmillan: 'I don't think this is right but I naturally have not tried to get Soskice to alter this conclusion.'[49] The bizarre situation arose in which the government's principal legal adviser, who believed that Kennedy was acting unlawfully, and having been consulted by the Opposition legal adviser who believed that the American action was not necessarily unlawful, contrived to mislead the Opposition front bench. As Dilhorne recognised, 'it would be very embarrassing to me and to Soskice if the fact that we knew his advice were revealed'.[50]

There were of course Labour MPs who went much further in their condemnation of American action. The veteran left wing MP, Konni Zilliacus, called for the removal of American bases from the UK and the withdrawal of British forces from West Germany and Berlin.[51] During the week of the Cuban crisis, Labour Party headquarters received some sixty resolutions from Constituency and District Labour Parties (CLPs and DLPs) on the crisis.[52] Many protested against the 'provocative use of force against Cuba in the imposition of a blockade by the US'.[53] Others went further. Crawley Labour Party urged the NEC to use the situation to work for the 'removal of American bases from Britain';[54] Wednesbury DLP called for Britain's withdrawal from the alliance with the United States. Few of the resolutions condemned Khrushchev's secret deployment of the missiles.

Such sentiments reflected feeling within the anti-nuclear movement, many of whose members were, of course, active in local Labour parties. In London there were several demonstrations mainly, though not exclusively, targeted at the American embassy. Amidst the diplomatic wining and dining, and worrying over disturbed centrists and doubting journalists, Ambassador Bruce also had to cope with protesters besieging his embassy. On Tuesday it was picketed all day by protesters bearing such signs as 'Cuba Si, Yankee No'. Bruce recorded in his diary:

> The Embassy sustained a massive assault this evening. About 2 000 people had gathered in Grosvenor Square, amongst them tough elements probably belonging to the Communist Party. The manifestation was ostensibly the work of the Committee of One Hundred (Lord Russell's anti-bomb people). The crowd attempted to break through the plate glass doors of the ground floor, but were repulsed by the Police . . . Had the demonstrators succeeded in breaking in we might have had a nasty time.[55]

In Washington Dean Rusk remarked wryly that the mobs of protesters 'we had simulated turned up in London instead of Havana'.[56] The following morning Bruce spent his time organising the protection of the embassy. Supplies of tear gas were sent from Germany, with which the embassy 'expected to repulse any attempt by rioters to penetrate above the first floor of the building'.[57] Strict instructions were given to the marines defending the embassy that 'under no circumstances are they to use pistols, even if attacked'.[58] Bruce nevertheless recorded: 'I do, however, want to reconsider whether for the protection of the code room we should not, as a last resort, open fire.'[59]

Throughout Britain there were protests against the super-power confrontation and the risk of nuclear war. In London the Committee of 100 organised a rally on Saturday 27 October, while CND's protest was arranged for the following day. Both attracted crowds of some 5 000, which barely compared with previous anti-nuclear demonstrations of over 100 000. According to Richard Taylor, the missile crisis also marked a growing anti-Americanism, both within CND and the Committee of 100.[60] As noted above, the American embassy in Grosvenor Square was besieged by protesters, though according to *Peace News*, at one point 'it looked as if there might be a fight between the anti-Americans and the Against-all-Missiles group'.[61] Nevertheless, while the American Ambassador was concerned with the protection of his embassy, demonstrations outside the Soviet mission were peaceful and of only token size.

The National Council of CND met on Saturday 27 October. Resolutions were passed calling on the government to de-nounce the blockade of Cuba and declare Britain neutral in the event of war. The TUC was urged, 'to resolve that, in the event of an armed attack upon or invasion of Cuba the TUC would, if the British Government did not oppose such action, call for a General Strike'.[62] Such statements and protests were easily brushed aside by the government. One action of some note was the role of Bertrand Russell, the Cambridge philosopher and luminary of the radical Committee of 100. Upon hearing of the American block-ade on 22 October Russell issued a press statement de-claring that it 'seems likely within a week you will all be dead to please American madmen'.[63] On 23 October he sent telegrams to Kennedy and Khrushchev, as well as to Macmillan, Gaitskell and the Acting Secretary-General of the United Nations, U Thant. Russell had previously de-scribed Kennedy and Macmillan as being 'much more wicked' than Hitler.[64] Now he cabled the President: 'Your action desperate. Threat to human survival. No conceivable justi-fication. Civilised man condemns it. We will not have mass murder. Ultimatum means war. I do not speak for power but plead for civilized man. End this madness.'[65] Russell's representations on behalf of Civilized Man to Premier Khrushchev were rather different in tone: 'I appeal to you not to be provoked by the unjustifiable action of the United States in Cuba. The world will support caution. Urge condemnation to be sought through United Nations. Precipitous action could mean annihilation for mankind.'[66] Robert Kennedy recounts that the President took time from his other responsibilities to compose an answer: 'I think your attention might well be directed to the burglar rather than to those who caught the burglar.'[67] When Russell congratulated Khrushchev's 'courageous stand for sanity' and asked Kennedy if there was anything he could do, Kennedy apparently fulminated: 'He asked if he could do something for me. He can. He can go and soak his head. The last person in the world I want to talk to is that son of a bitch.'[68]

The ninety-year old philosopher spent the week issuing statements to the press from his home at Penrhyndeudraeth, in North Wales, and sending off further telegrams. According to his biographer, he himself was under no illusions about the importance of his action.[69] Nonetheless, Khrushchev's reply to Russell's first telegram on 24 October was seen as diplomatically significant – Khrushchev was conciliatory in tone, promised not to make any reckless decisions, and proposed a top-level meeting to settle the dispute.[70] Within the Foreign Office, the message was also seen to signal a measured Soviet reaction to any incident at sea – war would only begin 'when the rockets' were fired, suggesting an opportunity to avoid war even after a naval clash.[71]

As Khrushchev's reply to Russell became known, the blockade was coming into effect and it was soon apparent that Soviet ships were avoiding confrontation. By the time Parliament discussed the crisis on Thursday 25 October, therefore, the initial shock had dissipated. The potential for Parliamentary opposition was limited, as Parliament was due to prorogue on Thursday 25 October, thus constraining opportunity for debate and criticism. After agreement between the front-benches, the prorogation of Parliament was delayed by half an hour so that Macmillan could make a statement. Macmillan's description of the occasion was that:

The Conservative benches were packed. Opposition pretty full, especially *below* the gangway. Statement well received on all sides. Gaitskell, as usual, said he would ask two questions and proceeded to ask ten. But his tone was helpful. By the time (after one or two Conservatives, including Selwyn Lloyd) we got to the Communists or Fellow Travellers it was getting on to 11.30 . . . There was a mild demonstration but it amounted to very little.[72]

The previous evening, Kennedy had emphasised two particular points to Macmillan for use in Parliament: his unambiguous statement of 13 September that offensive weapons would not be tolerated, and Soviet assurances that they were not deploying offensive weapons in Cuba.[73] In Macmillan's view, 'Parliament, the Press and the public remained remarkably calm, at least at this stage.'[74] The State Department's judgement was that the Prime Minister had made 'a strong statement to [the] Commons on October 25 condemning the Soviet action as a deliberate provocation designed to test the determination of the US and supported the US decision not to accept this Soviet move'.[75] The West, Macmillan had made clear, could not rely on words. On the other hand, the State Department also noted, that in addition to Ormsby-Gore's representations about POL, there were reportedly some British officials 'who do not understand why we should be less ready to live in the shadow of Soviet missiles in Cuba than they have been to accept the presence of Soviet missiles pointed toward them from the USSR.'[76]

The Cabinet met again for its scheduled meeting on the afternoon of 25 October.[77] Macmillan's statement to Parliament had been well-received. The Foreign Secretary reported on developments in the Caribbean, and also on a meeting he had held with the Soviet *Chargé d'Affaires* that morning (discussed in Chapter Six). Macmillan recounted his discussion with the President on the evening of the 24th and explained that:

He had suggested that the Acting Secretary-General's proposal for a standstill might be accepted provided that work on the missile sites in Cuba ceased, under United Nations inspection, and that United Nations observers were stationed in Cuban ports to examine incoming cargoes. He had also suggested the need to set any conference in as wide a context as possible. In general, the situation remained extremely serious. He would himself be ready to take any opportunity of intervening if he felt that by doing so the prospect of a settlement could be advanced, but it would be necessary to avoid at all costs the temptation of reaching a settlement by lowering the resistance of the free world to aggression. It was equally necessary to avoid driving those who felt they had been victims of aggression to desperation. It must be the object of all those who had any influence on the present pattern of events to find a middle course.[78]

As the crisis reached its climax in the ensuing days, Macmillan was increasingly exercised over where, and how, this middle course might be plotted and what role he should play. The Prime Minister also pondered over how to respond to Soviet feelers inviting a British initiative.

The Cuban missile crisis raised the twin issues of nuclear weapons and Britain's relationship with the United States in an acute form. Potentially the domestic political consequences were considerable. Within the Labour Party Gaitskell had already re-asserted his authority on nuclear weapons, and re-established party unity. The Cuban crisis might have triggered dissent and disunity, but several factors assisted the leader: Gaitskell took a firm line on Kennedy's lack of consultation and the role of the UN; second, within the party, the Chinese attack on India muted voices on the Parliamentary Left. Gaitskell himself thought 'that their inhibitions about the Asian war partly explained why they caused little trouble about the missile crisis'.[79] Privately the Labour leader thought it would be 'a pretty good exchange' to get rid of both the missiles in Turkey and the missiles in Cuba.[80] His public position was nevertheless supportive of Kennedy, though critical over consultation. Apparently he told Denis Healey that the Americans were entitled to prevent the installation of a Soviet missile base in Cuba by invasion just as Britain would be entitled to invade Ireland in similar circumstances.[81] The consequence of such attitudes was that a bipartisan consensus

obtained. Lord Home was able to tell the Soviet *Chargé
d'Affaires* on 25 October, that 'Her Majesty's Opposition fully
understood the American position and were just as alarmed
as Her Majesty's Government by the introduction of these
terrible weapons into another theatre.'[82] As with most of
Europe, early doubts and criticisms of American action did
not provide the Soviets with opportunities to use western
opposition parties against their governments.

Macmillan was sensitive to the charge that Britain should
have acted during the crisis, and the impression that he
had not been consulted by Kennedy may have damaged
him both within his party and in public. Soon after the
crisis, however, attention turned to the much more serious
political threat posed by the fiasco over Skybolt. The short
term effects of the missile crisis on the Labour Party appear to have reinforced existing trends. The achievement
of unity, and agreement on a coherent defence and foreign policy, was followed by Gaitskell's death in January
1963. At the 1963 party conference Cuba was barely mentioned.[83] The missile crisis had occurred at a time when
the party leadership had reasserted itself on defence, and
fratricidal tendencies within the anti-nuclear movement were
becoming apparent. The changes that took place in East–
West relations, including the nascent détente between
Kennedy and Khrushchev, together with the test ban treaty
agreement in which Britain participated, reinforced intra-
party developments and provided a context in which CND's
policy of unilateral nuclear disarmament was marginalised.
For CND itself, Richard Taylor argues, the crisis fuelled
the trend toward radicalisation, and away from working
within the Labour Party to achieve change.[84]

For the Conservatives the outcome could be seen to vin-
dicate nuclear deterrence and a strong relationship with
Kennedy's America. Although Labour was still opposed to an
independent British deterrent, the move away from unilateralism meant that Conservative exploitation of the defence
issue would be limited. Notwithstanding Labour's commitment to rid itself of an independent deterrent, domestic
issues became the focus of the political battle in the period up to the general election. There was, however, one
specific domestic legacy of the crisis, discussed in the next

chapter, concerning the role and persona of Captain Yevgeny Ivanov, the Assistant Soviet Naval Attaché. By design or fortune, Captain Ivanov was to have a considerable impact on British politics in the period after the crisis, and in undermining the fortunes of Harold Macmillan and his party.

6 Diplomatic Initiatives and Devious Approaches

The missile crisis presented the Macmillan government with a major diplomatic problem. American action in the Caribbean could provoke the Soviets in Europe, and Macmillan himself had doubts about the course of action chosen by Kennedy. Yet the unity of the West required public British support for the blockade. Macmillan and the Foreign Office remained anxious to engage in any diplomatic action that might forestall escalation to world war. However, unless such an initiative was carefully co-ordinated with Washington, independent British action risked splitting the alliance and alienating Washington.

Until very recently, discussion of Britain's diplomatic role was an almost exclusively British concern. American scholars and other writers have exhibited little interest in British actions and involvement. Nevertheless, Macmillan's conversations with Kennedy, and Ormsby-Gore's access in Washington, afforded Britain a unique position in NATO. Macmillan had chosen Ormsby-Gore as Ambassador to Washington in part because of his close childhood friendship with the Kennedys. The President stated that he 'would trust David as I would my own Cabinet',[1] and also considered him the brightest man he knew.[2] During the crisis, Ormsby-Gore had unrivalled access to the President amongst the Washington diplomatic corps. He saw Kennedy four times during the week from 21 October, 'on three occasions for long periods', and in addition conducted several telephone conversations with him.[3] Described by David Bruce as a man of 'transcendent qualities and unimpeachable character',[4] Ormsby-Gore was also criticised as having gone native and indeed become Kennedy's man.[5]

While certainly prepared to distance himself from his government,[6] Ormsby-Gore's independence of mind had positive features during the crisis. One Foreign Office misconception, for example, was that Kennedy might 'reconsider his present contention that the crisis arises from a conflict between the Soviet Union and the United States.'[7] The Foreign Secretary believed that if the President made clear that his concern was directed against Cuba and Castro 'and need not necessarily involve the vital interests of the two major powers, this might well take the heat out of the situation and prepare the way for a conference'.[8] The idea of dealing directly with Castro had also initially appealed to Dean Rusk.[9] By this stage, however, after the President's televised speech, the British proposal completely misread Kennedy's approach, and Ormsby-Gore decided not to put the idea forward: 'The whole American case is built upon the fact that this is a clear challenge by the Soviet Union and that Castro is a mere cypher in the game. They could not possibly now reverse themselves. Mr Rusk made this clear to me earlier in the afternoon. I know, therefore, that this idea is a non-starter.'[10] Privileged access was not, however, without difficulties. As shown in Chapter Three, Ormsby-Gore had to consider carefully how, and when, he reported back his conversations to Macmillan. As Ormsby-Gore informed Macmillan, he was hesitant to report Kennedy's views on Berlin, Turkish missiles and negotiations because of the frankness of the statements.[11] What Ormsby-Gore may have decided not to disclose is a matter for speculation.

What was reported to Macmillan showed the intimacy and trust between the President and the British Ambassador. On Tuesday 23 October, Ormsby-Gore explained that Kennedy was looking for a diplomatic settlement. He hoped and expected that the crisis would be resolved through discussions, which he believed would include Berlin, foreign bases and disarmament.[12] This statement, together with Kennedy's remarks about the obsolescence of the Turkish Jupiters, could carry very significant implications for Britain and Europe. Yet Ormsby-Gore did not immediately report this information back to Macmillan.

Ormsby-Gore was also able to provide the Prime Minister with insights into Kennedy's attitude toward Berlin. The West German Foreign Minister, Gerhard Schroeder, had just visited Washington, and Kennedy expressed his exasperation that:

like other Germans, [Schroeder] refused to face up to
the realities of the situation. One day, and it might be
soon, they would have to do so. He was disappointed
that some other European Power, perhaps Italy had not
tried to open their eyes. He of course understands our
dilemma with the Common Market negotiations at a critical
stage . . . There were other comments he made in the
Berlin context which I could not possibly put on record,
but I know you would be reassured by them. If you thought
it worth while, depending on events over the next few
days, for me to fly home for twenty-four hours, I would
gladly do so.[13]

Macmillan demurred at this suggestion, recognising the value
of having his Ambassador in place at this crucial time.[14]
Before the crisis, Ormsby-Gore had explained the political
pressures on the President to the Foreign Office. On 23
October, he reported his overwhelming impression 'that
Americans of every persuasion regard the President's action as the absolute minimum required to meet what all
see as a deliberate Russian challenge to test the will and
resolution of the United States.'[15]

In his rather exasperated message to Ormsby-Gore of
22 October, Macmillan had made clear that he would take
action to prevent war. On 24 October Home reiterated the
government's willingness to act: 'I do not wish to lose any
opportunity that may present itself of taking a useful initiative.'[16] Ormsby-Gore was asked to establish whether
Kennedy envisaged some kind of international conference,
and, if so, what its scope and purpose should be. Home
also wanted to know whether the initiative for such a conference should come from the US, the UN Acting Secretary-
General or 'other governments'.[17] Ormsby-Gore met Bundy
later that day in preparation for the phone conversation
between the two leaders in the evening, and raised the
question of the conference.[18] The Foreign Office was much
exercised with the most promising issue for such negotiations, and Home made clear to Ormsby-Gore that: 'A straight
bargain about bases has obvious disadvantages. It might
strike the neutrals as cynical and involve us in serious difficulties with some NATO countries, quite apart from Ber-

lin. It strikes me that a more favourable field from the
Western point of view would be that of disarmament and
the paramount need for reducing the dangers of nuclear
confrontation.'[19] The potential pitfalls of protracted and
complex negotiations were not lost on the British, though
it is clear that the Foreign Office believed that such an
approach was, at this stage, preferable to a simple deal
involving missiles in Europe.

What is (perhaps) extraordinary is that Ormsby-Gore made
clear to Bundy his own view that a summit was 'not a good
idea because the two sides are too far apart and because it
leaves no room for the French.'[20] He then told Bundy that
the President 'should make it very plain' to the Prime
Minister 'that this is not an acceptable position and that
the U.S. cannot stand down its blockade without progress
toward the removal of the missiles'.[21]

THE BLOCKADE AND AFTER

At 10 am (Washington time) on 24 October, the quarantine came into effect, and SAC moved to DEFCON-2. In
September Khrushchev had told the Austrian Vice-Chancellor
that an American blockade of Cuba would be 'an act of
war' – he 'had given instructions that Soviet ships bound
for Cuba were not to obey the orders of blockading American
ships and that if fired upon they were to fire back'.[22] On
Wednesday 24 October Khrushchev told a visiting American businessman, William Knox, that Soviet submarines would
sink US Navy ships which stopped and searched Soviet
merchantmen.[23] Khrushchev's public message to Bertrand
Russell that day, however, signalled a willingness to avoid
conflict and resolve the impasse through negotiation.

Now the world waited to see what would happen. Robert
Kennedy recounted that 'this Wednesday morning meeting [of ExComm], along with that of the following Saturday, October 27, seemed the most trying, the most difficult,
and the most filled with tension'.[24] The President heard at
10.25 am that some Soviet ships had stopped dead in the
water. It soon became clear that the six Soviet ships near-
est to the quarantine line had stopped or were turning

around.[25] Sixteen of nineteen Soviet ships en route to Cuba slowed, halted or reversed their course.[26]

Kennedy telephoned Macmillan at 11 pm (London time) and explained that some of the ships, 'the ones we were most interested in', had turned round but others were coming on.[27] He would not know whether the blockade had succeeded until the following day. If the quarantine was indeed working, then the immediate problem was the continuing work on the missile installations. Kennedy said that:

> if they respect our quarantine then we've got this prob-lem of the rockets on Cuba and the last 24 hours' film show that they are continuing to build those rockets, and then we're going to have to make the judgement as to whether we're going to invade Cuba taking our chances or whether we hold off and use Cuba as a sort of hostage in the matter of Berlin. Then any time he takes an action against Berlin, we take action against Cuba. That's really the choice we now have. What's your judgement?[28]

Whether the British were consulted during the crisis has excited much debate. Yet the President's direct question to the Prime Minister on *the* critical decision is a clear and unambiguous example of consultation. Whether Macmillan's answer in any way influenced the President is a separate question. Macmillan replied that he would like to think about it.

Kennedy reflected further on the central dilemma and the implicit linkage between Cuba and Berlin: 'He has Cuba in his hands, but he doesn't have Berlin. If he takes Ber-lin, then we will take Cuba. If we take Cuba now we have the problem of course of these missiles being fired or a general missile firing and we certainly will have the prob-lem of Berlin being seized.'[29] It is also clear from this ex-change (and became clearer in the ensuing days) that the operational state of the missiles was a key factor in when a decision to attack Cuba was deemed necessary. Kennedy made clear that American forces were mobilising, and that if a decision was taken to invade, they would be in a posi-tion to do so within a few more days.

Kennedy reformulated the central question to Macmillan:

The question I would like to have you think about, Prime Minister, is this one. If they respect the quarantine, then we get the second stage of this problem and work continues on the missiles. Do we tell them that if they don't get the missiles out we'll invade Cuba? He will then say that if we invade Cuba that there's going to be a general nuclear assault and he will in any case grab Berlin. Or do we just let the nuclear work go on figuring he won't ever dare fire them and when he tries to grab Berlin, we then go into Cuba. That's what I'd like to have you think about.[30]

Macmillan replied the following day counselling diplomatic, rather than military, action: 'I have been thinking over the 64 000 dollar question which you posed on the telephone. After much reflection, I think that events have gone too far. While circumstances may arise in which such action would be right and necessary, I think that we are now all in a phase where you must try to obtain your objectives by other means.'[31] Horne argues that, 'the famous Kennedy telephone calls were purely informative, and in no way seeking advice, only the comfort of affirmation'.[32] However it seems clear that here Kennedy asked Macmillan's advice on a crucial issue.

Macmillan recognised that given Soviet duplicity, 'we cannot rest on mere words in any arrangements, we must have verification and confirmation'.[33] A system of inspection was therefore essential if the quarantine was to be lifted, and while negotiations lasted. This

would enable you to say that you had in fact obtained your objectives. For if there are no ships arriving, then the purpose of the quarantine is served; and if there is no more construction the purpose of largely immobilising this threat is also served. In other words, such an approach as I suggest fits in with the answer to last night's question which I feel I must give. At the same time you will no doubt continue with your military build up for any emergency. This may be as important a factor for persuading the Cubans to accept inspections as in other directions.[34]

For Macmillan, the question of a British diplomatic initiative was a vexing one. On 25 October, he told the House of Commons that:

> I would always be ready to take an initiative at the moment at which I thought it valuable and when it would serve a useful purpose. But I cannot do so merely for the sake of appearing to do something. Rather I must do so in order to achieve something useful . . . it may be better at the moment to use the United Nations as an instrument, under the Acting Secretary-General's approach, rather than for there to be any initiative by me or the head of any other allied Government.[35]

This was welcomed by the Opposition, reflecting widespread British support for, and expectations of, the UN. At the outset of the crisis there was criticism of Kennedy across the British political spectrum for acting before taking the matter to the United Nations. 'Would it not have been better to state his case to the United Nations and to the Organisation of American States before instead of after, so far reaching a pronouncement?', asked the *Daily Telegraph*.[36] 'Even if the bases ARE in fact being built', the *Daily Herald* argued, 'President Kennedy would surely have done better if he had first reported this to the United Nations Security Council as a dangerous threat to peace before risking the incalculable consequences of a blockade.'[37] Harold Wilson also stated that the United States should have taken the evidence to the UN before taking action.[38] Some years later, David Owen even suggested that 'strictly speaking, the United States had acted in contravention of the United Nations Charter by failing to submit notice of a threat to peace to the Security Council before taking action'.[39]

Macmillan's expectations of the UN, however, expressed in his message to Kennedy on 22 October, were not high. If the Security Council resolution was vetoed, the only appeal would be to the General Assembly: 'What the result will be there no one can tell but I doubt whether they will be in favour of any conclusive action or even if they are I do not see how they will enforce it.'[40] Others, including the Labour Party NEC, held higher hopes and saw UN diplomacy as the alternative to military confrontation. In addition to its potential diplomatic role, the UN Security Council was also a public arena and the scene of dramatic confrontations between the American and Soviet representatives, Adlai Stevenson and Valerian Zorin.[41] The most famous moment came on 25 October when in the face of a continuing Soviet refusal to admit to the presence of the missiles, Stevenson produced aerial photographs of the bases.

On 24 October U Thant had made an 'urgent appeal' to Kennedy and Khrushchev asking them to 'refrain from any action which may aggravate the situation'; in the Security Council he called for all parties to enter into negotiations, and to gain time for these, he proposed 'the voluntary suspension of all arms shipments to Cuba and also the voluntary suspension of the quarantine measures'.[42] This was not acceptable to Kennedy because it would suspend the blockade while work continued on the missiles already in Cuba. Macmillan described U Thant's proposal as 'a very dangerous message' when Kennedy read him U Thant's letter late on the 24 October.[43]

In the Security Council Britain supported the United States. On 24 October the British Ambassador to the UN, Sir Patrick Dean, declared that, by 'a deliberate and deceitful act of provocation, the Soviet Union is introducing into the Western hemisphere nuclear missiles of mass destruction'.[44] Quoting the Foreign Secretary the previous evening, he emphasised that:

> We have never denied the right of the Cuban people to choose their own political regime or of the Cuban Government to take such defensive measures as they think necessary for their own defence. We do not dispute that a sovereign State is entitled to call for military aid from another government... But no one Mr President can fit the installation of these missile sites in Cuba into that picture. Legitimate defences are one thing, nuclear missiles with ranges from 1 000 to over 2 000 miles are quite another.[45]

Dean sought to distinguish between Soviet deployments in Cuba, which had been 'installed in secrecy and behind a mask of duplicity', and 'the open attitude of the Governments of NATO who have not attempted to hide the establishment, by mutual agreement, of their bases for the defences of the Free World.'[46] The British government was 'forced to conclude that these bases in Cuba are not for defensive purposes only', he argued.[47] British declarations in the Security Council gave no hint of disquiet about the legality of American action nor of any possible independent British role.

CAPTAIN IVANOV

After Kennedy's television address the British government, and the world, waited to see what would happen when the quarantine came into force. At the outset Macmillan had informed Ormsby-Gore that he could not allow escalation into war without taking action. He made this willingness to act clear to the Cabinet the following day. It was, however, the Soviets who made the first approach to the British. In his memoirs, Macmillan recounts that, toward the end of the week, 'there were some signs of Russian weakening', involving 'some rather devious approaches . . . to the Foreign Office'; the suggestion was that 'if the British Government would issue an appeal for a Summit conference to settle the issue, the situation might still be saved'.[48]

The story of these devious approaches and their diplomatic context has long been known, though recent evidence provides further detail. In the absence, however, of authoritative Soviet sources, key aspects remain open to speculation. Much information is available, in part because British–Soviet diplomacy during the crisis received unprecedented publicity following the resignation of the Secretary of State for War, John Profumo, in 1963. In July 1963 Macmillan made a statement to the House of Commons about the Profumo affair concerning, in particular, Captain Yevgeny Ivanov, the Assistant Naval Attaché. Ivanov had attempted to persuade the British government that, if they proposed a summit, then Khrushchev would respond and the crisis would be defused. Lord Denning's report into the Profumo scandal in September 1963 cast further light on the events of 1962.[49] The more recent release of PRO material provides details about the events and the diplomatic dialogue between Britain and Moscow. In addition a memoir, based on the recollections of Ivanov himself, was published in 1992.[50] These various disclosures have also been augmented by accounts describing the role of the London osteopath, Stephen Ward, who was at the heart of the Profumo scandal.[51] However, key aspects of the Soviet side of the story remain unclear, and it is therefore still difficult to fully assess the diplomatic and political significance of the events.

A good deal of evidence has emerged about the role of Soviet intelligence services at this time and how they served as diplomatic back-channels. Georgi Bolshakov, a GRU officer, was used as a channel of communication between Robert Kennedy and Khrushchev.[52] Bolshakov also passed disinformation to Kennedy, providing reassurances from the Soviet premier that offensive nuclear forces would not be deployed in Cuba.[53] Perhaps the most interesting and significant role played by an intelligence officer was that of the KGB *Resident* (or Head of Station) in Washington, Aleksandr Feklisov (known as Aleksandr Fomin).[54]

In 1992 an account of Ivanov's life as a GRU officer appeared, written by a journalist, Gennady Sokolov, based on taped recollections with Ivanov and apparently published in defiance of his former service.[55] The account included details of his posting to London under diplomatic cover as Assistant Naval Attaché, and presented 'new facts' about the Profumo affair and the events of October 1962. According to Ivanov, he was summoned by the GRU *Resident*, General Pavlov, 'early in the week', and ordered 'to establish unofficial contacts with the British political leadership with the aim of settling the Cuban crisis'.[56] Apparently, the GRU *Resident* was sceptical of the approach, telling Ivanov that 'the British will never undertake actions on the sly from the Americans, even with the noblest peace-making aims'.[57]

Questions inevitably arise about the credibility of Ivanov's memoir, produced thirty years after events without recourse to documents and written second-hand by a Novosti Press Agency official. Nevertheless, some of Ivanov's recollections can be corroborated from the British records. The parliamentary debate on Profumo and Lord Denning's report in 1963 illuminate Ivanov's activities, and give some indication as to how his approaches were viewed in Whitehall. Macmillan gave Parliament details of Ivanov's activities, some of which Stephen Ward had disclosed to the Opposition shortly after the missile crisis. Ward wrote on 1 November 1962 to Harold Wilson, outlining the proposal Ivanov had made to the government the previous week.[58] Wilson believed that Ward was probably some kind of 'madman' and took no action.[59] When the Profumo scandal began to break in March 1963 Ward spoke to Wilson's parliamentary colleague, George Wigg, raising *inter alia*, the Soviet approaches during the Cuban and Berlin crises.[60] Wilson then sent Ward's letter of 1 November and a note of the meeting between Ward and Wigg to the government Chief Whip, Martin Redmayne, who passed it to Macmillan. Wilson and Macmillan then met to discuss the security aspects on 27 March 1963.[61]

According to Macmillan's account to the House of Commons in July 1963, Ward telephoned the resident clerk at the Foreign Office on 24 October 1962 and gave him, to pass to Sir Harold Caccia, an account of a conversation he had just had with Ivanov. The Soviet official said 'that the Americans had created a situation in which there was no opportunity for either the Americans or the Russians to compromise and that the Soviet Government looked to the United Kingdom as their one hope of conciliation'.[62]

Caccia responded quickly to Ward's phone call. In 1961 Ivanov had used Ward's friend, Sir Godfrey Nicholson, a respected back-bench Conservative MP, to pass information to the Foreign Office concerning Soviet proposals on disarmament and Berlin.[63] This action was apparently designed to reassure the British government. In October 1962 Caccia cabled the British Ambassador to Moscow, Sir Frank Roberts, asking for an urgent evaluation of Ivanov's suggestion and various statements he had communicated to the government.[64]

The suggestion of a British diplomatic initiative carried considerable implications. While the British government had an obvious interest in helping avert catastrophe, there was the risk of a public split within NATO, and between Washington and London. Roberts' reply to Caccia the next morning, 25 October, was dismissive both of Ivanov's approach and the idea of a British initiative:

I am sceptical both about the information and the initiative. So far as I can judge from many recent contacts with Soviet officials and from [the] public attitude of Khrushchev the mood here altogether is not desperate and helpless as Ivanov suggests. Nor can I see why this junior official in London should have complete and up to date information on matters of highest policy outside his competence and on a situation which has developed so fast in [the] past 48 hours.[65]

Roberts does not appear to have known that Ivanov was a GRU officer, nor that he had attempted to act as an intermediary over Berlin.[66] According to Lord Denning, the Security Service (MI5) knew that Ivanov was a 'Russian Intelligence Officer',[67] and told the Foreign Office in June 1962.[68] Several accounts state that MI5 identified Ivanov as a member of the GRU when he arrived in March 1960, and that this was subsequently confirmed by Oleg Penkovsky, the West's spy in the GRU, in 1961.[69] Ivanov himself believed that Penkovsky betrayed him.[70] Whether Ivanov's identity as an intelligence officer would have lent greater credibility to his proposal is not clear. Nevertheless, his professed knowledge of Soviet missile deployments on 24 October was in contrast with the *Chargé d'Affaires*, V.A. Loginov.

For Ambassador Roberts, the Soviet advantage in dividing the West was nevertheless clear – 'I have no doubt that the Russians see good prospects of dividing [the] UK from [the] US over Cuba and they might like us to take some initiative, which could help them and certainly could not hamper them.'[71] He wondered why, if Ivanov was putting forward the real Soviet view, he had not been approached during various recent informal contacts. His conclusion was that:

The major danger in [the] present situation seems to me to be that Khrushchev cannot accept without excessive loss of face that Soviet ships be searched. He as well as President Kennedy is under inescapable pressures. But his response to Lord Russell's message (published prominently today) suggests that he would like to find a way out and to avoid action further endangering peace. The Russians have hitherto followed the simple rule that they do not wittingly risk provoking war on the other side of the East–West divide and count upon us to follow the same rule in reverse. While Khrushchev therefore needs to be faced with a firm Western front (hence my doubts about any spectacular British initiative) it is also important to leave him possible paths of retreat, preferably with the help of the United Nations and uncommitted countries. For this US restraint and some change in US position is also essential. U Thant's proposal surely offers better prospects than a British initiative and I hope we can put our weight behind it.[72]

By Thursday 25 October it looked as though Soviet ships did not intend to run the blockade. It was still far from clear to everyone involved how the stalemate was to be broken. In London Ivanov continued his efforts to interest the British in mediation, making use of the contacts he had developed through Ward.

Meanwhile, Loginov asked to see the Foreign Secretary to deliver a message from his government. According to Macmillan's account to the House of Commons:

> The next day, 25th October, my hon. Friend the Member for Farnham (Sir G. Nicholson) informed Sir Hugh Stephenson, then Deputy Under-Secretary of the Foreign Office [and Chairman of the Joint Intelligence Committee] . . . that Ivanov had been to see him to give a somewhat similar story and to ask for some indication that the British government were considering working towards negotiations at the Summit. This was the same day as that on which the Foreign Secretary had seen Mr Loginov; and later the same afternoon Mr Ward spoke to Sir Harold Caccia's private secretary to convey similar information.[73]

Loginov handed over the Soviet government statement of 23 October and then, on instruction, added that:

> the Soviet government considered that an extremely dangerous situation had been created by the United States in establishing a blockade off Cuba and in taking other actions outlined in President Kennedy's speech. They considered it necessary therefore to make the statement, a copy of which he had given me, and to raise in the United Nations the question of violation of the United Nations

Charter and the threat to peace by the United States. The Soviet Government hoped that Her Majesty's Government would do all in their power to avert developments in Cuba which could push the world to the brink of military catastrophe.[74]

On 24 October Home had told the Polish Ambassador that the initiative for any conference would have to come from either Kennedy or Khrushchev, and he also downplayed the suggestion that Macmillan might fly to Washington.[75] Loginov pressed the Foreign Secretary on whether the British government would use its influence to calm the present situation. 'I replied that we would and that we were watching developments very closely', Home recorded.[76] Later that afternoon, he told the Cabinet that Loginov's object had been to suggest that the government should intervene.[77] British officials immediately appraised the US Ambassador of the Soviet message, and Bruce duly reported back to the State Department.[78] In Washington, Dean Rusk telephoned Ormsby-Gore for details of the meeting.[79]

According to Macmillan:

> On the following day, 26th October, Mr Ward telephoned Lord Arran and asked to bring Ivanov to his house for a discussion the next morning. Lord Arran agreed and Ivanov and Mr Ward came to see him on 27th October. Ivanov again stated that he wished to get a message to the British government by indirect means asking them to call a Summit conference in London forthwith. Lord Arran reported this initiative at the time both to my office and to the Foreign Office, and later sent in a full report.[80]

Macmillan told the House of Commons:

> It is thus clear that at the time of the Cuba crisis Ivanov was using all the methods at his disposal to try to persuade the British Government to take some initiative. But he was not alone in this. Nor were we in any doubt about the motives of these approaches, which must have been to drive a wedge between ourselves and the United States at this very crucial moment. It is not uncommon, at a moment of crisis, that a lot of worthy people should be used to see whether they could be of some assistance.

That has often happened. Ivanov's approaches were, therefore, only a small piece of the jigsaw; they were a natural part of the Soviet attempt to weaken our resolution. Our reply at the time was that the ordinary diplomatic channels were open.[81]

As Macmillan told the House of Commons in 1963, the issue of a British initiative was something that had to be considered. The government took seriously Ivanov's entreaties, and as Macmillan's statement to the House of Commons indicates, the approach was not rejected out of hand. The provenance of Ivanov's mission is not yet clear. When news of his role was made public, TASS vigorously denied that, 'Ivanov either undertook or tried to undertake some sort of negotiations with British representatives about British mediation in the settlement' of the Caribbean crisis.[82]

If Aleksandr Feklisov's actions in Washington are any kind of precedent, it is conceivable that Ivanov's mission was conceived in the London embassy. Ivanov's own account implies that it was not, and certainly Lord Arran recorded that 'I believe that Commander Ivanov was speaking the truth when he said that he had been entrusted with a mission from his Embassy. Others, including the Counsellor, were I understand given the same task. I also believe that the Embassy and, *a fortiori* the Commander, were acting on definite instructions from Moscow.'[83] According to Ivanov's account, 'I was not the only one who was turned down. The Soviet Foreign Ministry instructed its London-based diplomats to act in similar fashion.'[84] Loginov, however, did not explicitly invite a British-sponsored summit either in his meeting with the Foreign Secretary on 25 October, or at a second meeting on 27 October.[85] While Loginov's statements were certainly consistent with Ivanov's approach, it is unclear from British records whether the Soviet Foreign Ministry was engaged in the overt side of a Soviet diplomatic manoeuvre or was circumvented, in the same way the Washington embassy was usurped by Bolshakov. The available evidence suggests the former.

Nor is it clear whether Ivanov was providing reassurance about Soviet deployments in Cuba or deliberate disinformation. Two of Ivanov's claims are of note in this context. First, he told Ward on 24 October that there were no nuclear warheads in Cuba.[86] The CIA had been unable to find evidence that warheads had arrived in Cuba, though it was made clear to the British and to NATO that Washington was operating on the assumption that warheads were present.[87] Recent evidence from Soviet sources makes clear that Soviet nuclear warheads *had* arrived both for M/IRBMs and tactical weapons deployed on the island.[88]

The second dubious claim concerned the range of the missiles. Ivanov stated that the 'missiles in Cuba were of very limited range; they might be able to strike North Florida but could certainly not reach Washington'.[89] American intelligence correctly believed that the IRBMs had not arrived in Cuba. Initially there had been some debate about whether the MRBMs were the 630 nm SS-3 rather than the 1020 nm SS-4, and the British intelligence community had not discounted the possibility that they could be the shorter range weapons.[90] The Americans were in no doubt that the missiles could strike further, including at Washington. Ivanov's claim that the missiles could only reach North Florida, (i.e. they were the SS-3 or the 350 nm range SS-2) might well suggest that he was serving as a conduit of disinformation on this potentially critical matter. On Saturday 27 October he was still adhering to this story, telling Lord Arran 'that the Russian missiles in Cuba were purely defensive in the sense that they would not carry further than the Northern borders of Florida and that they had no missiles of the size described by the Americans'.[91]

The fact that Ivanov was telling people that the Soviets had missiles in Cuba capable of striking the United States was nevertheless in contrast to statements by Soviet diplomats elsewhere. While the veracity of some of Ivanov's statements may be in doubt, he did acknowledge that there were Soviet missiles in Cuba capable of reaching the United States. This was at a time when Ambassador Zorin was refusing to admit to the UN Security Council that the Soviets had nuclear missiles in Cuba, and when Georgi Bolshakov was still trying to reassure the Americans that the deployment was purely defensive.[92] When Robert Kennedy visited Dobrynin on 23 October, the Ambassador repeated that there were no long range missiles in Cuba.[93] On Friday evening, Paul Nitze told key NATO Ambassadors in Washington that he 'thought that Mr Zorin's continued refusal to admit the presence of nuclear weapons in Cuba was designed to preserve a measure of flexibility for the future. There were signs that Russian diplomats all over the world were floundering on this particular point, and it was doubtful whether they had received adequate guidance from Moscow.'[94] Elsewhere, however, Soviet officials did appear to have received instructions. On 26 October the French Ambassador to Washington, Hervé Alphand, told Paul Nitze and Roger Hilsman that 'Russian diplomats in London had been speaking to the Italians about a possible deal over missile sites in Turkey',[95] and the Soviet Ambassador to Indonesia spoke to the Indian Ambassador in similar terms.[96] Most importantly, when Khrushchev met William Knox on 24 October he stated that there were ballistic missiles in Cuba which were equipped with nuclear warheads.[97] One purpose of Khrushchev's statement to Knox was to emphasise that 'the Cubans were unstable people' and that the missiles were wholly under Soviet control.[98]

Loginov and Ivanov appear to have consulted each other over their approaches to the Foreign Office. Apparently Ivanov relayed details of Loginov's meeting with Home to Stephen Ward.[99] Loginov was unforthcoming on the missiles. When asked by the Foreign Secretary why 'the Russians had put these missiles in Cuba', the *Chargé d' Affaires* replied that he 'did not know what missiles were there'.[100] The British record gives no indication that Loginov explicitly confirmed the presence of the missiles, but nor did he attempt any denials in the face of numerous assertions by Home about the missiles and their implications.

Ivanov's mission thus appears to have had several purposes, including disinformation. The main, diplomatic, purpose was to invite the British to play the role of intermediary:

> President Kennedy had created a situation in which there was absolutely no opportunity for either the Russians or the Americans to compromise; the Soviet Government regarded this as incomparably the most serious situation which had arisen in the history of the USSR; The Soviet Government therefore looked to the United Kingdom

for their one hope of conciliation. This was the only way out; there was no other loophole; A compromise might be achieved by inspection. Unilateral inspection of Cuba would never be permitted. But some form of reciprocal inspection might be open to agreement within hours e.g. the Soviet Union might be permitted to inspect Scotland in return for inspection of Cuba. (This idea was thrown out in response to a question about the form conciliation might take).[101]

There was no explicit attempt to link the inspection issue to the Thor bases (which were all in eastern England). This may have been because the British government had announced, in August 1962, that the missiles would be withdrawn in 1963. Nor did Loginov raise the Thors on 25 October, other than with a general reference to 'weapons in the United Kingdom directed against the Soviet Union'.[102] The 60 Thor IRBMs, 20–25 minutes flying time from the Soviet Union, provided a suitable comparison to the 36 MRBMs in Cuba, certainly in political terms.[103] Yet the Soviets did not raise the Thors as part of a face-saving formula either through Ivanov or Loginov.

On one hand, Ivanov offered some reassurance that the Soviet Union 'had no intention of taking retaliation by e.g. a blockade of Norway or Turkey'.[104] On the other 'Soviet reactions to the crisis were therefore negative. The Russian ships had been told not to submit to search. There was nothing the Russians could do; the ball was in the American court. The Embassy had, on instructions from Moscow, destroyed all unnecessary documents. The atmosphere was one of complete idleness and wait-and-see.'[105] In the absence of authoritative Soviet sources, an element of conjecture remains about the Ivanov episode. It seems reasonable to conclude that the GRU *Residentura* was engaged on a mission from Moscow. Whether the principal aim was to secure a way out of the crisis using London, or, in the words of Lord Home, 'to drive a wedge between ourselves and our American allies', cannot be answered from available Western sources.[106] Whether or not the primary mission was surrogate diplomacy, a secondary aim was almost certainly disinformation concerning Soviet nuclear forces in Cuba. Whether Macmillan should have seized the opportunity proffered by Ivanov is a separate question, and one to which the Prime Minister gave serious consideration as the crisis reached its climax. This is further explored in Chapter Nine. 'Some people thought that we should have taken the initiative. It was not a very easy decision to make and hon. Members must remember our close discussion all the time with the President of the United States', he told Parliament somewhat defensively in 1963.[107]

Macmillan clearly took the idea of hosting a summit seriously. His Foreign Secretary was more doubtful, and later stated that in addition to driving a wedge into the alliance, the Soviet approach was designed 'to test our resolve and lay a bait to our vanity'.[108] Whatever the appeal to Macmillan's vanity, it was his recognition of the catastrophic consequences of American (and Soviet) miscalculation that informed his thinking. Despite initial doubts about Kennedy's chosen course of action, his preference was to work with the United States and to preserve the cohesion of the western alliance. As the week of the crisis progressed, the British government sought to accommodate its support for the US, its doubts about the prudence and legality of American action, and its desire to avoid war, while preserving the solidarity of NATO. That it emerged with all these goals achieved is a measure of Macmillan's handling of the crisis, the degree of convergence between Kennedy's and Macmillan's views, and above all the element of luck, without which events could have escalated into military conflict and nuclear war.

7 Ormsby-Gore and Penkovsky: British Contributions?

The consensus amongst British students of the 'special relationship' has been that the role of the British government in the missile crisis was of minor significance.[1] These views tend to ignore several British contributions. These are of interest, not least in understanding the 'special relationship' and in the study of particular diplomatic, military and intelligence aspects of the crisis. Various claims about British actions during the crisis have been advanced, and this and the following chapter examine and adjudicate upon their significance. This chapter explores diplomatic and intelligence issues, and focuses on two very different individuals: David Ormsby-Gore and Oleg Penkovsky. Chapter 8 analyses British military preparations, including the alert and readiness posture of RAF Bomber Command.

MOVING THE QUARANTINE

Unquestionably the best informed, and arguably most influential, British figure in the crisis, David Ormsby-Gore, is credited with several contributions to American decision-making. The most noteworthy concerns where the quarantine line was to be established by the US Navy from 24 October. Several accounts describe how Kennedy accepted Ormsby-Gore's suggestion to move the quarantine line from 800 miles to 500 miles from Cuba,[2] and how Kennedy agreed, ordering McNamara to change the quarantine line in the face of 'emotional navy protests'.[3] It has also been suggested that these orders were not implemented as a result of what Graham Allison terms the 'organisational process' subverting the intentions of the President.[4] In 1978 Dan Caldwell argued, contra Allison, that Kennedy originally set the quarantine at 800 miles which he then moved to 500 miles.[5] British, American and Soviet sources now enable these accounts, and Ormsby-Gore's role, to be reassessed.

British records show that on the evening of 22 October Paul Nitze, the Assistant Secretary for International Security Affairs, convened the quadripartite Berlin military sub-group, and explained how the quarantine would work: 'Action would be taken quite far from Cuba. Mr Nitze said 'up to 500 miles'. Every effort would be made by signals to turn back ships approaching Cuba, or get them to permit examination. If this failed, a shot would be fired across the bows. If this failed, a disabling shot would be fired, and the ship would be brought into a United States port.'[6] The ambassadorial group met again on the afternoon of Tuesday 23 October, and Ormsby-Gore asked:

> whether the Americans had set any limit on how far out from Cuba interceptions could take place, adding that it seemed to me that it would be more understandable to public opinion if ships were stopped nearer rather than farther away. Mr Nitze replied that no limit had been set in the American minds, but whilst they agreed that interception should not take place too far away, equally if they took place too near there was the added danger and complication of Cuban air intervention. The Americans had therefore come to the conclusion that 'a considerable distance out' was wise.[7]

Later that evening, Ormsby-Gore and his wife were dinner guests at the White House and he took the opportunity to discuss the matter with Kennedy. According to his report to Macmillan:

> I suggested that there might be some disadvantage in the Americans apparently going out of their way to make an early interception of a Russian ship sailing to Cuba. The Russians were evidently carefully considering their future course of action. Even a few extra hours might enable them to take decisions which would avoid a serious clash. In these circumstances I could not quite see why it was necessary to intercept at seven or eight hundred miles from Cuba. The President said that the main

consideration was that they should intercept a ship containing a cargo of an offensive military nature. There was one ship which was apparently in this category and it was at present some way from Cuba. He also wondered whether there was any great advantage in delaying the confrontation but he took the point that the Americans should not look over eager to make their first interception.[8]

According to Ormsby-Gore, the President then telephoned McNamara:

> and discovered from him that one of the reasons why they wished to intercept at least five hundred miles from Cuba was because they were worried about the intervention of Cuban aircraft which had a radius of action of this order. The President was unimpressed by this argument. He said that he thought it in the highest degree unlikely that Cuban aircraft would try and intervene at this long range and if they did so, they would certainly be shot down and in the circumstances he did not think this would add in any way to the gravity of the situation. He told McNamara that he was against a strict application of the five hundred mile rule, but accepted that there were other factors which had to be taken into account with regard to the interception of the specific ship they had their eye on and he recognised that it might be better to contact it outside the five hundred mile radius.[9]

The Pentagon had decided by 20 October to establish the quarantine at 500 miles, to keep beyond the range of Cuban aircraft.[10] In EXCOMM on 22 October, however, McNamara had made clear that 'we intercept any place where it appears that the ship is moving toward Cuba.'[11] The following morning there was further discussion about where ships would be intercepted and boarded. McNamara suggested 'something in the order of 800 miles', as this was beyond the range of the 740 mile range Ilyushin-28s.[12] It was this idea to which Ormsby-Gore addressed himself, later that evening.

Schlesinger argues that Kennedy's heeding of Ormsby-Gore's advice 'was of vital importance in postponing the moment of irreversible action'.[13] This, however, assumes that Soviet shipping would have been intercepted and boarded had the larger quarantine area been adopted. It has been suggested that Khrushchev's initial reaction was to order the ships to run the blockade,[14] as he threatened when he met William Knox on 24 October.[15] Indeed, it now appears that the Presidium received Kennedy's speech at 1 am (Moscow time) on 23 October and agreed that, while most of the 30 ships in transit were not to continue, five ships carrying nuclear cargoes would proceed, as would preparations at the missile sites.[16] Four submarines armed with nuclear torpedoes would also continue.[17] By the time the blockade came into effect, all Soviet surface ships had apparently been ordered to halt or turn back.[18] Thus, however laudable Ormsby-Gore's intervention, it made no difference to the quarantine, as Khrushchev decided to avoid a conflict at sea. Moreover, even if Khrushchev had decided that the ships would run the blockade, Ormsby-Gore's proposal would not have bought any significant amount of time. This was because the Americans intended to stop and search the ship to which Kennedy had alluded in his conversation with McNamara, the *Kimovsk*, which reached the 500 mile quarantine limit at about 10.40 am.[19] The *Kimovsk* was scheduled to be stopped between 10.30 am and 11 am, no more than an hour after the quarantine came into effect.[20] Ormsby-Gore's suggestion would have made no real difference to the *Kimovsk*.

PUBLISHING THE PHOTOGRAPHS

A second intervention by the British Ambassador concerned publication of aerial photographs of the Soviet bases. As noted in Chapter Three, Macmillan's reaction when shown the evidence of the missiles was that European opinion needed careful handling. Publishing the photographs was one way of assisting the American cause, as well as easing the British government's domestic problem. When Chet Cooper left the meeting with Macmillan on 22 October, the Prime Minister's Private Secretary, Philip de Zulueta, immediately 'expressed serious concern about the reception any strong Government statement would have in the absence of incontrovertible proof of the missile build-up'.[21] Macmillan's press secretary, Harold Evans, telephoned his counterpart in the White House, Pierre Salinger, to urge their release.[22]

Kennedy had discussed publication of the photographs with Art Lundahl, Director of the National Photographic Interpretation Center (NPIC), at the outset of the crisis.[23] Lundahl was sceptical at the impact of high altitude photography on public opinion, but endorsed the idea that low altitude photography would have an effect. Ormsby-Gore raised the photographs with the President on 23 October:

> I said that I thought it was most important that the Americans provide really convincing evidence to the general public of the Soviet offensive build-up in Cuba. He quite understood, and after he had sent for a batch of photographs he gave instructions as to which of them should be published and he emphasised the importance of clear explanatory notes being attached to them. I had pointed out that without such explanatory notes the uninitiated would have no means of telling whether the missiles depicted were six feet long and therefore defensive or sixty feet long and therefore offensive. The President said that they had carried out a very low level photo-reconnaissance flight during the course of the day and they hoped that this would provide them with some useful close-up pictures of the missiles.[24]

Horne states that 'Ormsby-Gore pressed Kennedy to take Macmillan's advice and have the photographs immediately released to the press. This was done with telling effect.'[25] Macmillan, however, does not appear to have pressed Ormsby-Gore about the photographs. In a cable to the Ambassador earlier that day, he explained that the Press today is 'not too bad', though they were 'of course a little sceptical about the facts of the Soviet build-up in Cuba'.[26] His telegram made no reference to photographs, but instead emphasised that he needed to use the facts given him by Bruce the day before: 'It was definite figures rather than vague statements which struck home and this is what we need for the general public.'[27]

Moreover, the various accounts, including Ormsby-Gore's

contemporaneous record, provide a misleading impression of events. By the time Ormsby-Gore spoke to Kennedy, high-altitude photographs had already been given to the British media in London.[28] The responsibility for releasing them was variously ascribed, though the White House press corps, aggrieved at being 'scooped' by the British media, was told that it was the fault of an 'errant press officer' in the London embassy.[29] Roger Hilsman blamed Chet Cooper: 'I got Kennedy's permission sort of in my back pocket . . . to use them, but in the meantime . . . Cooper just without asking permission or getting anybody's permission gave them to the press of Britain.'[30] Ormsby-Gore believed that 'Ambassador Bruce had released them to the BBC in London without authority.'[31] Brugioni claims that after Kennedy's conversation with Ormsby-Gore Macmillan spoke to the President, who said that he would authorise the release of the photos but did not specify when; Macmillan assumed the release would be immediate and called Ambassador Bruce who then asked Cooper to arrange for the release of the photographs to the British press and media.[32] This does not, however, explain how the photographs came to be released in London on Tuesday evening *before* Ormsby-Gore dined at the White House.

Chester Cooper's contemporaneous account, and other evidence, helps provide an explanation. Following his briefing of the Prime Minister, Cooper was warned by de Zulueta about the likely public reception in Britain in the absence of proof of the missiles. This judgement was vindicated by the 'almost universally sceptical' reaction of the press to American claims, which together with confusion over whether the Pentagon had released the photographs, led Cooper to conclude that they should be published.[33] The London embassy was also keen to have the pictures released. Cooper records that: 'I received permission to have the pictures shown on television on the basis of the Ambassador's urgent request. The localities of the sites were to be removed and the press and the television audiences were to be told that these were *typical* sites but were not to be informed of the *number* of sites.'[34] Permission was obtained from the Deputy Director for Intelligence, Ray Cline, at 3 pm (GMT) to allow the photographs to be shown at a press conference at 5 pm.[35] According to Cooper: 'After consultation with Embassy officials, I agreed that since the pictures were going to be shown on television (it subsequently developed that ITV as well as BBC was going to have a special Cuba program) we could release sanitised versions of the photographs to the press for publication Wednesday morning.'[36] Cooper attempted to obtain authority for this decision, and advised both the CIA and the White House that unless he was instructed otherwise, he would release the photographs to the press. The deadline passed without a response from Washington and so decided to proceed, subsequently despatching a telegram to Washington to inform them of his actions.[37] He then informed headquarters at his first opportunity (after the briefing with Gaitskell at 9 pm), and then sometime after midnight explained the circumstances of the release after an irate call from Michael Forrestal, of the NSC, at the White House. The president was 'disturbed' about the release of the photographs and demanded an explanation from David Bruce.[38] When Cooper returned to Washington later in the week he expected to be sacked.[39]

It is thus clear that publication of the photographs was the result of a CIA official's initiative, acting with the cooperation and encouragement of the London embassy. Publication of the photographs on 23 October may have 'scooped' Adlai Stevenson's dramatic unveiling of the pictures in the UN Security Council on 25 October, and rather embarrassed the Pentagon (and McNamara), who denied requests for publication on grounds of security, just as the pictures were appearing on British television.[40] However, the impact on British public opinion clearly vindicated Cooper, Bruce, *et al*. As Roger Hilsman noted: 'the US aerial photographs of the missile sites proved invaluable in convincing Britons that there was justification for US action'.[41] The photographs did not convince everyone. The Labour NEC's statement of 24 October implied that the identity of the missiles was not proven. When Robert Kennedy was shown the photographs he later confessed that he had taken the word of the experts ('what I saw appeared to be no more than the clearing of a field for a farm or the basement of a house') and was relieved to hear later that others, including the President, had reacted similarly.[42] As Sherman Kent observed: 'of the millions of people of many nations who saw the pictures that fourth week of October, only a handful, and these were [Photo Interpreters], knew exactly what it was they were looking at . . . never have so many taken so much on the say-so of so few'.[43]

OLEG PENKOVSKY: THE SPY WHO SAVED THE WORLD?

According to Alistair Horne, Ormsby-Gore's proposal to move the quarantine was one of two important British contributions during the crisis; the other was the espionage of Oleg Penkovsky.[44] A GRU Colonel, between August 1960 and August 1962, Penkovsky supplied the West with some 10 000 pages of classified material from General Staff files.[45] In addition, Penkovsky was a confidant and protégé of the Chief Marshal of Soviet Artillery, Marshal Sergei Varentsov, responsible for Soviet tactical missile forces, and had cultivated a relationship with the head of the GRU, General Serov. He was therefore able to supply 'gossip and reports of the leadership's private meetings',[46] as well as information on Soviet intelligence operations.

The view that Penkovsky's espionage was of crucial importance in the missile crisis has received wide circulation.[47] A recent study based on scrutiny of American archives has, moreover, endorsed these judgements: Schecter and Deriabin contend that 'during the Berlin crisis of 1961 and the Cuban missile crisis in 1962, Penkovsky was the spy who saved the world from nuclear war.'[48] Very different views have also emerged. Some writers dispute the significance of Penkovsky's espionage for western policy-making. McGeorge Bundy argues that 'Penkovsky had no discernible relation to the real assessments and actions of the United States government in the missile crisis',[49] and his own account of October 1962 makes no reference to Penkovsky.[50] Similarly Raymond Garthoff, who was, before moving to the State Department in 1962, a CIA analyst responsible for appraising Penkovsky's material, describes the 'tremendous amount of important military information', but argues that this was merely 'useful background information during the crisis'.[51]

It has also been suggested that far from providing valuable intelligence, Penkovsky was a Soviet-controlled agent of disinformation. The initial source of this claim was the KGB defector, Anatoly Golitsyn, who persuaded some senior western intelligence officials that Penkovsky was working for the Soviets. These included James Angleton, the CIA's chief of Counter-Intelligence, who after initially endorsing Penkovsky's bona fides,[52] came to believe that Penkovsky may have been a double agent. These doubts were shared by some British officials, including Peter Wright of MI5.[53] The views of Wright (and other British officials) also became public.[54] A variation on this theme is the suggestion that Penkovsky could have been an 'unwitting medium in a Soviet intelligence operation', designed by 'Soviet doves', to communicate that Khrushchev was bluffing.[55]

Various accounts, including two by Greville Wynne (the British businessman used by SIS as an intermediary), describe operational aspects of SIS's involvement,[56] and senior British officials have commented on the importance of the case. Sir Frank Roberts believed that Penkovsky's information 'was almost more important than any other intelligence either way', while Sir Nicholas Henderson, erstwhile secretary of the JIC, has stated, 'that the intelligence he provided was of crucial importance to us in assessing the state of Soviet preparedness and intentions'.[57] According to Alistair Horne, Sir Maurice Oldfield, then SIS liaison officer in Washington, believed in the 'supreme importance' of Penkovsky's espionage, a view apparently shared by Harold Macmillan.[58] Yet, although some senior British and Soviet officials have spoken publicly of Penkovsky's role, evidence of how material was used in British policy-making is negligible. Whatever the actual importance of Penkovsky's material, British officials clearly believed that Britain made a significant contribution through the joint operation.[59]

Similar statements about the importance of Penkovsky's espionage have been made by senior American intelligence officials. It is clear both from US officials and recently declassified US documents that Penkovsky's intelligence was accepted and used by the West. The CIA has, for example, published various documents containing information from Penkovsky.[60] The significance of such material for western policy-making is a more contentious issue. However accurate and potentially important the material Penkovsky supplied, its significance depended, first, on how it was integrated into the intelligence analytical process, and then how such assessments were used by decision-makers. It is now possible to trace what Penkovsky passed to the West through this analytical and political process in the US, and scrutinise various claims about the importance of his intelligence.

MISSILE WARNINGS

Chapman Pincher asserts that, at his first debriefing, Penkovsky's

> most startling news was his statement that missiles of the type described in the [SS-4] manual [which Penkovsky supplied to his handlers] were shortly to be established in Cuba, only two hundred miles off the American shore, where they would be capable of threatening many cities . . . There is no doubt that Penkovsky's information not only provided President John F. Kennedy with advance information about the Cuban missiles but gave him confidence in taking a tough stand with the Kremlin.[61]

The suggestion that Penkovsky warned the West about the missiles in Cuba is repeated by Peter Wright,[62] and is wholly misleading. The declassified transcripts of Penkovsky's debriefings in the West reveal that at his first meeting with his SIS and CIA case officers in London on 20 April 1961, Penkovsky said that: 'Today [Khrushchev] will not begin a war. He will rant and rave and even send arms here and there just as he did to Cuba and possibly even send small-caliber rockets there. In fact there was talk about this with Castro and possibly a few rockets are already there.'[63] This equivocal statement clearly did not refer to MRBMs or IRBMs.

In July 1960 Khrushchev had publicly warned that Soviet intercontinental missiles would protect the Cuban people,[64] and in November there is evidence that Che Guevara 'probed'

Khrushchev on the idea of deploying nuclear missiles.[65] Various authoritative accounts of Soviet decision-making, however, make clear that Khrushchev only decided to install nuclear missiles in Cuba in the spring of 1962.[66] The decision to deploy short range missiles was taken in September 1962.[67] As Raymond Garthoff states: 'Colonel Penkovsky did not provide any information with respect to the stationing of missiles in Cuba.'[68] Indeed by September the CIA was increasingly anxious to learn whether the Soviets were sending missiles to Cuba, and the last message from Penkovsky's case officers specifically requested 'concrete information as to military measures being undertaken by the USSR to convert Cuba into an offensive military base. In particular we would like to know if Cuba is to be provided with surface to surface missiles'.[69] Despite several attempts to make contact in Moscow, these urgent requests failed to reach Penkovsky before his arrest.

Penkovsky did warn his CIA and SIS case officers about Soviet tactical nuclear missiles in East Germany. At his first debriefing in London in April 1961 he explained that with the exception of Albania, all 'People's Democracies were being provided with ballistic missiles, including the R-11 missile.'[70] Moreover, he stated that, 'in the DDR we now have four [rocket] brigades, and of these two brigades already are equipped with nuclear warheads'.[71] Further details were provided, including at subsequent meetings.[72] Apart from the military significance to NATO, this challenged the existing belief that the Soviets had never deployed nuclear warheads outside Soviet territory.

The American intelligence community believed that because the Soviets had never deployed 'offensive' nuclear weapons outside their own territory they would not do so in Cuba.[73] It is not clear whether the British JIC was tasked with evaluating the subject, though in September the British official responsible for liaising with the Pentagon, Iain Sutherland, told the US Latin American military intelligence section that:

> our feeling was that the Soviet Government probably did not have sufficient confidence in the future of Cuba to commit themselves to supplying weapons of this category

[ground to ground missiles and sophisticated fighters], that they had not supplied such weapons to other countries outside the Bloc and also that they must be well aware, particularly following the President's statement, of the very serious repercussions which the supply of offensive weapons would have on United States policy.[74]

As noted in Chapter 3, in October 1962, the Director of the JIB, Sir Kenneth Strong, and Sir Burke Trend, told their CIA host that the Soviets would not put missiles into Cuba – shortly before it was disclosed to them that Khrushchev had done just that. It is therefore clear that Penkovsky's information on Soviet nuclear deployments outside the USSR did not materially affect either CIA or British estimates of the likelihood of Soviet 'strategic' deployments in Cuba.

THE MISSILE GAP

The second, most widespread, claim about Penkovsky's intelligence concerns his role in dispelling the 'missile gap' – the belief that the Soviets were moving ahead in the development of ICBMs. During the 1950s it is now clear that the American intelligence community exaggerated and distorted the potential threat posed by Soviet strategic nuclear forces. The 'bomber gap' (1955–8), and then the 'missile gap' (1957–61), arose because of the paucity of western intelligence, and the analytical failures of the American intelligence community. The advent of aerial photography, afforded by the U-2, played a critical role in dispelling the bomber gap. By 1960, when Eisenhower suspended U-2 overflights of the USSR, there were growing divisions among the various intelligence bureaucracies over the scale of Soviet ICBM deployment. Satellite photography portended a transformation in the assessment of Soviet strategic forces.[75] There were, however, various problems with the US satellite programme, the first successful mission of which took place in August 1960. This meant that the differences within Washington had not been resolved when Penkovsky appeared. In February 1961, however, Robert McNamara, recently arrived in the Pentagon, told journalists his opinion that there was no missile gap (a major political *faux pas*, given Kennedy's exploitation of the issue in the Presidential election campaign). Although it was not until autumn 1961 that the issue was resolved within the American government, McNamara's public remarks indicate that growing scepticism about the missile gap at the highest levels in Washington preceded Penkovsky's espionage.

Various writers contend that Penkovsky's intelligence was critical in dispelling 'the missile gap', and in guiding Kennedy's handling of the crisis from a position of strength.[76] Recently declassified American documents show how and when Penkovsky's information was used in the American National Intelligence Estimating (NIE) process,[77] and illustrate, as Schecter and Deriabin observe, that 'integrating Penkovsky's reporting and documents into the intelligence community bureaucracy was a difficult and delicate matter'.[78] Of greatest potential interest was Penkovsky's information about Soviet ICBM capabilities, and in particular the SS-6 programme (NATO designation).[79] The information he supplied, indicated that the SS-6 was in considerable difficulty,[80] and that Soviet ICBM capabilities were well below American estimates. This information, circulated under the CHICKADEE classification, included his recollections of Marshal Varentsov's statements on the programme's progress, and does not appear to have included corroborative documentary material. Yet although his report was both significant and very useful, it did not have an immediate effect on the NIE 11-8-61 estimate agreed in June 1961.[81] When the United States Intelligence Board discussed the NIE in June, Penkovsky's information on the Soviet ICBM programme 'was not mentioned, or even reflected, in the body of the Estimate, and none of the participants at the meeting referred to it'.[82] Despite CIA assessment that Penkovsky's material called for the withdrawal and revision of NIE 11-8-61, senior officials were unwilling, for security reasons, to disseminate further details which might disclose their source.[83]

Although Penkovsky's information did not affect the June NIE, it was nevertheless clear that disagreements, in particular between USAF intelligence and the other organisations, including the CIA, were intensifying.[84] Between June and August 1961 photographic intelligence from the Corona satellite programme was received and included coverage of the ICBM field at Plesetsk.[85] This satellite intelligence was crucial to the revised estimate of Soviet ICBM strength and development, NIE 11-8/1-61.[86] In September, the US intelligence community significantly revised its estimate, although USAF intelligence remained wedded to a more worse case analysis.

Penkovsky's material certainly assisted CIA analysts in corroborating and explaining what they saw. It was not in itself decisive in changing the US National Intelligence Estimate. Although NIE 11-8/1-61 shows that by September 1961 Penkovsky's information was accepted, it was satellite photography which enabled a more realistic assessment of the Soviet strategic arsenal. By the autumn of 1961 the debate within the intelligence community was effectively resolved, and after careful consideration President Kennedy decided to make known that his government was now aware of US nuclear superiority.

The argument that Penkovsky's role was vital hinges not just on the claim that his information was instrumental in changing US perceptions of the military balance, but that this was crucial to Kennedy's handling of the missile crisis. The argument that Kennedy's recognition of American nuclear superiority was crucial is challenged by those studies which contend that nuclear superiority was of secondary importance to fear of nuclear war in Kennedy's management of the crisis.[87] Whatever Kennedy's perceptions, those of Nikita Khrushchev are also potentially significant. There are those, including within SIS, who believed that the KGB's discovery of Penkovsky's espionage alerted Khrushchev to the fact that Kennedy now knew he was bluffing, and this influenced his climb down. Sir Frank Roberts has written that Penkovsky's espionage 'was an important factor which must have influenced Khrushchev's thinking, as it did that of Kennedy in Washington'; it 'meant that the West knew the limitations of Soviet nuclear rearmament and Khrushchev knew that we knew ... Penkovsky's information ensured that Khrushchev could not indulge in diplomatic nuclear blackmail.'[88] When, and how, Khrushchev was told of

Penkovsky's arrest is not known. Indeed what he told his interrogators is a matter for speculation. What is clear is that, long before the missile crisis, the US government made publicly clear its recognition of American nuclear superiority. In October 1961 Roswell Gilpatric, McNamara's deputy, delivered a speech revealing that the United States was well ahead in the arms race, and that, therefore, the West knew Khrushchev was bluffing.[89]

THE MISSILES IN CUBA

A third claim about Penkovsky's intelligence, emphasised in recent literature, focuses on US assessments of the missiles in Cuba. Although Penkovsky did not alert the West to the deployment of missiles in Cuba, he did supply technical information, including the manual for the SS-4. This information was helpful to analysts at the NPIC in identifying the missiles, as the Deputy Director of Central Intelligence, General Marshall Carter, told the President and his advisers on 16 October.[90] Other sources of information were also important, in particular photographs taken by military attachés at Red Army parades. As Lundahl told the President, the CIA knew the missiles were MRBMs because of their length.[91] Initially there was some doubt over whether the MRBMs were the fixed base SS-3s or road mobile SS-4s.[92] Further U-2 overflights and analysis based in part on Penkovsky's material firmly identified the SS-4 MRBM.[93] Identifying the type of missile was important: 'the SS-3 had a range of some 630 nm, enabling coverage of seven SAC bomber/tanker bases; the 1020 nm SS-4 could target 18 bomber/tanker bases (plus one ICBM complex),[94] and some 58 cities with a population of over 100 000, including Washington, accounting for 92 million people'.[95] More significant was that Penkovsky's data enabled accurate assessments of the readiness state of the missiles. This became a critical issue for American decision-makers, some of whom believed that the operational status of the missiles would determine when a decision to destroy them had to be taken. Within the White House on 16 October there was disagreement over the implications of the operational condition of the missiles. McNamara argued that if an air strike was to be launched it had to take place 'prior to the time these missile sites become operational'.[96] This assumption was challenged by Dean Rusk who questioned whether the Soviets would automatically retaliate against the United States in the event of an American attack on the Cuban bases.[97] McNamara remained concerned whether the decision to launch would be taken in Moscow or Cuba. Soviet command and control arrangements, and associated technical aspects of launch procedure, were therefore of great importance to senior US officials. McCone told McNamara on 17 October that CHICKADEE reports, 'indicated considerable autonomy in hands of field commanders',[98] which may well have contributed to the Defense Secretary's fears of unauthorised use and inadvertent nuclear escalation.

The operational status of the missiles was a major concern to the US government. Schecter and Deriabin argue that Penkovsky's information on the technical details of the SS-4 missile system was his vital contribution.[99] Richard Helms, CIA Deputy Director for Plans, believed that Penkovsky's material on the SS-4 enabled American decision-makers to know exactly when the missiles would become operational. In Helms' view, the information gave Kennedy three extra days.[100] This 'gave President Kennedy time to manoeuvre. I don't know of any single instance where intelligence was more immediately valuable than at this time. Penkovsky's material had a direct application because it came right into the middle of the decision-making.'[101] Helms' claim raises interesting and still controversial issues, including whether, and under what circumstances, Kennedy would have attacked Cuba. The President's initial reaction to the discovery of the missiles was certainly belligerent, though this quickly gave way to a more sober and pragmatic disposition. The CIA's technical intelligence on the SS-4 may have informed his understanding of when a decision was necessary. Whether he would have opted to destroy the missiles in the absence of such material is a separate matter. In the absence of Penkovsky's intelligence, a combination of worse case analysis and mirror imaging (based on western IRBM launch procedures) would have provided a rough and ready guide to

Soviet command and control arrangements. Moreover, technical questions about launch protocol did little to alter the strategic logic of Dean Rusk's argument that Soviet use of the missiles would be deterred by US retaliation against the USSR.

The CIA told the President on 19 October that two MRBM sites were operational, though they could not confirm whether the warheads were present (or were even in Cuba.)[102] By 27 October all six MRBM sites were reported to be operational. Lebow and Stein conclude that: 'From the beginning, the situation was one of gradually diminishing advantage because at least some missiles became operational shortly after their discovery'.[103] The only 'window of opportunity' therefore existed between when the President was told of the missiles and when some became operational – at most a matter of days. Whether Helms' claim that Penkovsky's information was vital in dissuading Kennedy from taking precipitous military action is far from proven, and based on a contested and unsubstantiated reading of Kennedy's attitude when the missiles were discovered. On balance, it seems unlikely that Penkovsky's material was decisive. Yet, American attitudes were guided by psychology rather than logic, as McGeorge Bundy has conceded.[104] American leaders behaved as though the operational condition of the missiles was an indicator of Soviet intent, and therefore of importance to the decision whether or not to attack them. The implications of this for the final phases of the crisis are dealt with in Chapter Nine.

Finally, the question of whether Penkovsky was genuine remained a concern for the American and British intelligence communities. As McCone told the US Intelligence Board in 1963, the possibility that Penkovsky was a plant 'was something that we always feared. We had checked his bona fides extremely carefully, and help up dissemination of reports in order to ensure their validity. After most careful checks with all other types of intelligence, we came to the conclusion that this was authentic.'[105] The British were convinced perhaps more wholeheartedly, and at an earlier stage than their US counterparts, though fear that their agent might be turned was an inevitable concern. It is extremely difficult to equate Penkovsky's disclosure that he was under

KGB surveillance from early 1962 with a disinformation operation. Moreover, it is even more difficult to plausibly suggest that, if Penkovsky was a conduit of disinformation, he would have been discontinued at the precise moment when communication channels between the leaderships were so crucial. The available evidence overwhelmingly suggests that Penkovsky was genuine. As Schecter and Deriabin argue, 'he told too much, and what he provided was too damaging to Soviet interests'.[106] Nevertheless, that Britain made a contribution to the American conduct of the crisis in this context is clear. Equally, the significance of this contribution should not be exaggerated.

The contributions of David Ormsby-Gore and Oleg Penkovsky provided the most significant British contributions to the unfolding of the crisis, and have excited much interest amongst a variety of writers. Recent historiography and archival disclosures suggest that these have frequently been exaggerated and distorted. Nevertheless, Ormsby-Gore and Penkovsky illustrate different aspects of the 'special relationship', and suggest that the diplomatic and intelligence dimensions of British–American relations are both intrinsically crucial to understanding that relationship, and equally, dependent on the individuals involved.

8 Thor and Vulcan: British Gods of War

When I joined Peter Thorneycroft, the Minister [on Sunday 28 October], I learnt that the crisis was over, and that the Russians had accepted the American's terms without loss of face. We sat around the table just looking at each other. Dickie [Mountbatten] broke the silence. 'Well what would we have done if the Russians had not pulled back? Do we know? We've got to work this out.' No-one knew, but he was the only one to put the question. To the best of my knowledge, neither he nor anyone else has yet provided an answer. Perhaps there is none.[1]

The Cuban missile crisis was (probably) the closest the world has come to nuclear war. If there had been all-out war, hundreds of millions of people would have been killed in Western Europe, the communist world and (possibly) North America. If hypotheses about the climatic effects of nuclear war are correct, life itself could have been extinguished in the Northern Hemisphere. In October 1962, the United States had some 5 000 nuclear weapons that could strike the USSR, compared with a Soviet force estimated to comprise 300 weapons.[2] What this meant in practice for American and Soviet decision-makers, together with what lessons could be learned for the conduct of nuclear deterrence, remain matters of interpretation and debate. Did the United States possess an effective first-strike capability, ie. the capacity to destroy the Soviet ability to retaliate? How far did Soviet fear of such an attack pressure them to 'get their retaliation in first'? These are crucial questions in assessing the risk of war in 1962. There were senior American military officials who believed that the US possessed the ability to destroy the Soviet strategic arsenal with only limited risk of retaliation against the United States, though there is no evidence that Kennedy or his closest advisers had begun to discuss how such a nuclear war would be waged.

The idea that either the United States or the Soviet Union would initiate nuclear war as a rational act of national policy was one fear, though recent historiography has strongly suggested that fear of such a war drove both Khrushchev and Kennedy to seek accommodation.[3] Risk of inadvertent nuclear war also exercised American and Soviet officials. Yet evidence has emerged to suggest that the arrangements for the command and control of American nuclear forces were not what many imagined. Scott Sagan has concluded that, 'the US nuclear command system clearly did not provide the certainty in safety that senior American leaders wanted and believed existed'.[4] Together with recent evidence about Soviet tactical nuclear deployments and nuclear alert activities, there is now reason to believe that the risk of inadvertent nuclear war was greater than hitherto realised.[5] The United States government, for example, was unaware that the Soviets had deployed a panoply of tactical nuclear weapons in Cuba, and had Kennedy decided to invade there was some risk that Soviet commanders might have fired these weapons.[6]

Most 'scenarios' of nuclear war in 1962 envisage conflict in Europe as a Soviet response to US action in the Caribbean. The link between Cuba and Berlin was drawn by Kennedy and Macmillan (and their advisers). Soviet actions against Berlin would have triggered a NATO response, which, in the event of armed conflict, would have quickly required a NATO decision on whether to use nuclear weapons. There were fundamental differences within NATO over contingency planning for the defence of West Berlin, and indeed in the development of NATO force planning and strategy. The British Chiefs of Staff, for example, were adamant that NATO should not respond in Berlin with a ground probe against overwhelming Soviet superiority (see below). If the Soviets had taken action against Berlin (or Turkey), NATO would have been faced with escalation or abandoning not simply an ally, but the very foundation of the Atlantic alliance. Yet, for NATO planners, war in Europe meant nuclear war – armed conflict would escalate across the nuclear threshold, quickly involving attacks by US strategic nuclear forces against the USSR. The Soviets also had a panoply of nuclear and other weapons of mass destruction, which could have brought carnage and destruction to Europe on an all but unimaginable scale.

This chapter focuses on the UK military role and the nuclear relationship with the United States. The alerting of nuclear forces in Britain and Europe illuminates the military dimension of the 'special relationship'. Crucial differences between the British and American governments about the role of military preparations and the value and risks of mobilisation are also examined. In addition, specific issues are discussed, in particular the preparations involving the Thor IRBMs. It is worth noting that the crisis was reaching its climax in part due to how American leaders saw the state of preparations of 36 Soviet MRBMs in Cuba, which could be prepared for firing in a matter of hours. During the crisis, 59 British Thors were ready to be fired in no more than 15 minutes. The state of readiness of the Soviet MRBMs led American decision-makers to the brink of hostilities. The state of readiness of the British and European IRBMs has generally passed without comment.[7]

LESSONS OF HISTORY?

Not long before the Cuban missile crisis, John F. Kennedy read Barbara Tuchman's account of the outbreak of the Great War.[8] He 'was tremendously impressed' by her description of how 'the miscalculation and misunderstanding' of European leaders had led to war, and became determined 'that no comparable book would be written on the miscalculations' of October 1962.[9] According to Horne, Harold Macmillan was also 'profoundly affected' by the book.[10] In 1914 political leaders had not been in control of events and 'tumbled' into a war which few wanted. Yet for Kennedy the lessons of 1914 had to be measured against other 'lessons of history', such as those of 1939 and 1941.[11] The view, for example, that resolve discouraged aggression became a prevailing assumption of Western policy toward the Soviet Union in the Cold War and a key factor in Kennedy's initial response to the discovery of the missiles.[12] Nuclear alerting was the modern day equivalent of mobilising mass armies. Whereas it had taken the Imperial Russian

Army weeks to mobilise, the missiles of the Soviet Strategic Forces (or the Strategic Air Command) could be ready in hours or indeed minutes. Mutual misperception could lead to catastrophe far greater, and far more quickly, than had occurred in 1914. Yet there is little evidence that Kennedy and his senior officials agonised over raising the DEFCON alert states. On 16 October, when McNamara was discussing military action against Cuba, he suggested that, in such circumstances, SAC should be alerted to deter the Soviets. This would probably include an airborne alert and other alert measures. 'These bring risks of their own, associated with them', he warned.[13] Yet, neither the President nor his colleagues appear to have been particularly exercised over whether the Soviets might misinterpret the signals and mistake resolve for aggression.[14] Harold Macmillan, however, took a very different view, both with regard to preparations by NATO and by Bomber Command.

NUCLEAR ALERTS

As President Kennedy appeared on television on 22 October, American military forces world-wide were moving to the heightened alert state of DEFCON-3.[15] SAC immediately increased the number of nuclear bombers on ground alert from 652 to 912, and 183 medium range B-47 bombers were dispersed to civilian airfields. The scale of the B-52 airborne alert was increased from 12 training missions to 66 sorties a day.[16] ICBMs were placed on alert and all available Polaris SSBNs were operationally deployed. On 24 October SAC moved to the unprecedented and unrepeated state of DEFCON-2, just short of full readiness for war, which it maintained until 21 November. According to Sagan, SAC more than doubled its nuclear capability. At its highest level, on 4 November, alert bombers increased from 652 to 1 479; ICBMs on alert went from 112 to 182; the total SAC-alerted nuclear weapons peaked at 2 952, compared to 1 433 before the crisis; in addition, by October 24, Polaris SLBMs on alert increased from the regular peacetime level of 48 to the full force of 112 missiles.[17]

It is now also clear, in the words of Air Chief Marshal

Slessor, 'that Bomber Command . . . including both V bombers and the Thor missile squadrons, was brought quietly but quickly to an advanced state of readiness'.[18] Slessor argued that there 'can be no grounds for criticism of the resolute loyalty to the Alliance shown by the British Government during that grim week'.[19] In the words of the Commander in Chief of Bomber Command, Air Marshal Sir Kenneth Cross: 'we very quickly brought the whole [V-bomber] force to [readiness] without any fuss or without any bother'.[20] Furthermore, 'the Americans knew exactly' that they had a 'friend at their side . . . fully at readiness'.[21] In October 1962 Britain was one of three states with operational nuclear weapons (France had tested an atomic device in 1960, but did not deploy operational weapons until 1963). The British were probably capable of targeting as many nuclear weapons on the Soviet Union as the Soviet Union could target on the United States. Air Vice-Marshal Menaul has stated that in 1962 the RAF's IRBMs and V-bombers were capable of visiting 230 megatons on 230 separate targets in the USSR.[22]

The pattern of American alerting in Britain in 1962 reflected the arrangements for the four main categories of nuclear forces operated from the United Kingdom, each of which had different command and control procedures. SAC deployed B-47 medium range nuclear bombers at British and European bases, and during the crisis some 30 B-47s were despatched to British and Spanish bases.[23] In addition, the USAF in Europe operated various dual-capable fighter-bombers (F-100, F-101s, F-104s, F-105s). Third, American Polaris submarines were based at Holy Loch in Scotland and during the crisis, the USS *Abraham Lincoln* and the Polaris tender ship USS *Proteus*, put to sea. The most significant form of bilateral co-operation was the deployment of 60 Thor Intermediate Range Ballistic Missiles (IRBMs).

The British had their own strategic and tactical nuclear forces deployed in Britain, Western Europe and at certain overseas bases, in addition to atomic bombs deployed on two carrier borne squadrons of Buccaneer aircraft.[24] These forces operated under differing command arrangements, which affected their state of alert and readiness during the crisis. In February 1962 Bomber Command had introduced

Quick Reaction Alert (QRA) designations for aircraft that would be airborne within 15 minutes. Some of the QRA aircraft were assigned to SACEUR, and during the crisis American and British QRA aircraft remained at this state of alert. What QRA meant in practice is described by a Vulcan squadron commander:

> I spent most of that period on Quick Reaction Alert (QRA) in a flight hut on 'B' Dispersal at RAF Waddington. My Vulcan was parked about 20 yards away, fully fuelled, and loaded with a nuclear weapon. All the switches in the aircraft were set for a rapid start on the four engines, the aircraft was locked, and I carried the key to the door on a string around my neck. My crew and I were not permitted to leave the dispersal, so food was brought out to us, and we slept fully-clothed on camp beds. Although we were nominally at 15 minutes readiness, we could have been airborne day or night within half that time.[25]

As the crisis was reaching its climax, Bomber Command adopted a higher alert posture, though this did not extend to dispersal of aircraft or any airborne alert. Bomber Command's heightened state of readiness fell well short of SAC's posture. The reluctance to adopt measures that might be viewed as provocative accorded with the approach of SACEUR, General Lauris Norstad. As Commander in Chief of US Forces in Europe (CINCEUR), General Norstad could change the alert status of US nuclear forces in Europe, without prior consultation of his NATO colleagues. When the US Joint Chiefs of Staff ordered all US forces worldwide to DEFCON-3 on 22 October, Norstad was given discretion in implementing the command.[26] Norstad, however, decided to take less obtrusive action so as not to alarm Western Europeans and undermine political support for the United States.

Norstad's judgement did not reflect any formal consultation within NATO. An emergency North Atlantic Council (NAC) meeting was arranged for the evening of Monday 22 October and Dean Acheson, assisted by the CIA's Sherman Kent, briefed the Council about the missiles and the American response.[27] Under the NATO treaty there was an obligation for parties to consult together whenever the territorial integrity, political independence or the security of any party was threatened. Earlier in the year both the American and British governments had undertaken 'to consult with the North Atlantic Council, if time permits, concerning the use of nuclear weapons, anywhere in the world'.[28] Recent evidence about Soviet tactical nuclear weapons in Cuba suggests that the risk that American conventional attacks could escalate to regional nuclear war were higher than understood. Cuba was itself outside the NATO area, though areas north of Cuba inside the blockade were covered by the provisions of the treaty. This technicality did not detain the Kennedy administration, and although Acheson addressed the NAC several hours before Kennedy appeared on television, there can be no question that NATO was informed, rather than consulted.

European anxieties that an alert might be provocative surfaced in the NATO Council. The Belgian Ambassador to NATO complained strongly about announcements that, without any consultation, NATO air forces had been put on a state of alert.[29] General Moore, SACEUR's Chief of Staff, explained that measures taken amounted neither to a state of simple alert nor to a state of vigilance, and that subordinate commanders 'had been asked to do this in an unprovocative manner and as far as possible without exciting public notice'.[30] Norstad recommended that no measures should be taken 'which could be considered provocative or which might disclose operational plans'; these included: intensification of intelligence collection; increased security and anti-sabotage measures; review of alert procedures and emergency plans; manning of operational centres at reduced strength; checks of equipment and supplies.[31]

By coincidence, that same evening, Monday 22 October, Norstad dined with Harold Macmillan at Admiralty House, as part of a pre-arranged visit to mark his departure as SACEUR (due to the crisis he agreed to stay on until the end of the year). For the Prime Minister, mobilisation raised powerful memories of the calamity of the Great War (perhaps fortified by Tuchman's account), in which he had been wounded and had lost so many of his generation.[32] Privately he believed that the American reaction was 'rather panicky'.[33] The dinner with 'an old and valued friend' was a 'tiresome distraction', but it did give Macmillan a chance of a private talk with General Norstad:

> Washington . . . have been urging a NATO 'Alert', with all this implies (in our case, Royal Proclamation and call-up of reservists) I told him that we would *not* repeat *not* agree at this stage. N. agreed with this, and said he thought NATO powers would take the same view. I said 'mobilisation' had sometimes caused war. Here it was absurd, since additional forces made available by 'Alert' had *no* military significance.[34]

Norstad sent a private letter to Kennedy after dining with Macmillan, reporting that the Prime Minister 'appeared to favor strong but quiet and deliberative approach. He emphasised the need for positive and successful action should further still be necessary.'[35] Norstad, presumably, also made clear Macmillan's views on mobilisation.[36] When Norstad called on the Prime Minister the following day, Macmillan noted that the General had little to say, 'except the good news that he had persuaded Washington to be more reasonable'.[37]

Washington already knew of British concerns about mobilisation, before Norstad met Macmillan. By Monday afternoon the Foreign Office believed that the Americans might want to increase the state of NATO alert in case of trouble in Berlin and made clear to the State Department, ahead of the emergency NAC that night, they thought this 'most unwise'.[38] Ormsby-Gore conveyed this to Dean Rusk that evening, who assured him that American proposals 'would introduce no visible action' and 'only amount to an increased degree of vigilance'.[39] Norstad's views were made known to the NATO Council while he was dining in London, and these reflected his own judgement about the impact of military action on Western European political support for the US. As Raymond Garthoff comments 'It was a wise move, and a good example of political "feedback" in decision-making.'[40] Notwithstanding the significance of Macmillan's views (discussed below), the main responsibility for the lower NATO alert posture was that of General Norstad.

It now appears, however, that actions by subordinate commanders somewhat undermined SACEUR's intentions.

According to Sagan, General Truman Landon, the Commander of the United States Air Forces Europe (CINCUSAFE), 'pushed his individual authority for alerting his forces to its limits', and 'despite the Norstad prohibition against a formal DEFCON-3, numerous operational activities fully commensurate with such an alert status were instituted'.[41] According to Sagan:

> Most dramatically, Landon ordered an increased in the number of nuclear QRA aircraft on alert throughout his command, on October 24 or 25. Some of these extra nuclear QRA were alerted in Great Britain, to compensate for U.S. aircraft in West Germany, which were taken off nuclear [QRA] on 24 October and placed on conventional QRA status in anticipation of a potential Soviet attack on Berlin.[42]

For the Soviets, NATO's QRA aircraft were a factor in the military equation. The greater threat, however, was posed by SAC and Bomber Command's medium and strategic bombers, and the Thor and Jupiter IRBMs, all of which were capable of attacking targets deep inside the USSR. The 45 Jupiters were targeted at Soviet M/IRBM launchers aimed at Western Europe.[43] Under the co-ordinated British–American nuclear strike plan adopted in August 1962, Bomber Command targeted 28 Soviet IRBM sites.[44]

The relationship between SAC and Bomber Command had grown, formally and informally, in the years preceding the Cuban crisis. Since 1958, British and American targeting plans had been co-ordinated;[45] British Canberra and V-bombers were adapted to carry American nuclear weapons;[46] and from 1959 Thor IRBMs were deployed in England under dual-key arrangements. In February 1962 the introduction of the QRA system into Bomber Command meant 'an integration with SAC rather than mere co-ordination', according to Air Marshal Cross.[47] By the time of the Cuban crisis the relationship between SAC and Bomber Command was therefore an intimate one, and occurred, as Menaul explained, 'just when [Bomber] Command was reaching the peak of its operational efficiency'.[48] Kennedy and Macmillan did not discuss preparations for nuclear conflict. As the Foreign Office subsequently noted:

'The Cuban situation did not reach a point, as far as we know, at which the early use of nuclear weapons might have been contemplated or the President required to fulfil his undertaking to consult H.M.G. on their use.'[49]

The issue of military mobilisation did arise in the Macmillan–Kennedy conversations, although in the Caribbean context. Despite his remarks to Norstad about mobilisation, Macmillan advised Kennedy 'that you will no doubt continue with your military build-up for any emergency', as 'this may be as important a factor for persuading the Cubans to accept inspection as in other directions'.[50] Mobilisation may sometimes have caused war. It could also signal resolve, and deter or compel an adversary. Nevertheless, in Europe the Prime Minister remained opposed to mobilisation, including involving nuclear forces, and was to make this clear to his military commanders.

The issue of consultation, both in general political terms and over the use of American nuclear weapons, was of concern in Whitehall and Westminster. In February 1961 Kennedy had reaffirmed the undertakings given by Eisenhower to 'take every possible step to consult with Britain and our other allies'.[51] Changes in the USAF alert status had been an issue of public concern when it emerged that during the 1960 U-2 crisis SAC engaged in a practice alert without the British government being consulted. Within Whitehall this was believed to contain an element of American 'sabre-rattling'.[52] 'Special confidential planning channels' were used to pass news of the alert from SAC to Bomber Command, though this was not made public.[53] Subsequently, Eisenhower's Defence Secretary undertook to inform his British counterpart when American political authorities or military commanders decided to alert US forces in the UK.[54] According to Menaul, Bomber Command learned of the DEFCON-2 alert from SAC, presumably through these confidential planning channels, on 25 October.[55]

HOLY LOCH

Since 1960, the United States Navy had also based strategic nuclear forces in the United Kingdom at Holy Loch in

Scotland. The firing of Polaris missiles from British territorial waters was a matter for joint decision, and the 'deployment and use of the submarine depot ship and associated
facilities' would be 'a matter of joint consultation between
the two governments'.[56] However, this did not involve consultation with the British government on the deployment
or use of the submarines outside British territorial waters.

The United States Navy declared DEFCON-3 at 3.46 am
on 23 October, at which point there was only one Polaris
SSBN, USS *Abraham Lincoln*, in Holy Loch.[57] According to
a US naval staff officer, Vice-Admiral Beshany, there were
three Polaris submarines at Holy Loch at the start of the
Cuban crisis, which were moved 'out of Holy Loch as a
precaution without orders from above'.[58] The decision was
then at once communicated to higher authorities and 'immediately endorsed, embraced, there was no argumenta-
tion'.[59] Both the submarines and the submarine tender, USS
Proteus, were deployed from Holy Loch: 'The first ship went
out almost immediately and the second one went out within
24 hours and then there was a third one alongside and
she went out like 36 hours later, followed by the tender,
which was really a remarkable achievement.'[60] If this account is accurate, two of the boats were 'flushed' before
the declaration of the DEFCON-3 alert state. The USS
Abraham Lincoln left Holy Loch at 2 pm on 23 October.[61]
American political authorities were then informed of the
Polaris deployments. The Joint Chiefs situation report to
the White House and State Department for 25 October
showed that 112 Atlantic Command SLBMs were on alert,
indicating that all seven available SSBNs were on station;
it was also made clear that the 'submarine tender Proteus
is dispersing to Clyde Op[erational] Area'.[62] Hence, there
was adequate time for the US authorities to meet the formal
requirement to consult on the deployment of *Proteus* after
the military decision to deploy the submarines. Naval channels of communication, and possibly the Royal Navy's own
monitoring team at Holy Loch, presumably enabled the
Admiralty to learn of events in the same way Bomber Command was told of changes in SAC's DEFCON alert state.

The American government did not ask the British government to raise the alert status of British nuclear forces.[63]

According to Sagan: 'There is also no indication in the available records that high-level American political or military authorities in Washington were aware that Britain's nuclear forces were being put on a higher state of alert'.[64] However, SAC headquarters would have been aware of the changes in the Thor force, through 7th Air Division HQ in Britain.[65] Direct communications between SAC HQ and Bomber Command HQ, and between their respective commanders, Air Marshal Cross and General Tommy Power, were normally regular, if not daily; curiously, however, 'once the Cuban missile crisis started, there was no one on the other end of the phone and there was no one on the other end of the phone until the crisis was over'.[66] The alert state of three Valiant and four Canberras on NATO-assigned QRA was reported to senior American political authorities.[67] Nevertheless, despite considerable American anxiety about the Jupiter IRBMs, there was apparently no concern about the Thor IRBMs in Britain.

The change in the alert and readiness postures of British nuclear forces during the crisis is now clearer. It first became known when an article appeared in the *Daily Mail* in February 1963;[68] Menaul published his account in 1980;[69] more recent evidence has been produced by Scott Sagan.[70] The extent of the alert caused some consternation in 1963 when it became known, and when it was even claimed that the V-bombers had been airborne.[71] In his memoirs Macmillan alludes to 'certain precautions affecting the Royal Air Force',[72] though in Parliament in 1963 he downplayed suggestions that anything dramatic had occurred, while nevertheless emphasising that precautions were taken: 'Naturally, if the deterrent is to play its role it is always kept at a state of readiness. During a period of tension certain additional steps were taken, but they are of a kind which is merely intended and normal and were no more than normal.'[73]

As Macmillan explained, whatever the alert condition of British nuclear forces, the credibility of a British deterrent depended on a high state of readiness under any conditions. The ability of the V-bombers and Thors to attack Soviet targets depended on not being destroyed on the ground. With the emergence of the Soviet ballistic missile threat in the late 1950s, a policy of dispersal and warning was increasingly critical to the survivability and credibility of the British nuclear force. The Soviets were believed to possess some 700 Soviet M/IRBMs,[74] and had 129 M/IRBM launchers capable of striking Western Europe.[75] With the advent of Soviet submarine based missiles, warning time was further reduced and Bomber Command arrangements for scrambling bombers and launching missiles were constantly under review. Alert and readiness postures were practised and revised. In October the Soviets were estimated to have some 97 'short range' submarine based missiles on 35 diesel and nuclear submarines.[76] According to Garthoff, these 'were all in Soviet waters and unavailable for early commitment [against the US], in addition to being highly vulnerable'.[77] British bases were therefore likely to have been a high priority for these weapons.

Menaul mistakenly claims that when SAC moved to DEFCON-2 Bomber Command was already in the middle of a regular alert and readiness exercise.[78] According to this account, Air Marshal Cross decided on 26 October to prolong the exercise, on his own authority. Then, in the early hours of Saturday morning, 27 October, and in response to American and Soviet statement, 'the C-in-C decided to increase the readiness of the force, purely as part of the training exercise'.[79]

Air Ministry records present a different picture. It was at 1 pm on Saturday 27 October that Bomber Command HQ initiated Alert Condition 3.[80] This state of readiness remained in force until 5 November. It had been designed to enable C-in-C Bomber Command 'during a period of political tension, to take certain precautionary measures short of the full and specific measures involved in the calling of higher Alert Conditions'.[81] All key personnel were required to remain on stations, Operations Room Staff were to be available at short notice. The record of No. 1 Group Headquarters states that 'although no generation of aircraft was ordered, some preparations were made to ensure rapid generation if necessary. All measures were to be unobtrusive'.[82] No aircraft were dispersed or on any form of airborne alert, although a detachment of Vulcans was recalled from an exercise in the Middle East.[83]

On 28 October orders were given to increase the number of aircraft on QRA. At No. 1 Group the number of QRA bombers was to increase from six to 12.[84] At RAF Waddington the QRA force would have doubled from three bombers to six, but the 'tigerish' station commander increased it to nine.[85] The Bomber Command order to increase the QRA force was given at 3.47 pm, on Sunday 28 October, to come into operation at 8 am, the following morning.[86] This order, it should be noted, was given *after* Macmillan and the rest of the world learned that Khrushchev would withdraw the missiles from Cuba. By Tuesday 30 October, however, tension had lessened such that one Group Captain, Ian Campbell, felt that, 'shades of Drake', he could spend several hours shooting partridges on a local estate.[87]

In addition to the medium bombers, the RAF's Thor missiles were also made ready. Sixty Thors were deployed under a bilateral agreement between the British and American governments.[88] To conform with American legal and political requirements the weapons were deployed under dual-key arrangements, whereby the missiles were owned and operated by the RAF and the warheads held under USAF custody. The principal features of this dual-key system were replicated in the arrangements for the Jupiters in Italy and Turkey.[89]

When the first Thors arrived in 1959, the warheads were kept separate from the missiles. Under these circumstances, it would have taken between 24 and 57 hours to prepare and fire the weapons.[90] Under American pressure, British ministers accepted that this was militarily inadvisable and arrangements for mating missiles with warheads were accelerated.[91] By October 1962 the normal state of readiness for the missiles was 15 minutes.[92] By August 1961 modifications meant that the 'total countdown time' was 13 to 14 minutes.[93] This could also be reduced. If the missiles were kept in the vertical unfuelled position they could be launched within seven minutes.[94] Some modifications to the Thors appear to have made during 1961–2, and, according to one source, some missiles at the Driffield complex were adapted to be fuelled during erection, reducing launch time from fifteen to nine minutes.[95] These times refer to the firing sequence and do not include time for the two governments to consult on their joint decision to launch. Under normal peacetime conditions 65 per cent of the Thor force (39 missiles) was kept at standby (30 minutes readiness).[96] During the missile crisis, 59 of the 60 Thors were at a readiness state of 15 minutes or less.[97]

The possibility of inadvertent nuclear war, arising from the use of nuclear weapons by subordinate or host country commanders was an issue that greatly exercised President Kennedy, and has attracted recent attention from American scholars.[98] There has been speculation about whether the American veto on the Thors could have been overridden *in extremis*.[99] Safeguards were procedural rather than electronic: no Permissive Action Links (PALs) were installed, and it is possible that British crews could have armed their missiles during the crisis. Conversely, as only one American serviceman was involved in the launch procedure it is virtually inconceivable that the British veto could have been overridden. While there is no suggestion that any RAF crew contemplated such action (or that the British authorities had any contingency plan for seizing control), fear of unauthorised use of the Jupiters IRBMs worried ExComm, and the President.

Since Menaul's account there has been speculation concerning the change in Bomber Command's alert posture, and whether ministers were involved in, or indeed aware of, the decision. Menaul doubts whether more than 'a handful of people' outside Bomber Command knew of what happened.[100] Sagan quotes senior MOD officials, including the Chief Scientific Adviser, Lord Solly Zuckerman, who have indicated that MOD did not order Cross to change the alert posture of his force.[101] Sagan's preliminary conclusion is that senior civilian officials, including the Prime Minister, 'were not fully cognizant' of increased alert activities, and he argues that 'Air Marshal Cross's actions are another example of how the military commander's interests in combat readiness can cut against civilian authorities' interests in safety.'[102] This conclusion has been challenged by the head of the MOD Air Historical Branch, Ian Madelin,[103] and by archival disclosures.

According to his own recollections, Cross did act on his own initiative, though he also sought sanction 'up the line', without success.[104] His 'first contact upwards' did not take place until the afternoon of Sunday 28 October, when he was summoned to White's Club to meet the Chief of the Air Staff, Sir Thomas Pike, and the Secretary of State for Air, Sir Hugh Fraser.[105] He was asked for his opinion on what measures should be taken. The previous day, Saturday 27 October, Cross had raised Bomber Command to Alert Condition 3. This however, was specifically designed to be authorised by C-in-C Bomber Command (without recourse to higher political authority), and to involve discrete and unobstrusive measures. Further action, such as dispersal, would have been obtrusive and potentially provocative (and would have required political authorisation). Cross was very much aware of the operational constraints under Alert Condition 3, and later explained to the VCAS that: 'when despite having everything ready to bring 75% of the aircraft in the Command to readiness, we could not give the order for fear of the effect it might have (if it became known) on the very tense negotiations being carried on by Mr Kruschev and Mr Kennedy'.[106]

Second, records of key decision-making now indicate that Cross' actions accorded with government wishes. On the morning of 27 October Sir Thomas Pike was summoned to Admiralty House at 11 am when he was appraised by the Prime Minister on the latest developments in the Caribbean.[107] Pike then reported to other service chiefs at 2.30 pm. The previous evening, the Chiefs of Staff were told, President Kennedy had warned the Prime Minister that if he did not receive adequate assurances, the United States would attack the missiles, or invade, or both.[108] Pike briefed Macmillan on the RAF's current alert posture. Although there were indications of diplomatic progress at this time, the situation was very tense. The Prime Minister, however, was 'adamant' that:

> he did not consider the time was appropriate for any overt preparatory steps to be taken such as mobilisation. Moreover, he did not wish Bomber Command to be alerted, although he wished the force to be ready to take the appropriate steps should this become necessary. If the situation deteriorated further the Prime Minister

intended calling a Cabinet Meeting on the next afternoon at which the Chief of the Defence Staff and the three Chiefs of Staff would be in attendance. At the moment, however, he did not wish the Chief of the Defence Staff to be brought back to London, since his intention was that matters should be played in as low a key as possible.[109]

Macmillan's remarks invite speculation about how far he grasped the details of Bomber Command's alert and readiness plan. It was nevertheless clear that the Prime Minister did not want Bomber Command to disperse, though it was to take appropriate precautionary measures. Whether Macmillan understood that bombers at main bases were fifteen minutes or less from take-off is not clear, although in September the government took part in the NATO FALLEX command post exercise which should have exposed the Prime Minister to Bomber Command's operational procedures.

Following his conversation with the Prime Minister, the Chief of the Air Staff contacted Air Marshal Cross: 'Sir Thomas Pike said that as a result of his conversation with the Prime Minister, he had warned the Air Officer Commanding-in-Chief, Bomber Command that he should be on the alert and that his key personnel should be available on station. There were ten bombers overseas at present, but he felt that it was not desirable to recall these aircraft at the moment.'[110] Thus, Cross' actions fell within the provisions of Alert Condition 3, which, as noted, was instituted at 1 pm on Saturday, and which Cross was entitled to order without seeking political authority from the Air Ministry. Which ministers were told, and when, is still not clear, though the immediate political authority for Bomber Command was the Air Ministry rather then MOD, which may help explain the statements of MOD officials.[111]

The government's military advisers clearly did not share the bellicosity of their American counterparts, who, as General William Smith, then aide to the Chairman of the Joint Chiefs of Staff, General Maxwell Taylor, has noted, 'were consistent and united in recommending the use of overwhelming military power against the Soviet and Cuban military on the island'.[112] The Chief of Staff of the US Army, General Wheeler told the US service chiefs on 20 October: 'I never thought I'd live to see the day when I would want to go to war.'[113] General Curtis Le May, USAF Chief of Staff, even argued for an American attack on Cuba *after* Khrushchev had agreed to withdraw the missiles.[114] President Kennedy later remarked that the American military were mad.[115] By contrast, the British Chiefs of Staff were deeply concerned about the prospect of escalation and, for example, believed that in the event of Soviet action against Berlin, overwhelming Soviet conventional superiority meant that 'it would be useless to launch any of the ground access probes at present planned on a tripartite basis. The Prime Minister should be advised of this in order that he may urge the President to restrain General Norstad from undertaking any such operation.'[116] On Sunday 28th October Chiefs of Staff made clear to the Defence Secretary and the Chief of Defence Staff that such action would be 'foolish'.[117]

By Saturday 27 October the crisis was still a Caribbean affair. At the outset the government decided that there would be no British involvement in the blockade. As noted in Chapter Two, the air base at Mayaguana was to be made available for USAF operations against Cuba, but elsewhere British frigates were ordered to stay clear of the quarantine area.[118] The Secretary of State for the Colonies, Duncan Sandys, cabled St Lucia that requests from Cuban or Warsaw Pact ships for facilities were to be treated like those from any other county: 'it is NOT (repeat NOT) our intention to offer the Americans any special help in enforcing the blockade', he emphasised.[119] There is, however, some evidence that three squadrons of Shackleton Reconnaissance and Anti-Submarine Warfare aircraft were due to fly to Nassau 'to show the flag' at the weekend, but the deployment, whose exact purpose is unclear, was cancelled shortly before the aircraft were due to leave.[120] British intelligence gathering during the crisis, especially through the Havana embassy, and in the monitoring of Soviet shipping, was a further aspect of British involvement, whose scope and significance is beginning to emerge.

Adjudication of the significance of British military activities during the Cuban crisis involves the unresolved question of how the Soviet authorities perceived Western action. The issue of whether Western nuclear alerts were a deterrent or a provocation is of central importance in assessing broader issues of nuclear deterrence. How the Soviets saw British nuclear operations is also important to debates about an independent British deterrent. The British authorities were keen to maintain a low-key approach. Nevertheless, among former senior RAF officers there was a clear belief that Bomber Command's actions had contributed to deterrence and the prevention of war: 'The Kremlin would undoubtedly have known of the Command's response and put this factor in their scales of what to do next';[121] 'the knowledge that there was a mass of nuclear-armed bombers standing-by on numerous airfields must have served to tilt the balance in favour of peace. This is one time when nuclear deterrence was clearly seen to work'.[122]

Little has yet emerged about Soviet intelligence activity in Europe during the crisis. It is believed that both the GRU and the KGB depended upon a network of base watchers to provide warning of nuclear attack.[123] Oleg Penkovsky had made clear to CIA and SIS that warning of a nuclear attack was the priority of the GRU.[124] Soviet military attachés were a potential source of intelligence, and the War Office 'received numerous requests from Soviet attachés to visit air bases, particularly those on which USAF units are based; the requests were refused'.[125] An interesting vignette is provided by Captain Ivanov (of the GRU) who recalls touring the main US and British Air Force bases, using the car of a Bulgarian colleague. Ivanov claims to have seen 'pilots mindlessly drinking beer and flirting with local girls. I did not detect any alarming signals, and duly reported this to Moscow Centre.'[126]

Had the Soviets detected the change in the British alert posture, their analysis of its significance would have depended, among other things, on what they knew of British procedures. The previous month, for example, Bomber Command held its second 'no notice' alert and readiness exercise, which entailed dispersing the Medium Bomber force, and raising the Alert State to Conditions 1 and 2.[127] Aircraft were sent to their dispersal airfields and practised scrambling. Assuming that Soviet intelligence monitored these activities, military authorities would have recognised the limited scope of British action in October. Of greater concern to the Soviet authorities at this time was the alert state, and the intentions, of US forces in Europe. While those assigned to SACEUR were at a lower level of readiness, SAC's bombers in Europe, as elsewhere, were at the unprecedented state of DEFCON-2. Whether the Soviets made any meaningful distinctions between British and American nuclear forces under such circumstances remains an interesting question.

Western military alerts were taken to deter Soviet action, not in response to any Soviet measures. The Chairman of the JIC, Sir Hugh Stephenson, told the Chiefs of Staff on 25 October that the only measures known to have been taken so far were those consistent with a 'State of Readiness'.[128] The CIA's retrospective analysis in December 1962 concluded that there 'was no evidence of any significant major redeployments of forces or any readiness measures by the Soviet Long Range Air Forces'.[129]

Whether the Cuban missile crisis marked the triumph of deterrence or a hazardous exercise in nuclear brinkmanship remains a key debate about October 1962. Within the British defence establishment there was no reassessment of British defence policy. The central tenets of nuclear deterrence and British–American co-operation continued as before, only to be shaken shortly after by the Skybolt crisis. Some military consequences did follow. The Cuban crisis, Air Marshal Cross believed, had 'amply demonstrated that what really counted was the number of aircraft at readiness',[130] and he was unhappy at what the V-force had achieved. Subsequently procedures were reviewed to bring a higher proportion of aircraft to a higher state of readiness under Alert Condition 3, unobtrusively. The performance of the Thor squadrons on the other hand, was praised by Cross: 'the Cuban crisis had really shown the value of this missile', he told his officers, for, 'without visible change 59 of the 60 missiles had been made serviceable and ready simply by use of the telephone'.[131] An attempt was made to prolong the deployment of the Thors. Cross outlined the advantages of the weapons to the VCAS, Sir Wallace

Kyle: first, as their normal state of readiness was 15 minutes, the whole force could be alerted inconspicuously, and second 'this well proven weapon enables a high proportion of missiles to be brought to readiness at will'.[132] In the 'eyes of the American professional, as represented by SAC it was systems at readiness that count', he argued; Cross recommended that the phase-out of the Thors be 'retarded' and 'the reduction planned to start on April 1st 1963 be postponed until at least April 1964'.[133]

The view of the C-in-C Bomber Command was shared within the Air Ministry. Immediately after the crisis the Secretary of State for Air, Hugh Fraser, suggested to Defence Secretary Thorneycroft that 'there are arguments for slowing down the programme' of withdrawal 'and retaining at least some of the missiles for rather longer'.[134] Thorneycroft, however, was not convinced, both on grounds of cost and because 'with its operational limitations it could never be a really satisfactory second strike weapon'.[135] Thorneycroft's reaction reflected the government's decision in the summer of 1962 that given its operational limitations, Thor would not be cost-effective when American financial support finished at the end of the initial deployment agreement. Had the British government given serious consideration to delaying their withdrawal, this might also have complicated the diplomatic position and the withdrawal of the Jupiter missiles from Turkey and Italy. As will be seen in Chapter Nine, whatever the military role of the missiles, the diplomatic side of the European IRBMs was significant in the unfolding and denouement of the crisis. For the British government, the Thor missiles were to become the basis of an initiative designed to assist President Kennedy to resolve the crisis by diplomatic means.

The Cuban missile crisis illuminates the complex and intimate relationship involving the nuclear forces of the United Kingdom and the United States. Yet, in terms of consultation, the crisis had not reached the stage at which Kennedy was obligated to consult the British (or other allies) on the use of nuclear weapons. Moreover, it seems clear that Kennedy consulted Macmillan (and Ormsby-Gore), not because Britain was a nuclear power, but because she was a political ally with crucial common interests (not least in Berlin). Notwithstanding its intrinsic fascination, therefore, the military aspect of the crisis is of limited value in addressing the central issues concerning Britain's nuclear relationship with the United States.

The missile crisis nevertheless demonstrates important differences between American and British leaders over the manipulation of nuclear force in pursuit of political goals. Macmillan and Kennedy had both read Barbara Tuchman's *Guns of August*. Both recognised that lessons should be learned from 1914. Yet, in practice, Macmillan refused to disperse the V-bombers or mobilise his forces, while under Kennedy the USAF adopted an unprecedented alert posture. Differences in perception were also apparent at the military level. The British Chiefs of Staff were clearly horrified that NATO might consider moving against Berlin should the Soviets seize the city. The missile crisis did not challenge British attitudes toward deterrence in general or to a British deterrent in particular. Nevertheless, recognition that nuclear war would be a disaster for all, and that measures of arms control and disarmament were a necessity, was, diplomatically, the more important lesson and one that the British and American governments strove, successfully, to implement by negotiating a ban on atmospheric nuclear testing.[136]

9 'The Frightful Desire to *Do* Something'[1]

On the morning of Friday 26 October President Kennedy told ExComm that by itself the quarantine would not remove the Soviet missiles from Cuba. There were only two ways: trading them out or 'to go over and just take them out', he believed.[2] At the United Nations U Thant was about to begin exploratory talks with the Cubans, Soviets and Americans. With the crisis reaching its climax, Kennedy and his colleagues debated the diplomatic and military options. With recognition that action against Cuba was likely to provoke a Soviet response against Berlin, the British, French and German Ambassadors in Washington were kept closely in touch with developments, and a North Atlantic Council meeting was scheduled for Sunday 28 October. Kennedy spoke to Macmillan on the telephone and Ormsby-Gore held conversations and meetings with senior administration officials, including the President. The British government was actively, if not intimately, involved in the Kennedy administration deliberations. This chapter explores relations between Washington and London as the crisis reached its climax, and how Macmillan reconciled his impulse to act (and to be seen to act) with his desire to support Kennedy. How far, and in what ways, British–American consultation would have extended to the decision to use force against Cuba is also considered.

On Friday 26 October Ormsby-Gore was unable to see the President, though they spoke on the telephone. Ormsby-Gore asked Kennedy 'how long he felt they could give U Thant to try and produce a satisfactory and verified standstill'; the President 'said that the evidence was that the Soviets were pushing ahead preparing the missile sites and the United States could not, therefore, wait very much longer'.[3] Ormsby-Gore did meet Dean Rusk, who explained that U Thant had been given an assurance that, if the Soviets and Cubans accepted effective UN verification of a standstill, the United States would not attack Cuba for the two or three weeks while talks went forward.[4]

Adlai Stevenson would be meeting U Thant later that afternoon to make clear three immediate US requirements: no further shipments of offensive weapons; standstill of construction work on the missile sites; existing missiles must be made inoperable.[5] Rusk told Ormsby-Gore that work on the missile sites was being accelerated, and emphasised that 'a very serious situation would arise if any of the weapons were moved into a firing position or if it were discovered that they were being fitted with nuclear warheads'.[6]

In the absence of a settlement, Ormsby-Gore warned the Foreign Secretary:

> As to what 'the other action' that the President mentioned might be, I have little doubt that it would entail the bombing of all the known sites for long-range missiles in Cuba. I cannot see that a simple extension of the blockade would meet their main objective which is to prevent these long-range offensive missiles coming into a state of immediate readiness for firing. The Americans are in no doubt by this time also in a position to invade, but if they were to invade before first of all carrying out a missile strike this would be inconsistent with their policy up to now of using the minimum force necessary to achieve what they regard as their essential objective. Nevertheless, I suppose that bombing Cuba would very likely result in a series of engagements and perhaps Cuban action against Guantanamo. The situation could then quickly arise in which the Americans would see little alternative to an all-out invasion.[7]

Later that day, however, the first indications emerged of Soviet willingness to withdraw the missiles in return for American concessions. Over lunch Aleksandr Feklisov, a counsellor at the Soviet embassy and KGB *Resident* in Washington, discussed a possible deal with an American journalist, John Scali. The 'deal' conveyed to the President was that 'bases would be dismantled under United Nations supervision and Castro would pledge not to accept offensive weapons of any kind, ever, in return for [a] US pledge not to invade Cuba'.[8] The Americans believed that this suggestion had come from the Soviet government and that they had established a new back-channel to Khrushchev. It now seems clear that both these assumptions were mistaken: Feklisov had initially acted on his own initiative, and reports of his meetings did not reach Khrushchev at the appropriate time.[9]

At 6 pm (Washington time), the first section of a letter from Khrushchev arrived, which was verbose and highly personalised, but appeared to make a similar proposal to Feklisov's,[10] although McNamara later described the letter as 'twelve pages of fluff'.[11] Other members of ExComm worried that Khrushchev was exhibiting signs of instability. Macmillan later described it as characteristically 'impulsive and highly emotional'.[12] Nevertheless, Khrushchev indicated that if Kennedy gave assurances not to invade and recalled his fleet, 'this would immediately change everything'; if there was no threat then 'the question of the destruction . . . of the armaments which you call offensive' would look different.[13] When taken in concert with Feklisov's approach, a deal began to look possible.

On Friday evening Rusk summoned the British, West German and French Ambassadors, David Ormsby-Gore, Wilhelm Crewe and Hervé Alphand. Khrushchev's message was still arriving and, with Feklisov's approach, was being analysed. The Ambassadors were told by Roger Hilsman that 'there could be no doubt some of the MRBMs were operational', and that 'it was fair to assume that the warheads were there for those of the MRBMs which were operational'.[14] Paul Nitze emphasised that in the UN negotiations the Americans must obtain their three objectives within 48 hours.[15]

Rusk emphasised that continuing Soviet preparation at the missile sites 'was the most serious element in the situation'.[16] Moreover

> When asked what further action the United States might take if they failed to obtain a satisfactory outcome in the talks with U Thant, [Rusk] indicated that they would have to consider destroying the sites by bombing. He did not expect to be faced with such a decision for two or three days and in the view of the world wide repercussions

which might result he assured us that *our countries would be consulted before the decision was taken.*[17]

Ormsby-Gore's messages to London clearly convey Washington's intention to take military action if the Soviets did not halt work on their MRBMs. It was made clear that the US was preparing to act on Monday morning, though Ormsby-Gore later told the Foreign Secretary that, in his view, 'the Americans would have waited until Tuesday morning, 30th October, before taking military action, unless of course there had been some new element introduced such as a Cuban attack on Guantanamo or a serious air battle over Cuba'.[18] Why the Kennedy administration believed that it was necessary to attack if the missiles became 'ready' remains a critical issue.[19] In retrospect, Macmillan endorsed Kennedy's brinkmanship. In his diary, he praised Kennedy for having 'played a firm *military* game throughout – acting quickly and being ready to act *as soon as* mobilised. This was Eden's *fatal* mistake – in which we share the responsibility. You cannot keep an 'army of invasion' hanging about. It must invade or disperse. President K. did not bluster – but everyone knew that (if no other solution was found) there would be an invasion.'[20] With an American decision on military action looming, the diplomatic options were under intense scrutiny.[21] In London the FO's Northern Department assessed likely Soviet reactions to an American attack on the missiles or a US invasion:

> Our assessment is that the Russians acknowledge American nuclear superiority and recognize therefore that they cannot survive a nuclear exchange. They would go to almost any lengths to avoid nuclear annihilation and we believe, in relation to China, that they would allow China to be destroyed rather than risk involvement on her behalf. This calculation would apply equally to Cuba. The Russians would of course know that to back down would be a blow to their prestige from which it is hard to see how they could recover.[22]

In the face of American military action the key questions for the Soviets would be whether the Americans had taken 'the final decision to have a nuclear show-down', and whether

the time had 'come for the Russians to consider a first
strike against American nuclear installations both in the
United States and elsewhere'.[23] As noted, Khrushchev had
signalled in his reply to Bertrand Russell that war would
only be unleashed when missiles were fired. The Northern
Department believed that while such thinking might guide
Soviet reactions to an American attack on Cuba, 'it would
be a very near thing: there would be at best a 50–50 chance
that the Russians would conclude that there was no option
to them but to get their strike in first'.[24]

Kennedy spoke again with Macmillan on Friday.[25] Kennedy
thought that he would know by 'tomorrow morning or noon'
whether the Soviets had a serious proposal.[26] Macmillan
warned Kennedy that 'at this stage any movement by you
may produce a result in Berlin which would be very bad
for us all. That's the danger now.'[27] When Kennedy then
said that, 'if at the end of 48 hours we are getting no
place, and the missile sites continue to be constructed then
we are going to be faced with some hard decisions',
Macmillan rejoindered that, 'in making those decisions one
has to realise that they will have their effect on Berlin as
well as on Cuba'.[28] Kennedy promised that, 'in any case
I'll talk to you on the phone before we do anything of a
drastic nature'.[29]

As the crisis now reached its climax the Prime Minister
and his close colleagues considered whether British diplomatic action was necessary. The idea of using the Thor
missiles in some form of reciprocal arrangement with Soviet MRBMs in Cuba was already being explored by the
Foreign Office. The Americans were giving active consideration to the withdrawal of the missiles from Turkey, though
the issue had not yet been raised by Khrushchev. On 26
October Ormsby-Gore was informed by London that it might
be less invidious for the Turks if Britain was also prepared
to accept United Nations observers on 'proper conditions'
at the Thor missile sites: 'If it might help to persuade the
Russians and Cubans to accept something on these lines
by introducing the idea of reciprocity, we might be ready
to consider some similar arrangements for the Thor missile sites in this country.'[30] The Foreign Office had not yet
consulted the Ministry of Defence or obtained Governmental

authority for a definite proposal on these lines but intended
to do so, if Ormsby-Gore thought it helpful. The Foreign
Office, nevertheless believed that, 'it would be disadvan-
tageous if the Cuban problem were resolved in the context
of bases overseas alone'.[31] A broader agenda was preferable,
possibly involving anti-surprise attack measures, in particular,
static observation posts at danger points, including outside
the Caribbean.[32] The idea of British sponsorship of a
conference to broker a settlement had been put to the British
government by Captain Ivanov. The Foreign Office was
anxious to learn whether Kennedy was still seriously
interested in a broader conference and whether Washington
had given any thought to what form, sponsorship and place
they might prefer.[33]

On Friday evening, 26 October, Macmillan floated the
idea of immobilising the Thors to the President (before
Khrushchev had publicly raised the Turkish Jupiters). After
Kennedy had spoken of possible guarantees for Cuba's
security, Macmillan asked whether if, 'we want to help the
Russians to save face would it be worthwhile our undertaking
to immobilise our Thor missiles which are here in England
during the same period – during the conference?'[34] Kennedy
promised to 'put that into the machinery', and be in touch
later; and then said: 'I think we don't want to have too
many dismantlings but it is possible that proposal might
help; they might also insist on Greece, on Turkey and Italy
but I will keep in mind your suggestion here so that if it
gets into that it may be advantageous.'[35] Macmillan then
wrote to Kennedy, confirming the main points of their
conversation, and outlining the three possibilities they had
discussed: that the inviolability of a demilitarised Cuba could
become subject to international guarantee; that in the absence
of a settlement U Thant should go to Cuba himself, secure
immobilisation of the missiles and prevent further work
on the sites to allow discussions to open; and third:

> the proposal that it might be helpful to save the Rus-
> sians' face if we undertook during the same period to
> allow the immobilization of our Thor missiles, of which
> there are 60, under United Nations supervision. This
> has, of course, the disadvantage that it brings in the

concept of bargaining bases in Europe against those in Cuba. Nevertheless if it would turn the scale I would be willing to propose it to U Thant and it might be less invidious for us to take the lead rather than place the burden on the Turks. You said you would have this idea looked at.[36]

There are no indications that Kennedy displayed any interest in the idea, and there was no discussion of the proposal in ExComm on the Saturday.[37]

BLACK SATURDAY

Among American officials 27 October became known as 'Black Saturday' and may well have been the closest we have come to Armageddon. Within ExComm the measured optimism of Friday was quickly dispelled by the broadcast of a second, formal, letter from Khrushchev in which he publicised the proposal to withdraw the missiles in return for guarantees of Cuba's security, but also added that 'analogous weapons' in Turkey should be withdrawn.[38] As ExComm debated the significance of Khrushchev's new demands, news came through that a U-2 had been shot down over Cuba, and the pilot killed.[39] There has long been speculation why Khrushchev sent two letters, and within the Foreign Office and the State Department there was conjecture about possible division within the Presidium. Sir Evelyn Shuckburgh shared the view of some Americans that the additional demand for the Jupiters 'argues divisions in the Soviet leadership'.[40] Reports from French diplomats suggested 'a greater state of disarray in the Kremlin than ours do'.[41] From Moscow, however, Sir Frank Roberts, argued that there was 'absolutely no evidence of disarray in the Kremlin', and suggested the alternative theory 'is simply that Khrushchev runs the show, and not always very well'.[42] Recent evidence from Soviet sources indicates that Roberts was correct, and that Khrushchev was responsible for both letters – the more discursive message was written after warnings from Soviet and Cuban intelligence that an American attack on Cuba was imminent.[43] Some of this intelligence concerned US activities in the Caribbean and Florida, where American military preparations were well advanced. The British Acting Consul in Miami described the atmosphere in Florida at the time as 'very much like Southern England before D-day'.[44]

The deployment of American nuclear missiles in Turkey had been a particular irritant to Khrushchev and may well have played a greater part in his Cuban policy than western historians have accepted.[45] The missiles had also exercised American officials well before Khrushchev raised them in his letter received on 27 October. President Kennedy saw little value in the Jupiters, but in the face of Turkish commitment continued the deployment, with the initial missile launch positions handed over to the Turkish Air Force in October 1962.[46]

In addition to the diplomatic aspects Kennedy was conscious that, notwithstanding dual-key control, unauthorised host-country use might be a short cut to nuclear catastrophe. On 22 October he therefore gave instructions that American commanders in Italy and Turkey were to 'take special precautions' to prevent unauthorised use of the weapons in the event of Soviet attack.[47] The Joint Chiefs instructed local commanders to destroy the missiles in the event of unauthorised attempts to fire them.[48] Nevertheless, the Jupiters were at 15 minutes readiness, with the warheads mated to the missiles, in the same manner as the Thors.[49] Electronic locking mechanisms had not been installed on the Jupiters,[50] and although American participation was still required to arm the warheads, Kennedy and his colleagues had anxiety about the procedures and mechanisms for preventing unauthorised launch. Within the American government, the Jupiters were seen as obsolete and vulnerable. Nevertheless, 80 per cent of them were normally kept at 15 minutes readiness.[51] By 25 October, 37 (of the 45) Jupiters (in Turkey and Italy) were reported to be on alert by the Joint Chiefs.[52] It should therefore be noted that the specific circumstances which Rusk said could provoke American military action – missiles in firing position armed with their warheads – were exactly those confronting the USSR from Europe.

The idea of trading the Turkish Jupiters for the Soviet missiles in Cuba emerged quickly in the first days of the crisis. Horrified at the 'incalculable consequences' of military action, Adlai Stevenson wrote to the President on 17 October, urging that 'the existence of nuclear missile bases anywhere [should be] negotiable before we start anything'.[53] Stevenson's views were dismissed by the President and afterwards leaked (by Kennedy) to a hostile press. Ormsby-Gore later characterised Stevenson's performance at this stage as 'lamentably spineless',[54] and argued that 'he showed little if any resolution in the discussions leading up to the President's original decision and . . . had no stomach for the part he had to play in the Security Council'.[55] By 19 October, however, Robert McNamara had suggested that some kind of trade on the Jupiters would be necessary, and on 21 October Robert Kennedy confided to Arthur Schlesinger that a deal would have to be made in the end.[56] President Kennedy quickly recognised that for much of world opinion, Soviet missiles in Cuba were equivalent to American missiles in Turkey, and within ExComm he emerged as the strongest proponent of a deal. The perception of Cuban–Turkish symmetry reflected a Soviet–American perspective that took no account of other Soviet forces facing NATO, including the 129 Soviet M/IRBM launchers targeted on Europe. Nevertheless, American consideration of a Turkish deal began well before Khrushchev formally raised the issue on 27 October.

Despite the importance of the Turkish missiles, Macmillan's advisers appear curiously ill-informed about their diplomatic and military status. On 28 October de Zulueta enquired of Bundy:

> If the question of missiles in Turkey should be revived in one form or another (as we gather from David Gore may have been in the President's mind) it would be very helpful to the Prime Minister to know what the position in Turkey actually is. Could you let me know what missiles there are actually operational and whether these are manned by the Turks or by the United States? Of course we realise that the war heads will be under the key of the cupboard. Also are these missiles regarded as part of the NATO forces or are they like the Thors in the UK, part of a separate Turko-American arrangement?[57]

This rather suggests that during the critical phase of the crisis, Macmillan and his government conducted crucial deliberations with the Americans in ignorance of the basic diplomatic and military circumstances of the Turkish deployment.

Kennedy had confided in Ormsby-Gore on 21 October that the IRBMs in Turkey and elsewhere were 'more or less worthless', and that he hoped and expected that the crisis would be resolved through discussions involving 'Berlin, foreign bases, disarmament, etc., in addition to Cuba.'[58] Before learning of these sentiments Macmillan had warned Kennedy that Khrushchev might trade his Cuba position against European goals, and that this was to be avoided at all costs. In the NATO Council on 22 October Dean Acheson made clear no such deal would be struck.[59] Macmillan later reiterated his resolve and, in his forward to Robert Kennedy's memoir, argued that: 'Perhaps [Kennedy's] most difficult decision was the refusal, against the advice of weaker brethren in America and elsewhere, to bargain the security of the Western world by yielding to the specious Russian offers of a face-saving accommodation at the expense of America's allies.'[60] His own position, he states, was 'one of complete support for the President at every stage',[61] and indeed the British Ambassador to Ankara, Sir Bernard Burrows, made clear to the Turkish government on 25 October, that 'the British government thoroughly appreciated the difference between existing bases in Turkey and what the Russians were now doing in Cuba'.[62]

Yet in Washington active consideration was being given to trading the Jupiters.[63] No formal approach was made to the Turkish or Italian governments but soundings were taken at NATO, and from the US Ambassadors in Ankara and Rome. The US Ambassador to NATO, Thomas Finletter, reported on 25 October that his Turkish counterpart had consistently made clear that the 'Turks set great store in Jupiters in Turkey'.[64] They were a symbol of the 'alliance's determination to use atomic weapons against [a] Russian attack on Turkey whether by large conventional or nuclear forces', even though the Turkish government had been most reluctant to publicly admit the presence of the IRBMs.[65] Finletter also raised the idea of trading American nuclear bases outside the NATO area for those in Cuba.

Both Finletter and the US Ambassador to Turkey, Raymond Hare, warned of the diplomatic consequences of a trade involving the Jupiters. Hare believed that a deal 'would present major problems not only in bilateral Turkish–American relationships but also [for the] NATO association'.[66] He nevertheless recognised the strong attractions of a deal involving a 'dubious and waning asset', and further argued that 'as a bargaining asset the Turkish Jupiters might be a more potent factor in Soviet eyes . . . for [the] simple reason that propinquity tends to magnify'.[67] The Turkish Foreign Minister, Mr Erkin, however, made clear to Hare on Thursday that his government deeply resented any coupling of Turkey and Cuba; the British Ambassador was told that the Turkish government was 'particularly annoyed' at comparisons in the British, French and American press between the bases in Turkey and those in Cuba.[68] Indeed, the Turks subsequently raised this press coverage in the NATO Council.[69]

As the debate in Washington over the political and military options developed, Ormsby-Gore gained further insights into Kennedy's thinking, and reported these back to London. On the Saturday morning he met the President and was shown a draft reply to Khrushchev's second letter.[70] Kennedy explained that the message from Khrushchev on Friday had made no mention of the Turkish bases. Ormsby-Gore suggested that in spite of the changed circumstances, it might still be useful for U Thant to go to Cuba. On the merits of Khrushchev's new proposal the President 'indicated that from many points of view the removal of missiles from Turkey and Cuba to the accompaniment of guarantees of the integrity of the two countries had considerable merit.'[71] However, the form and timing of the offer made things difficult. The President thought it might be helpful if the British Ambassador to Turkey could also give his opinion. Kennedy 'himself, felt that there was little military value to be attached to the missiles in Turkey, but one difficulty was that they had been handed over to the Turks, although the Americans of course controlled the warheads'.[72] Sir Bernard Burrows, the British Ambassador in Ankara, subsequently expressed similar views to his American counterpart. A trade would be 'repugnant' to the Turkish government.[73] The British embassy believed that within the Turkish foreign ministry there was opposition to a Cuban-Turkey trade, though recognition that Turkish bases could be discussed only 'after a suitable lapse of time and in a general NATO context'.[74]

Finletter was also concerned that withdrawal of the missiles from Turkey would be seen to weaken America's nuclear commitment to Europe. Nevertheless, in his view there was the possibility 'that some members [of the] alliance might be willing [to] accept [a] Cuba–Turk deal "to avoid nuclear war", i.e. Norwegians, Danes and maybe even [the] British'.[75] Various solutions were canvassed within the Kennedy administration, including deploying Polaris submarines in the Eastern Mediterranean and basing Polaris missiles on surface ships, in a NATO Southern Command, manned by crews of mixed nationality.[76] The State Department was already wedded to the idea of an alliance-wide seaborne force, which was under consideration within NATO. When the NATO Council met on 28 October Finletter was instructed to make clear the American determination to 'press on its present course'.[77] In Ankara, however, Hare told Burrows of his advice to Washington, that if the missiles in Turkey were eliminated (as part of a broader tension reducing agreement), then 'it would be desirable to offer the NATO countries some compensation e.g. a NATO nuclear force'.[78]

In Europe the idea of a Turkish trade was first expressed to American officials during General Norstad's visit to London. A senior British official raised the 'possible desirability of [a] trade of Turkish missile base for Soviet missiles in Cuba'.[79] The identity of this official is unknown, though one candidate could be Lord Mountbatten, the Chief of the Defence Staff, who attended the lunch at Buckingham Palace for Norstad on Tuesday.[80] Norstad's response was an 'emphatic and categoric "no"',[81] and he remained opposed to a deal, making this clear to the President in a letter on 27 October.[82] A trade between the Turkish Jupiters and the Soviet missiles in Cuba was privately supported by Gaitskell in his conversations with US officials on 23 October, and advocated in the British and French press.[83] It was also suggested in the *Washington Post* by the veteran

American columnist, Walter Lippman, on 25 October, and there was speculation that Moscow may have viewed Lippman's article as a 'trial balloon'.[84]

Despite Macmillan's earlier opposition to a deal which jeopardised the unity of the alliance, Roger Hilsman reported to Dean Rusk that 'a great many of our allies would probably favour such an agreement', including 'much of British public opinion, certain members of the Conservative government, and many members of the Labor Party'.[85] Senior diplomats, however, rejected the idea. Sir Frank Roberts described Khrushchev's demand of 27 October as 'an obvious but disingenuous try-on'.[86] Roberts, nevertheless, concluded that Khrushchev was 'now in a mood for horse-trading' – the Turkey proposal 'testifies to his talent and his methods', offering to trade 'something he does not really control for something long in the hands of his opponent'.[87]

Macmillan did not seek to dissuade Kennedy from a trade. Indeed, as the crisis reached its climax the British government sought ways to facilitate agreement by involving the Thors. The State Department planners had given little attention to the idea of using the Thors diplomatically, although Ambassador Hare suggested on 26 October that as one option 'British abandoning of Thors and possible Italian agreement [to] dismantle [the] Jupiters could be helpful' in approaching the Turks.[88]

CHICKENING OUT?

Meanwhile, Kennedy appraised Macmillan on Khrushchev's two separate proposals and on Stevenson's meeting with U Thant.[89] The President had publicly restated his position that work on the Cuban bases must stop before other proposals could be considered. He emphasised to Macmillan that the US should not negotiate on the individual security interests of NATO allies: 'Any initiatives in this respect, it seems to me, should come from Europe'.[90] He then asked for Macmillan's views, emphasising again 'we must secure the actual dismantling of the missiles currently in Cuba as the first order of business.'[91]

In London there was growing anticipation of American military action. As noted in Chapter Eight, after Macmillan spoke to the Chief of the Air Staff on Saturday morning, Sir Thomas Pike reported to the other Chiefs of Staff that 'the President had stated that unless he received [adequate assurances] within 48 hours he would take action to destroy the rocket sites either by bombing, by invasion, or by both'.[92] This was inaccurate, as Kennedy had not committed himself to military action. Nonetheless, Macmillan himself later recounted that 'it seemed therefore, that on Saturday the climax had now been reached, and that the Americans could have no alternative but to launch an attack, at least to destroy the SAM [Surface to Air Missile] sites... If the next thirty-six hours were agonising in Washington, they were almost equally so in London.'[93]

Kennedy's remarks to Macmillan on the Friday evening were taken by Sir Harold Caccia to indicate his willingness to act unilaterally. Caccia's brief for the Foreign Secretary, prepared on Saturday morning and shown to the Prime Minister, made clear the assumptions and calculations of the Foreign Office. Notwithstanding the prospect of nuclear war on 27 October, the Permanent Secretary was clearly focused on the demands of the 'special relationship'. Caccia explained that the President had indicated that military action could be imminent, though he had given the assurance that 'he would not act under 48 hours and that he would not take any drastic action, which presumably means bombardment or invasion, without telling the Prime Minister in advance'.[94] Caccia was clear that this 'does not mean that we shall be consulted', and 'as the Prime Minister is aware... only deals with the formalities and not the realities of the situation'.[95] This interpretation was at variance with Rusk's assurances to consult Britain, France and West Germany before any decision was taken.[96]

Caccia concluded that, given the President would have already taken such a decision when he contacted Macmillan

at that time it would be likely to be too late for any other initiative. If the Prime Minister were to ask for more time in order for instance to summon a meeting of Heads of States, the result could hardly change things at that stage. It would only have the consequence that the President would conclude that when it came to the crunch Britain had wanted to chicken out. If this is right we would not have been able to alter events and we would have done lasting damage to our relations with the United States.[97]

The Permanent Secretary's conclusion was that, while an 'independent British initiative should not cross the wires of what is now being attempted', it would have to come within the next 24 hours.[98] Caccia did not support a conference, which 'might only muddle things at a critical stage'.[99] Instead, he suggested that Sir Patrick Dean should raise the immobilisation of the Thors with U Thant.

In addition, Caccia advised that the Soviet *Chargé d'Affaires* be told by the Foreign Secretary, 'not as a threat but as a fact that the chance of negotiation hangs on the immobilisation of the missile sites in Cuba'.[100] Loginov was duly summoned, and in addition to increasing diplomatic pressure on the Soviets, Home laid the ground for the Thor initiative. The Foreign Secretary emphasised the 'extreme gravity' of the situation and explained that 'the key to the immediate future was the removal of offensive nuclear weapons or that they should be made inoperative, and that a scheme for either must be made in conjunction with the United Nations. Therefore Russia should cooperate in any proposal to this end put forward by U Thant. After that wider talks should be possible.'[101] Home emphasised that 'this was not a demand that we were making of the Russians but our assessment of the facts of the situation of which I wanted his Government to be made aware immediately'.[102] When Loginov was summoned, according to Ivanov, 'he really believed that he was to be told that Britain was prepared to make a deadlock-breaking gesture, and he was completely bouleverse' when he learned otherwise.[103]

Sir Patrick Dean was then briefed for his meeting with U Thant.[104] The government did not want to cut across the three-sided conversations, but if the talks were not getting anywhere, a critical point might be reached within the next 24–48 hours. One idea would be for U Thant, 'preferably with but if necessary without any special authorization from the United Nations', to take a team of inspectors to Cuba to verify that work on the missiles had stopped and no further offensive weapons were arriving.[105] Dean was also told to raise two ideas which were acceptable to Washington, namely, 'that the inviolability of Cuba might become a subject of international guarantee provided that it was demilitarised', and second, that Latin America should become a nuclear free zone.[106] Both had 'obvious merits against any idea for reciprocity in the European area', but 'if it would make all the difference and help both Khrushchev and Castro to agree you could say that for the short term and in order to enable negotiations to take place, we would be likely to respond affirmatively to any appeal from U Thant to allow during this period the immobilization of our Thor missile sites in the United Kingdom.'[107] Dean was instructed to obtain an assurance from U Thant that he would provide prior warning of any such appeal, and should let the government know, 'well before he finally gets stuck', in case London decided to announce a public initiative along these lines.[108]

Macmillan's press secretary, Sir Harold Evans, provides a rather more frenetic picture of events at the centre of British government as the day progressed.[109] He recounts being summoned back to Admiralty House on the Saturday night. Kennedy seemed 'hell-bent on destroying the missile sites', and Macmillan 'felt that he must intervene if it really looked like coming to that. He proposed to suggest immobilisation of the Thors in Britain in return for immobilisation of the Cuba missiles during a standstill period of negotiations at a London summit.'[110] The idea of a conference had been mentioned by Macmillan to Ormsby-Gore at the outset of the crisis and raised by Captain Ivanov on Wednesday. Now, on the Saturday afternoon, 'the proposal was repeated directly to [Macmillan] through a Conservative Member of Parliament of high character and standing [Sir Godfrey Nicholson]'.[111] Ivanov also canvassed Lord Arran on Saturday, who reported the approach to Macmillan's office and the FO.[112]

Harold Evans recalled that he

asked exactly how a London summit meeting would be handled. Home was already feeling that this particular proposition had a Diefenbakerish flavour to it, and faced with the hard questions he suddenly decided that it ought to be erased and jumped up to say so to the P.M. The P.M. agreed without argument, and I had to run down and get the paragraph struck out when the draft was already being typed on the teleprinter to the White House.[113]

Macmillan had floated the idea of offering the Thors as a *quid pro quo*, and now formally outlined this to the President, as a draft British proposal to Khrushchev. Macmillan declared that he was fully in accord with Kennedy's desire to avoid negotiating on the security of a NATO ally, and that any initiative on this had to come from Europe:

> Accordingly since I think it is very important for British public opinion, as well as such Commonwealth opinion as we could influence to have a good public position, I am proposing to send a message to Khrushchev ... If Khrushchev agrees you will have got a standstill which gets the missiles immobilised. If he refuses and more drastic action has to be taken at least we will have punctured his rather specious affectation of moderation.[114]

While denying comparisons between missiles in Europe and those in Cuba, Macmillan's aim was to gain 'at least a breathing space during which negotiations on all these matters might be undertaken'.[115] If, under UN authority, the Soviets stopped work on the sites, did not import more ballistic missiles, made the existing weapons inoperable, and if the United States lifted the quarantine and took no physical action against Cuba during the standstill, then the British government would make an offer to Khrushchev that was both 'symbolic and real':

> If a standstill on the above lines was agreed the British Government would be ready to agree that the Thor missiles, which form a considerable force in my country, should be immobilised under similar arrangements during the period of the standstill. This proposal is put forward in good faith in the hope, Mr Chairman, that you will accept it as a fair arrangement so that even if final settlements cannot now be reached nevertheless by the introduction of an immediate standstill, we can set about the task of discussion and negotiation.[116]

Macmillan was thus proposing to Kennedy an initiative from Europe, couched in terms of a good position for world opinion. This did not extend to removing the missiles from Cuba and Britain. The initiative on the Thors addressed the specific question of immobilisation. British experts believed that this could be secured by taking the missiles off the ramps and placing them apart under cover. 'Inspection of the ramps alone would then suffice to ensure that the missiles could not be used; at the same time, 'there would be no military disadvantage to the Russians or Cubans in this procedure since the period (normally four to eight hours) required to bring missiles to a state of readiness to fire would not be appreciably lengthened if the preparations began with the missiles off the ramps'.[117]

Macmillan did not propose withdrawal of the Thors, presumably because immobilising missiles was the vital question under consideration, and also as the decision to withdraw the Thors had already been announced. Kennedy, however, was not interested, at least at this stage and in this form. Ormsby-Gore reported:

> I have spoken to the President and as Bundy will have told Zulueta over the 'phone they are not happy about your initiative at this stage. They will be giving you a full explanation. The President did say that at the correct time there might well be something to be said for you and perhaps the President of Turkey making an offer with regard to the supervision or even dismantling of existing missile sites. He is most anxious that the US should not take the initiative over European bases as this would look as though the US would be prepared to trade the security of European nations for the US security in the western hemisphere.[118]

Sir Patrick Dean saw the UN Acting Secretary-General at 1 pm Washington time.[119] U Thant was more optimistic than he had been on Friday. Dean spoke as instructed, but omitting reference to the Thors.[120] The idea that U Thant should himself offer to go to Cuba if there was deadlock in the negotiations was apparently new to the Acting Secretary-General.

Meanwhile, Macmillan agreed 'that the use of any initiative by me is all a matter of timing.'[121] His colleagues were, according to Harold Evans, also having second thoughts about what Evans termed, the 'appeasement flavour which some would see in the Thors proposition.'[122] By the time Macmillan's colleagues (Home, Butler and Heath) reassembled at 9 am on Sunday, an overnight phone conversation between Bundy and de Zulueta had conveyed the American reaction.[123] Bundy made clear that Kennedy thought the proposal was 'not yet right'; Bundy's view was that the Thors were a 'card' which 'might be played in some way different from the one which the Prime Minister suggests', in the circumstances of a 'more tense situation in which conceivably our current efforts are so near breakdown and the prospect of major escalation so high that we would all revise our estimates of what we wanted to do'.[124] Despite this, according, to Evans, 'the P.M. retained a hankering to take the initiative on a summit meeting, but Caccia came up hard and strong against anything which might be construed as the British being the first to crack'.[125]

The Prime Minister cabled Kennedy that: 'The trial of wills is now approaching a climax. Khrushchev's first message, unhappily not published to the world, seemed to go a long way to meet you. His second message, widely broadcast and, adding the Turkey proposal, was a recovery on his part. It has made a considerable impact.'[126] Within ExComm, the idea emerged of replying only to the private letter, ignoring the public demand for a trade on the Turkish Jupiters.[127] This became known as the Trollope ploy, based on the apparent willingness of heroines in Trollope's novels to interpret innocuous compliments as proposals of marriage. It was this approach that was to provide the public basis on which Kennedy successfully resolved the crisis. On Sunday 28 October Moscow Radio broadcast that orders had been given to dismantle those weapons in Cuba which the Americans regarded as offensive, for return to the USSR.

The view that Khrushchev had decided on what Ormsby-Gore described as 'virtually a complete climb-down' spread quickly.[128] Kennedy and his officials were anxious not to appear triumphant, though the President was praised from all quarters for his calmness and resolution. The view of most historians and students of crisis management has echoed this view of Kennedy's statesmanship. New evidence from American and Soviet sources, however, has cast a rather different light on the events of the weekend of 27–8 October. It is now clear that contrary to the received wisdom, Kennedy contrived a secret arrangement with Khrushchev involving assurances to withdraw the Jupiters.[129]

The new evidence has significant implications for understanding Kennedy's handling of the crisis, and for lessons about the outcome. It refutes the idea that Kennedy simply stood firm while Khrushchev retreated, and as Lebow and Stein argue, requires revision of the belief that 'resolve discourages aggression and accommodation invites it.'[130] The revelations should not diminish Kennedy's reputation. They demonstrate his dexterity in squaring the circle of diplomatic accommodation and alliance cohesion. On the other hand, it is now clear that Khrushchev would have retreated without the 'sweetener' of the Turkish missiles.[131] Khrushchev's reputation is also enhanced, though why he did not make greater use of the deal to his critics (or later to posterity) is less clear.

There is no evidence that British officials learned of the secret arrangement.[132] McGeorge Bundy doubts 'if [Kennedy] would have told David [Ormsby-Gore] about his own Turkish assurance to Khrushchev; there was no need for that, and some risk in doing it.'[133] Bundy believed that Macmillan would have backed the Turkish assurance had he known about it. He also believed that, if Kennedy had opted for a public missile trade, Macmillan would have supported Kennedy, 'at least as strongly' as he supported rejection of the public deal.[134] Certainly in private, Macmillan felt that the 'Turkey–Cuba deal would of course have been greatly to the advantage of U.S. The Turkey base is useful, but not vital. Cuba was vital.'[135] Macmillan himself declared boldly in his memoirs, 'I should never have consented, in spite of the arguments which might be urged about the obsolescence of the missile base in Turkey, to this as a permanent deal'.[136] Bundy's reading of Macmillan is surely the correct one.

Kennedy's determination to reach a compromise invites speculation about why he did not express greater interest in Macmillan's Thor proposal. According to McGeorge Bundy:

'my guess would be that JFK would have wanted not to have any British action until he did want it, and not to pass any final judgement on any specific action until then.'[137] Kennedy may well have been suspicious of Macmillan's personal and political motives in seeking a role in the settlement. Nevertheless, had the Trollope ploy and the secret deal failed, Macmillan's initiative could then have been considered.

There is still great debate about what Kennedy would have done if a diplomatic settlement had not emerged by the weekend.[138] Some, like Bundy and McNamara, have argued that Kennedy would have chosen other options falling short of attack, such as widening the scope of the blockade. Others such as Sorenson and Schlesinger are convinced that Kennedy would have made further concessions. New evidence has been used to argue that Kennedy was determined to 'go the extra mile for peace', and would not have used force at this stage, even though he ordered the necessary military preparations for action against Cuba. In particular, in 1987 Dean Rusk disclosed that he had been instructed by Kennedy to contact the former UN diplomat, Andrew Cordier, and lay the foundations for a public trade on the Jupiters. According to Rusk he was instructed to telephone Cordier 'and dictate to him a statement which would be made by U Thant proposing the removal of both Jupiters and the missiles in Cuba. Mr Cordier was to put that statement in the hands of U Thant only after a further signal from us.'[139] This has been interpreted by some (including the author) to indicate Kennedy's determination to act diplomatically, rather than initiate hostilities with the Soviets.[140]

From British archives evidence has emerged to challenge this interpretation. On 25 October Sir Patrick Dean reported to the Foreign Office that he had heard from 'a most reliable source', that Cordier had been in touch with 'top-level persons in the United States Government' about U Thant's statement on Cuba.[141] According to Dean:

> Cordier says that if a United Nations Commission could be introduced to keep a watch on Russian bases in Cuba under satisfactory guarantees, the United States might

be prepared to consider allowing a similar United Nations Commission to look at some bases elsewhere, e.g. the United States bases in Turkey. If a satisfactory arrangement about Cuba could be reached they would be prepared for the United Nations Commission to go to other places but not to all the other American missiles and other bases around the world.[142]

Dean also reported that Adlai Stevenson had 'dropped a hint to this effect to me last night'.[143] If Dean's account corresponds to that of Rusk, this indicates that Rusk's recollection that Cordier was approached on 27 October is in error. Moreover, if the two accounts describe the same events then, as Mark White argues, 'Dean's telegram clearly renders all previous interpretations of Rusk's revelation obsolete.'[144] The establishment of a UN observer team, White argues, was separate to a public and reciprocal withdrawal, and on this basis he concludes that 'JFK did not consider trading away the Jupiters as part of a public quid pro quo'.[145]

However, it is not self-evident that the two accounts describe the same event.[146] Certainly if Rusk's statement that only he, Kennedy and Cordier knew of the ploy is true, the fact that Dean's source, and possibly Adlai Stevenson also knew, may indicate that Cordier had more than one conversation with American officials. Dean's reference to an observer team does not preclude that Kennedy considered an explicit deal, even assuming that Dean's source was privy to the exact terms of the message given to Cordier by Rusk. As the week progressed American officials were preoccupied with the operational status of the missiles. Macmillan's offer to immobilise the Thors under UN supervision, for example, was not aimed at the removal of the Soviet missiles from Cuba. Likewise, the 'Cordier ploy' of Dean's telegram may have focused on the specific problem of the continuing construction of the missiles. Observer teams in Turkey would have entailed linkage, though not at this stage reciprocal, withdrawal. What role Dean's report played in the development of British ideas on the Thors is a further dimension to the puzzle.

On Sunday Macmillan assembled his advisers. The government's senior military officials were also gathered to consider precautionary military measures, such as dispersing the V-force or mobilising.[147] The speed of the settlement took Whitehall by surprise. By the time ministers had agreed a message to Khrushchev, the Soviets had announced the withdrawal of the missiles from Cuba. The purpose of the government's message, Macmillan explained later to Parliament, was 'to range the British Government squarely and publicly with the President now that the climax had been reached'.[148] It stated:

> The essence of the position reached is that once the problem posed by the offensive missile bases in Cuba has been dealt with under effective United Nations control and the situation in the area normalised, the way would be open for us all to work toward a more general arrangement regarding armaments. For instance, we should be able to reach an early conclusion of an agreement about the banning of tests of nuclear weapons on which much progress has already been made as well as to give firm directives to settle the main elements in the first stage of disarmament. I would hope that this might mark a new determination to resolve the problems from which the world is suffering . . . I therefore ask you to take the action necessary to make all this possible. This is an opportunity which we should seize.[149]

Sir Frank Roberts, charged with delivering this message, realised that the crisis was over when he heard Soviet radio playing Beethoven's 'Ode to Peace' rather than martial music.[150] Macmillan's letter fell far short of any independent initiative. Harold Evans described it as a 'mouselike message', which was sent 'just in time for us to be able to claim that it had anticipated Khrushchev's caving-in reply.[151]

AFTERLIFE

Although Khrushchev's statement of 28 October marked the end of the thirteen days which for most people represented the Cuban missile crisis, the situation was not yet resolved. Castro was furious with Khrushchev over the removal of the missiles and refused to allow UN inspection of Cuban territory. Moreover, his opposition to the removal of the Ilyushin-28 bombers meant that the crisis did not formally end until after three weeks of intensive negotiations, and not before Kennedy gave consideration to renewing the quarantine and threatening further escalation. Khrushchev's decision to withdraw the missiles was taken without any consultation with Castro, who at one point had advocated pre-emptive nuclear attack against America.[152] Kennedy's assurances not to invade Cuba did not extend to actions which his government had adopted prior to the crisis. Castro therefore insisted that withdrawal of Soviet forces should be conditional on the following: the cessation of the economic blockade, all subversive activities and the end of 'pirate attacks' from American and Puerto Rican bases, no further violations of Cuban air and naval space, and withdrawal from the naval base at Guantanamo. Kennedy had no intention of acceding to such demands and remained determined to secure the withdrawal of the Ilyushin-28 bombers, which had been handed over to the Cubans.

Aerial reconnaissance had identified the Ilyushin-28 bombers by early October. Although potentially capable of carrying nuclear payloads, they had not caused alarm in Washington, mainly because the Soviets had also supplied them to countries like Indonesia and Egypt. McNamara nevertheless told Congressional leaders on 22 October that, 'without any doubt', the I1-28s were offensive weapons.[153] It now appears that six nuclear gravity bombs did reach Cuba for the bombers (though probably for tactical strikes against invading US forces rather than on American territory).[154] The Americans insisted on withdrawal of the bombers because Kennedy had included them in his speech of 22 October. His initial view in ExComm on 28 October was that 'a private approach to Khrushchev' should be used to remove them. He did not want to get 'hung up' on the bombers, but we should seek to include them in the Soviet definition of "offensive weapons" or "weapons we call offensive" . . . The I1-28 bombers were less important than the strategic missiles.'[155] The ensuing prolongation of the crisis was not simply a diplomatic imbroglio. SAC remained at DEFCON-2 until 21 November (Bomber Command remaining at Alert Condition 3 until 9.09 am on 5 November[156]). The possibility of inadvertent or accidental use of weapons during this period could not be discounted, and indeed one particular episode is an exemplar of how misperception during this period could still have led to disaster.

PENKOVSKY'S FINAL WARNING

According to the KGB, Oleg Penkovsky was arrested on 22 October. The emergency warning procedure, agreed between SIS/CIA and Penkovsky, was subsequently activated. Warning of 'a sudden development of a dangerous situation' was transmitted by two voiceless telephone calls on 2 November.[157] When the coded warning was sent, news was immediately passed to the Director of the CIA, who in turn briefed the President, on 3 November.[158] Why the KGB activated the DISTANT warning procedure remains a matter of speculation.[159] Raymond Garthoff suggests that Penkovsky could have deliberately tried to provoke a nuclear attack on the Soviet Union.[160] This would be consistent with his repeated suggestions to his CIA and SIS handlers that they furnish him with atomic demolition charges to plant at strategic points in Moscow to 'decapitate' the Soviet system at the necessary moment.[161] There are no indications of how and when the British authorities were informed of Penkovsky's warning and how it was interpreted by SIS or the JIC.

British policy on the Ilyushin-28s was to support the United States, though Sir Frank Roberts was concerned that Khrushchev's major retreat would make further concessions difficult, and within the Foreign Office there was some doubt over whether the Americans saw the bombers as a serious military threat or a pretext for withholding their guarantee not to invade.[162] When Kennedy spoke to Macmillan on 14 November, the Prime Minister recommended firmness with Khrushchev: 'You must not give in to him.'[163] The following day Macmillan advised, 'You must get the bombers out before you give any guarantee of non-invasion.'[164] Kennedy told Macmillan that he did not 'want to crank up the quarantine again over the bombers',[165] though as the situation continued, with little sign of a breakthrough, the US government considered how to exert pressure, if possible, on Castro rather than on Khrushchev. On 20 November, shortly before Castro succumbed to Soviet pressure, Kennedy sent Macmillan a message explaining that 'we are considering further actions, which may involve response from the air to any attack on our surveillance, or a reimposition and extension of the naval quarantine, or perhaps both in combination'.[166] The logical way of extending the blockade, Kennedy argued, would be to add oil products 'as these are directly related to the operation of the bombers'.[167] With the climb-down by Castro and Khrushchev, Macmillan was spared the problem of an embargo on oil.

The world drew back from the abyss in 1962 thanks to the decisions of Kennedy and Khrushchev and because, for whatever reasons, inadvertent, insubordinate or unforeseen actions did not undermine the efforts of the political leaders. Kennedy's handling of the denouement of the crisis focused on managing the NATO alliance as much as the Soviets. Macmillan was aware of much, though not all, of Kennedy's manoeuvres, and provided various kinds of support. Had the crisis continued he was well positioned to play a role, which he was in any case tempted to try. Wise counsels prevailed over Macmillan's political instincts. The 'frightful desire to do something' was subordinated to the imperatives of the 'special relationship', and exigencies of the crisis.

Conclusion

I am lost in admiration for the superb manner in which you handled the momentous events of the critical week we have just lived through. I know what a mass of conflicting advice you received and I can only say that looking back on it all you acted at each stage with perfect judgement. I mean it quite sincerely when I say that America and all of the free world must feel a deep sense of gratitude that you are President of the United States at this moment in history (Ormsby-Gore to JFK, 30 October 1962).[1]

The Cuban missile crisis reinforced British attitudes to security in the Cold War, while helping create conditions for limited East–West détente. Relaxation of tension brought the opportunity to agree the Partial Test Ban Treaty in 1963, in the negotiation of which the British government played a significant role. European security, and in particular what Lord Home called the 'tacit moratorium' on Berlin,[2] was preserved and enhanced. In the immediate aftermath of the crisis, Ormsby-Gore suggested explicitly linking the security of Berlin with that of Cuba[3] (and raised the idea in Washington[4]). Macmillan and Home, together with other senior diplomats, were sceptical.[5] The Prime Minister explained to the Foreign Secretary that he did

not think that these two places are of equal value to us and I fear that to make an explicit link between them might even encourage Mr Khrushchev to feel that he might take Berlin at the risk not of nuclear war but only of the loss of Cuba. It seems to me that the protection of West Berlin must continue to be assured by the full weight of Western and above all of United States power rather than just by the Cuban hostage. Apart from other considerations it is surely possible that Senor Castro may one day be overthrown by a spontaneous revolution, and we should not get ourselves into a position in which such a development might seem to justify the Russians in seizing Berlin.[6]

Such judgements were vindicated, not least as Khrushchev's Cuban adventure marked his last attempt to force the Berlin issue.

THE SPECIAL RELATIONSHIP: AN ACID TEST?

When the immediate crisis was over there was a fulsome exchange between London and Washington.[7] Yet the consequences of the missile crisis for Britain's international standing, and more specifically for relations with Washington, became the subject of animated debate. Labour made great play with Kennedy's failure to consult the government. Macmillan himself was anxious to emphasise that, 'it is not true that we in this country have played an inactive role in this great trial of strength'.[8] From Moscow Sir Frank Roberts (whose reading of Soviet actions during the crisis was highly prescient), cabled Home that 'your own strong warnings to [the] Soviet *Chargé d'Affaires* in London no doubt played a part in bringing Khrushchev to call a halt to his Cuba blackmail'.[9] Nevertheless, the view that Britain's role was nugatory clearly exercised officials and commentators. Robin Edmonds, erstwhile head of the FO's American Department, has suggested that, as Britain's influence in the crisis was marginal, 'by the end of 1962, the age of the superpowers had begun'; with the resignation of Macmillan and the death of Kennedy what he terms 'the long parenthesis in the Anglo-American relationship was drawing toward its close'.[10] David Owen has also argued that: 'The Cuban missile crisis demonstrated clearly – even to the reluctant dreamers of the Western Alliance – the harsh realities of the new super-power structure which had become increasingly apparent ever since the end of the Second World War.'[11]

Such a bipolar view of international relations, however, ignores the complexities of US foreign policy-making and, in particular, the requirements imposed by America's alliance obligations. In this respect, the British government played a useful role for Washington. Dean Rusk told Ormsby-Gore that, in addition to British advice and support to Washington, 'the lead that we had given from the start to the rest of our allies had undoubtedly much to do with the successful outcome of last week's events'.[12] A recent study of Canada's role in the crisis, for example, suggests that Macmillan's 'leadership' was a factor in persuading Prime Minister Diefenbaker to change his attitude and support the US position.[13] Macmillan himself believed that 'our complete calm helped to keep the Europeans calm'.[14] Shortly after the crisis, he reflected in his diary that the French 'were anyway contemptuous; the Germans very frightened, though pretending to want firmness; the Italians windy; the Scandinavians rather sour. But they said and did nothing to spoil the American playing of the hand'.[15]

The British role, both in NATO and in the Commonwealth, was helpful for Washington, but should not be exaggerated. The French were no less, and possibly more robust, within NATO. While de Gaulle was a growing diplomatic problem within the alliance, he nevertheless provided unambiguous support for Kennedy in October 1962. The British did provide a lead to the Italian government, which made two interventions with Moscow, one along the lines of Home's statement to Loginov on 27 October, and the other telling the Soviets they saw no future in a Cuba–Turkey deal.[16] Perhaps most importantly within NATO, the Turks adopted an uncompromising stance on trading the Jupiters, which owed nothing to anybody, certainly not to the British.

Other British contributions were seen in Washington to be of help. Ormsby-Gore's standing in Washington rose, and whatever the precise importance of Penkovsky's intelligence, senior CIA officials recognised SIS's role. Yet British–American disagreements over shipping and trade with Cuba quickly resurfaced. Moreover, whatever the positive consequences for British–American relations, the cancellation of Skybolt swiftly plunged the 'special relationship' into crisis. Did Macmillan's behaviour during the missile crisis affect Kennedy's decision to supply Polaris? Or was it the case, as McGeorge Bundy argues, that 'Macmillan could have been dull, and Ormsby-Gore just another diplomat, and the underlying imperative would still have been clear: Nothing could justify this kind of American damage to Anglo-American relations'?[17] Whatever the answer, if Macmillan had broken ranks over Cuba, and Britain was seen to 'chicken out' in October, the underlying imperative could well have been undermined. British solidarity over Cuba was a necessary, if insufficient (and unforeseen), condition for the supply of Polaris.

There was, and there remains, debate over what the crisis tells us about the 'special relationship'. In part this reflects differing interpretations of what occurred, as well as continuing dispute over its significance. Alistair Horne argues that, 'it was during the Cuban missile week that the 'Special Relationship' reached a new peak'.[18] Others have taken the opposite view, arguing that failure to consult over the blockade marked 'the death of Britain's "special relationship" with America'.[19] Close analysis of British–American relations during the crisis reveals different phases. Before the discovery of the missiles, Macmillan pursued a robustly independent approach to trade with Cuba in the face of increasing US pressure, including Kennedy's pleas that Britain should support an ally in difficulty. Macmillan, however, was prepared to stand alone within NATO on the grounds of principle and economic interest. When Soviet nuclear missiles in Cuba were discovered Kennedy decided to act without seeking counsel from Macmillan or other European allies. Had London supported Washington's policy toward Cuba before October 1962, Kennedy might well have sought British views on the new situation.

Fresh light has been cast on how British officials were told about the missiles, which provides an interesting vignette of British–American intelligence relations. Kennedy informed Macmillan of the missiles on Sunday 21 October, over a day before his televised speech. As with other key NATO allies, there was the opportunity to register dissent, so that there was a form of consultation. In reality, Kennedy had already decided upon a course of action which, as Ormsby-Gore explained, was the minimum that American public opinion required. Rusk's observation that Macmillan's formal reply contained nothing that the Americans had not thought of underlines that Kennedy would not have been swayed by European voices counselling inaction (or invasion). Macmillan's initial reflexes (like those of Kennedy) favoured military action. His more considered views (like those of Kennedy) favoured diplomatic negotiation. His exclusion from the initial debates in Washington was therefore probably fortuitous. One question is how far Macmillan's transition from hawk to dove reflected his own deliberation (and that of his advisers) or whether it reflected his knowledge (via Ormsby-Gore) of Kennedy's private feelings, and his calculations about how Britain might exercise influence in Washington.

What the archives in London and Washington show is that there was widespread recognition that events in the Caribbean were inextricably linked to the situation in Europe, and in particular to Berlin. Soviet action against West Berlin could have precipitated armed conflict and indeed nuclear war. Under such circumstances Britain, and indeed other NATO members, had every right to be consulted over American action against Cuba. For the United Kingdom, with its panoply of US nuclear bases and its growing and intimate military relationship with the United States, this right was even more apparent. Critics of the 'special relationship' have long argued that in a crisis the United States would act in America's interest, regardless of the views or interests of its allies. The early phase of the Cuban missile crisis provides support for this argument.

However, the subsequent phases of the crisis up to, and including, the weekend of 27–8 October, provide a different picture. Kennedy's relations with Ormsby-Gore and his transatlantic telephone conversations with Macmillan present a much more intimate, and in some respects, equal relationship. On the other hand, specific claims about British interventions have been misleading. Ormsby-Gore's suggestion to move the quarantine line was not decisive in the operation of the blockade. Similarly, Ormsby-Gore suggested publishing the aerial photographs *after* they had been given to the British press. Nevertheless, that Kennedy heeded Ormsby-Gore's advice is of note in debates about the 'special relationship', and endorses the view that Ormsby-Gore and Kennedy was 'a special relationship within the "Special Relationship"'.[20] How far did Ormsby-Gore act as his own man rather than Macmillan's? It is clear that his independence of mind extended to undermining his Prime Minister's proposals for a summit. May and Zelikow argue that

'Macmillan and Ormsby-Gore became de facto members of Kennedy's Executive Committee'.[21] In fact, Ormsby-Gore's role corresponds more closely to that of the inner circle of advisers whose influence on the President was more significant than the debates in ExComm. Kennedy's telephone calls with Macmillan remain of particular interest. H.G. Nicholas has argued that they meant that Britain was 'not merely consulted . . . but intimately involved' in the management of the crisis.[22] Several writers describe them as 'a sounding board' for Kennedy's thinking.[23] The most crucial conversation was that of 25 October. Kennedy twice asked Macmillan for his views on what the Prime Minister described as the '$64 000 question', namely whether the United States should invade Cuba or not.

There remains disagreement about whether Kennedy would have invaded Cuba had a diplomatic settlement not emerged over the weekend. The archival evidence shows that the British anticipated American military action the following week. London received (or interpreted) differing signals from Washington concerning whether they would be consulted over this. Rusk assured the British, French and West German Ambassadors that their governments would be consulted. Kennedy told Macmillan only that he would talk to him 48 hours before he did anything. What is clear, however, is that the British were kept informed, both on Soviet–American developments and on deliberations within the US government, including on a possible deal over the Turkish Jupiters. Indeed, it was through the range of contacts between London and Washington (and New York) that Macmillan devised his offer to immobilise the Thors. There is no evidence that the British knew, or subsequently learned, of the secret arrangement on the Jupiters, which, as McGeorge Bundy has admitted, involved misleading America's NATO allies.[24] Notwithstanding Macmillan's disclaimers to the contrary, it is difficult to envisage the Prime Minister or his colleagues opposing such a deal, which so brilliantly squared the circle of alliance cohesion and diplomatic accommodation.

The British government thus had a position of unrivalled access to the President. Ormsby-Gore's position was even closer. For students of the 'special relationship', the central question was whether this access provided influence, and if so at what cost. Assessing British influence on American policy-making is sometimes difficult. Assessing the costs of acquiring such access is more straightforward. Britain was constrained from attempting any independent British diplomatic action – as many American officials fully understood. Macmillan continued to give serious thought to a London summit, reflecting both his political instincts (which he made known to Ormsby-Gore on 22 October) and 'devious approaches' from the Soviets (which began on 24 October). When Sir Harold Caccia advised Lord Home on the morning of Saturday 27 October, he nevertheless emphasised the long-term political costs to Britain if an initiative failed to achieve anything, except show the President that, 'when it came to the crunch Britain had wanted to chicken out'.[25]

The central diplomatic lesson of the crisis for Britain was that the price of access in Washington was loss of political independence. Such access did not of itself guarantee influence, though Ormsby-Gore's personal relationship with the President was noteworthy. The true acid test of the 'special relationship' lay in what influence Britain could exercise in American decisions about war with the Soviet Union. The Foreign Office prognosis of Kennedy's willingness to consult about using force against Cuba was pessimistic, while highlighting a brief window of opportunity for British diplomatic action that did not undermine US diplomacy. Yet had the Trollope ploy and the secret deal proved insufficient, Macmillan had positioned the British government to play a role in the next, possibly final, diplomatic phase.

UNFLAPPABLE MAC?

So how well did Macmillan play his cards? Macmillan's role during the crisis was to provide support to Kennedy and the United States, even though the British government's legal advisers were convinced the quarantine was illegal, and despite his early feeling that it was imprudent. Macmillan's impulse to *do* something was driven by fear of escalation in Europe and desire to play a role on the world stage. Yet his impulses were kept in check, most notably by Home and Caccia (adding credence to D.R. Thorne's portrayal of Macmillan's relationship with his Foreign Secretary as that between Don Quixote and Sancho Panza[26]).

Yet does the missile crisis lend credence to the self-cultivated persona of 'Unflappable Mac'? On balance, the answer is yes. Macmillan deserves credit for his management, both of the diplomatic conduct of the crisis and of the military preparations. Politically he emerged with all that he might realistically have hoped for, save for domestic doubts about his relations with Washington. Moreover, in 1962 the most likely path to nuclear war ran through a concatenation of misperception, inadvertent and unauthorised action, with decision-makers quickly losing control of events. Recent historiography has shown examples of where subordinate activities increased the risk of inadvertent escalation (as well as a smaller number where subordinate activity reduced such risks). British records, and testimony from RAF personnel, indicate that British military preparations were not a problem in this context. British nuclear forces were placed on a higher alert condition than normal, though this fell well short of corresponding action by SAC. Macmillan exercised close political control over British nuclear forces and adopted a very different approach to military preparations to Kennedy. It is also clear that British military activities were conducted in accord with the wishes of British political authorities and within agreed procedures.

Notwithstanding Macmillan's calculations (domestic and international), there were understandable reasons for him wanting to do something. Indeed, for many, there were equally understandable reasons for wanting, in Caccia's phrase to 'chicken out', if the alternative was nuclear war. Western Europe could live with Soviet nuclear missiles. So, too, the United States could live with Soviet missiles in Cuba. The Soviets may have gained advantages at the margins of the military balance with their deployment, and posed new threats to some US targets, but these were essentially changes in the arithmetic, rather than the equations, of deterrence.

Subsequent British political debates about nuclear weapons

were influenced by the outcome of the crisis. The anti-nuclear cause suffered serious loss of support, and became increasingly marginalised in mainstream political life. Already, the anti-nuclear cause within the Labour Party had reached its high tide at the 1960 party conference. Thereafter, CND was unable to mobilise effectively within the party (until the 1980s). Moreover, within the anti-nuclear movement itself divisions over tactics and principles were growing, fuelled by personal antagonisms within the leadership. Nevertheless, the Cuban missile crisis was significant, and was seen to be significant by many of the activists. As one of them explains:

> up until Cuba in '62 I think it's true to say that the nuclear issue preceded *everything*, but just everything . . . Of course, Cuba changed all that: they could actually manage the thing intelligently . . . sooner or later they would make a mistake and the thing would go up . . . *But* it was not within the decade: I think we could well go on living like this for two or three hundred years . . . The whole kind of frenetic politics of total disaster of that period is difficult to recall.[27]

The events of October 1962 reinforced the orthodoxies of deterrence, while providing momentum for arms control. Bomber Command was seen to have reinforced deterrence, even though great care had been taken to avoid overt preparations. In the 1960s the strategic rationale for the British deterrent shifted from independence to a second centre of decision-making within NATO. Central to the credibility of this was the assumption that the Soviets might believe there were circumstances in which the British deterrent would be used when that of the United States would not. The Cuban crisis was, so far as we know, the moment in its history where Bomber Command was closest to mobilisation. Yet as US nuclear forces remained at much higher, and more conspicuous, states of alert, the relevance of the events of 1962 for debates about a Britain deterrent is limited. What is clear is that Kennedy's friendship with Ormsby-Gore, and his discussions with Macmillan, did not happen because Britain possessed nuclear weapons, but because of the complex of shared values, beliefs and concerns that have been the essence of the 'special relationship'.

The Cuban missile crisis defused anxiety about nuclear weapons, and provided reassurance that nuclear weapons and nuclear diplomacy could be managed. At the same time, in the post-crisis détente, fear of nuclear war subsided and the test ban treaty reduced environmental concern. It is a political irony that the test ban, whose negotiation owed much to Macmillan's government, helped defuse anxiety about nuclear war and thus assisted Labour in 1964, when it focused the election on domestic issues, where it was stronger. At one point in the midst of the crisis one man became convinced that *managing* nuclear weapons was not enough and that nuclear disarmament was necessary: John F. Kennedy. As Ormsby-Gore reported to Macmillan on 23 October: 'I had some indication of the scope of his thinking when he said with great seriousness that the existence of nuclear weapons made a secure and rational world impossible. We must somehow find a means to get rid of nuclear weapons.'[28] Whether these remarks were a transient aberration or a moment of deep insight depends on one's perspective. British officials drew rather less dramatic conclusions. While nuclear tests might prove a way forward, de Zulueta counselled Macmillan: 'The air of unreality which always lies heavy on disarmament negotiations is still very thick. Few people are able to take them seriously. There seems no chance of a full-scale disarmament agreement in the present state of international confidence nor have we had any success with the limited measures proposed. Is it really in our interest to go on playing this insincere charade?'[29]

The Cuban missile crisis was (almost) certainly the most dangerous confrontation of the Cold War. Kennedy's momentary embrace of disarmament passed as the intensity of his concern faded. 'Life goes on somehow', as Macmillan remarked about the Soviet threat in Europe. Avoiding nuclear confrontation and *managing* differences was the lesson learned from 1962, though as the collapse of East–West relations in the 1980s demonstrated, such education faded with time. Similarly, many in 1962 came to understand the dangers of deploying land-based nuclear missiles close to the territory of the other superpower. Such understanding did not survive the test of time. In 1962 the British Ambassador told the UN Security Council: 'Legitimate defences are one thing, nuclear missiles with ranges from 1 000 to over 2 000 miles are quite another.'[30] In 1979 the British government supported the NATO decision to deploy 108 1 800 km-range Pershing-2 and 464 2 500 km-range Ground Launched Cruise Missiles in Western Europe.

While historians draw lessons, as well as discern consequences, they are also conscious that events are singular. The dramatic nature of the crisis should not obscure the inherent implausibility of events, with the necessary corollary that drawing lessons (or predicting outcomes) are hazardous enterprises. The final word therefore falls to Ambassador Marchant, reporting from Havana on 10 November 1962:

> Any record of the story of these first two weeks of the Cuban crisis must necessarily read more like a wildly improbable sequel to 'Our Man in Havana' than a Foreign Office despatch. Indeed I doubt whether a month ago any reputable publisher would have given a moment's consideration to a story in which Soviet Russia was to be credited with shipping some four dozen assorted giant missiles, each one longer than a cricket pitch, across the Atlantic to Cuba, where, Russian military technicians disguised as agricultural advisers would set them up in secret on launching sites – some of them just off the main road less than 50 miles from Havana. Certainly no publisher could have accepted a Chapter II in which less than a week later the same missiles were feverishly dismantled, packed up and re-shipped back across the Atlantic. Yet this in brief is precisely what seems to be happening.[31]

Appendix: Nuclear Arsenals – The Cuban Missile Crisis, October 1962

	USA	USSR	UK
ICBMs	172	c24	
M/IRBMs		36[a] (Cuba)	60[b]
		c700 (USSR)	
Submarine-based Missiles	112	97	
Bombers[c]	1 450	155	140+

Sources: figures on American and Soviet forces are adapted from Garthoff, *Reflections*, p. 208; and Fursenko and Naftali, '*One Hell of a Gamble*', *passim*.

[a] The Soviet nuclear deployment in Cuba was intended to comprise 24 IRBMs, 36 MRBMs, 80 cruise missiles, six gravity bombs for some of the Ilyushin 28 aircraft and 12 short range battlefield nuclear missiles. Four submarines armed with nuclear torpedoes were also to be deployed. Owing to the US quarantine, while most of the tactical weapons reached Cuba, only the 36 MRBMs reached the island – none of the IRBMs arrived.

[b] The 60 British Thor IRBMs operated on the basis of dual-key control, whereby the British operated the missiles and the USAF retained formal custody of the warheads (which, by 1962, were nevertheless 'mated' with the missiles). The same arrangements were applied to the 45 Jupiter IRBMs in Italy and Turkey.

[c] Figures are for strategic and medium range bombers.

Notes

1 Improbable History

1. Oral History Interview (undated), Peter Thorneycroft, National Security Archive, *The Cuban Missile Crisis, 1962*, Microfiche Collection (Alexandria, Va.: Chadwyck-Healey, 1990) [hereafter NSA:CMC], Doc. 03338.
2. R.S. McNamara, *Blundering into Disaster: Surviving the First Century of the Nuclear Age* (Bloomsbury, 1987), p. 11.
3. Interview, BBC Radio *Today* Programme, 1 January 1993.
4. R.N. Lebow and J.G. Stein, *We All Lost the Cold War* (Princeton, New Jersey: Princeton University Press, 1994), p. 142.
5. B. Russell, *Unarmed Victory* (Penguin, 1963), p. 7.
6. A.M. Schlesinger, *A Thousand Days – John F. Kennedy in the White House* (Andre Deutsch, 1965), p. 700.
7. R. Taylor, *Against the Bomb: The British Peace Movement, 1958–1965* (Oxford University Press [OUP], 1988), p. 90 n.
8. The US Ambassador, David Bruce, noted the Queen's 'lively interest in the Cuban imbroglio' at a lunch for General Norstad on 23 October, David Bruce's Diaries, 23 October 1962, (NSA:CMC), Doc. 01623. She was 'fully and continuously informed' by the Prime Minister and the Foreign Secretary, Public Record Office, London [hereafter: PRO]: PREM 11/1369, Michael Adeane, Queen's private secretary, to Macmillan, 31 October 1962. Macmillan recounts that when he explained the dangers of the situation at his audience on 23 October, 'She was, as usual, calm and sympathetic', H. Macmillan, *At the End of the Day, 1961–1963* (Macmillan, 1973), p. 196.
9. Harold Macmillan's Diaries (HMD), 22 October 1962, quoted in Macmillan, *End of the Day*, p. 189.
10. Ibid., p. 195.
11. *The Times*, 27 October 1962, p. 13.
12. P.A.G. Sabin, *The Third World War Scare in Britain* (Macmillan, 1986), pp. 56–7.
13. K. Martin, London Diary, *New Statesman*, 26 October 1962, p. 562.
14. B. Boothroyd, 'Signs of a Crisis', *Punch*, 31 October 1962, p. 635.
15. *The Guardian*, 25 October 1962, p. 4; in a negotiated settlement, the pupils subsequently agreed to their headmaster's proposal to return early from half term to make up time, *The Guardian*, 26 October 1962, p. 12.
16. *The Times*, 1 January 1993, p. 6.
17. D. Nunnerley, *President Kennedy and Britain* (Bodley Head, 1972), pp. 72–3.
18. PRO: FO 371/162384, FO Minute, C.M. James, AK 1261/189/A, 24 October 1962.

19. Ibid.
20. *HC Deb.* vol. 679, 17 June 1963, col. 68.
21. *The Listener*, 30 January 1969, p. 142.
22. Oral History Interview (undated), Peter Thorneycroft, (NSA:CMC), Doc. 03338.
23. PRO: Air 8/2378, DC(55) 1st mtg. 15 January 1955.
24. E. Abel, *The Missiles of October, The Story of the Cuban Missile Crisis* (MacGibbon and Kee, 1966), p. 119.
25. C. Webster and N. Frankland, *The Strategic Air Offensive Against Germany, vol. IV*. (Her Majesty's Stationary Office [HMSO], 1961), p. 496.
26. S. Menaul, *Countdown – Britain's Strategic Nuclear Forces* (Robert Hale, 1980), p. 115.
27. Since the twenty-fifth anniversary, various important studies have appeared, including: B.J. Allyn, J.G. Blight, and D.A. Welch, *Back to the Brink: Proceedings of the Moscow Conference on the Cuban Missile Conference, January 27–28, 1989*, CSIA Occasional Paper No. 9 (Lanham, Maryland: University of America Press, 1992); M.R. Beschloss, *Kennedy v. Khrushchev, The Crisis Years 1960–63* (Faber and Faber, 1991); J.G. Blight and D.A. Welch, *On the Brink: Americans and Soviets Reexamine the Cuban Missile Crisis*, (New York: Noonday Press, 1990); J.G. Blight, B.J. Allyn, and D.A. Welch, *Cuba on the Brink: Castro, the Missile Crisis and the Soviet Collapse* (New York: Pantheon Books, 1993); D.A. Brugioni (Ed. R.F. McCort), *EyeBall to Eyeball: The Inside Story of the Cuban Missile Crisis* (New York: Random House, 1991); M. Bundy, *Danger and Survival: Choices About the Bomb in the First Fifty Years* (New York: Random House, 1988); R.L. Garthoff, *Reflections on the Cuban Missile Crisis* (Washington: The Brookings Institution, 1989); Lebow and Stein, *We All Lost the Cold War*, E.R. May and P.D. Zelikow (Eds), *The Kennedy Tapes: Inside the White House During the Cuban Missile Crisis* (Harvard University Press, 1997); P. Nash, *The Other Missiles of October: Eisenhower, Kennedy, and the Jupiters 1957–1963* (Chapel Hill, North Carolina: University of North Carolina Press, 1997); J.A. Nathan (Ed.), *The Cuban Missile Crisis Revisited* (New York: St. Martin's Press, 1992); S.D. Sagan, *The Limits of Safety – Organisations, Accidents, and Nuclear Weapons* (Princeton, New Jersey: Princeton University Press, 1993) and M.J. White, *The Cuban Missile Crisis* (Macmillan, 1996).
28. For discussion, see L. Scott and S. Smith, 'Lessons of October: historians, political scientists, policy-makers and the Cuban missile crisis', *International Affairs*, Vol. 70, No. 4 (October 1994).
29. Most notably, A. Fursenko and T. Naftali, *'One Hell of a Gamble': Khrushchev, Castro, Kennedy and the Cuban Missile Crisis 1958–1964* (John Murray, 1997); see also V. Zubok and C. Pleshakov, *Inside the Kremlin's Cold War* (Harvard University Press, 1996).
30. For European aspects, see M. Vaisse (Ed.), *L'Europe et la Crise de Cuba* (Paris: Armand Colin, 1993); F. Costigliola, 'Kennedy, the European Allies, and the Failure to Consult', *Political Science Quarterly*, Vol. 110, No. 1 (1995) and T. Risse-Kappen, *Cooperation Among*

Democracies: The European Influence on U.S. Foreign Policy (Princeton, New Jersey: Princeton University Press, 1995), pp. 146–82; for work on the British side, see P.G. Boyle, 'The British Government's View of the Cuban Missile Crisis', *Contemporary Record*, Vol. 10, No. 3 (Autumn, 1996); A. Horne, *Macmillan, 1957–1986, Vol. II of the Official Biography* (Macmillan, 1989); G.D. Rawnsley, 'How Special is Special? The Anglo-American Alliance During the Cuban Missile Crisis', *Contemporary Record*, Vol. 9, No. 3 (Winter, 1995); and D.R. Thorne, *Alec Douglas-Home* (Sinclair–Stevenson, 1996), pp. 231–52; see also Nunnerley, *President Kennedy*, pp. 71–90.

31. British nuclear activities are entirely neglected in key studies, for example, M. Trachtenberg, 'The Influence of Nuclear Weapons in the Cuban Missile Crisis', *International Security*, Vol. 10, No. 1 (Summer 1985) and *History and Strategy* (Princeton, New Jersey: Princeton University Press, 1991), pp. 235–60; Bundy, *Danger and Survival*, pp. 445–58; an important exception to this neglect is Sagan, *Limits of Safety*, pp. 111–13.

32. An important recent exception to neglect of British sources is May and Zelikow, *The Kennedy Tapes*, which, *inter alia*, reproduces the transcripts of the Macmillan–Kennedy conversations, pp. 283–7, 384–9, 427–30, and 480–4.

33. HMD, 22 October 1962, quoted in Macmillan, *End of the Day*, p. 184.

34. Nash, *The Other Missiles*, pp. 118–49, et seq.

35. See D. Brinkley, 'Dean Acheson and the "Special Relationship": The West Point Speech of December 1962', *The Historical Journal*, Vol. 33, No. 3, (1990).

36. Nunnerley, *President Kennedy*, p. 71.

37. Ibid., p. 79.

38. Oral History Interview (undated), Peter Thorneycroft, (NSA:CMC), Doc. 03338.

39. Ibid.

40. John Fitzgerald Kennedy Library (JFKL): Oral History Interview, McGeorge Bundy, 30 January 1970.

41. Horne, *Macmillan, 1957–1986*, p. 382.

42. D. Reynolds, *Britannia Overruled: British Power and World Policy in the 20th Century* (Longman, 1991), p. 214; Costigliola, 'Kennedy, the European Allies'; Rawnsley, 'How Special is Special'; for a more nuanced assessment, see Horne, *Macmillan, 1957–1986*; for a radical reassessment, see Risse-Kappen, *Cooperation Among Democracies*.

43. See in particular, J. Baylis, *Ambiguity and Deterrence: British Nuclear Strategy 1945–1964* (OUP, 1995); I. Clark, *Nuclear Diplomacy and the Special Relationship: Britain's Deterrent and America, 1957–1962* (OUP, 1994); J. Melissen, *The Struggle for Nuclear Partnership: Britain, the United States and the Making of an Ambiguous Alliance 1952–1959* (Groningen: Styx, 1993); and S. Twigge and L. Scott, *Fail Deadly? Britain and the Command and Control of Nuclear Forces, 1945–1964* (Aberystwyth: Nuclear History Program Report, 1997).

44. Taylor, *Against the Bomb*, p. 91.

45. T.C. Sorenson, *Kennedy* (Hodder and Stoughton, 1965), p. 719.
46. PRO: FO 371/168135, Marchant to Home, Cuba – Annual Review for 1962, 23 January 1963.

2 The Cuban Revolution and British–American Relations

 1. R.S. Churchill, *Winston S. Churchill, Vol. I Companion, part I, 1874–1896* (Heinemann, 1967), pp 616–18.
 2. A. Chayes, *The Cuban Missile Crisis* (OUP, 1974), pp. 116–17.
 3. Beschloss, *Kennedy v. Khrushchev*, p. 91.
 4. PRO: FO 371/168136, Profile of Fidel Castro by Bill Marchant, AK1012/3. Undermining Castro's political authority by removing his beard also occurred to the CIA, who planned to introduce depilatory powder into his shoes so that his beard would fall out. According to Henry Brandon the idea was originally that of the novelist and erstwhile British naval intelligence officer, Ian Fleming, the creator of James Bond. H. Brandon, *Special Relationships: A Foreign Correspondent's Memoirs From Roosevelt to Reagan* (Macmillan, 1988), p. 111. For a different version of the plot against Castro's beard, see Beschloss, *Kennedy v. Khrushchev*, pp. 134–5.
 5. PRO: FO 371/168136, Profile of Fidel Castro by Bill Marchant, AK1012/3.
 6. Ibid.
 7. Fursenko and Naftali, '*One Hell of a Gamble*', pp. 14–16.
 8. Y. Pavlov, *Soviet–Cuban Alliance 1959–1991* (Transaction Publishers, 1994), pp. 3–4.
 9. *The Guardian*, 17 April 1961, p. 8.
10. S.G. Rabe, *Eisenhower and Latin America: The Foreign Policy of AntiCommunism* (University of North Carolina Press, 1988), p. 124.
11. P.M. Williams, *Hugh Gaitskell: A Political Biography* (Jonathan Cape, 1979), p. 685.
12. A. Hennessy and G. Lambie (Eds) *The Fractured Blockade, West European–Cuba Relations During the Revolution* (Warwick University Caribbean Studies, Macmillan, 1993), pp. 6–8, 29–31.
13. H. Thomas, *Cuba or the Pursuit of Freedom* (Eyre and Spottiswoode, 1971), p. 1009; Blight, Allyn, and Welch, *Cuba on the Brink*, p. 167; T.G. Paterson, *Contesting Castro: The United States and the Triumph of the Cuban Revolution* (OUP, 1994), pp. 188–9.
14. A further irony was that some of the 12 Sea Furies eventually sold to Batista, helped in Castro's military victory over the émigrés at the Bay of Pigs.
15. PRO: FO 371/148178, Annual Review of Cuba for 1959, Fordham to Lloyd, AK 1011/1, 20 January 1960.
16. PRO: PREM 11/3622, Fordham, Tel. 31, 13 January 1959.
17. PRO: PREM 11/3622, Lloyd To Herter, Tel. 4678, 29 October 1959.
18. PRO: PREM 11/3622, Paris to FO, Lloyd to Herter, Tel. 331, 11 November 1959.
19. Ibid.

20. PRO: PREM 11/3622, Caccia to Lloyd, Tel. 2455, 24 November 1959. Dulles also imparted his view that, 'Castro was not only a bad man but had a streak of lunacy in his make-up which might have incalculable results. In other words, he was more like a Cuban Hitler than a Cuban version of Peron'.

21. PRO: PREM 11/3689, J.C. Thomas to de Zulueta, Shipping to Cuba, 27 September 1962.

22. PRO: PREM 11/3622, Paris to FO, Lloyd to Herter, Tel. 331, 11 November 1959.

23. PRO: FO 371/148178, Annual Review of Cuba for 1959, Fordham to Lloyd, AK 1011/1, 20 January 1960.

24. Ibid. This proved both the high point for British exports, and the last trade surplus. By 1960 British exports were down to £7 million, falling to less than £2 million by 1963, PRO: PREM 11/4695, Value of United Kingdom Trade with Cuba, [undated].

25. See in particular, Fursenko and Naftali, '*One Hell of a Gamble*'.

26. Rabe, *Eisenhower and Latin America*, pp. 122–3.

27. PRO: FO 371/148178, Annual Review of Cuba for 1959, Fordham to Lloyd, AK 1011/1, 20 January 1960.

28. PRO: PREM 11/3689, Home to Erroll, Trade with Cuba, FS/62/56, 15 June 1962.

29. Macmillan, *End of the Day*, p. 181.

30. Rabe, *Eisenhower and Latin America*, pp. 129–30; for analysis of the Bay of Pigs operations, see P. Gleijeses, 'Ships in the Night: The CIA, the White House and the Bay of Pigs', *Journal of Latin American Studies*, Vol. 27 (1995) and J.G. Blight and P. Kornbluh, *Politics of Illusion: The Bay of Pigs Reexamined* (Lynne Rienner, 1998).

31. Horne, *Macmillan, 1957–1986*, p. 298.

32. Ibid.

33. Ibid.

34. Ibid.

35. Ibid.

36. Beschloss, *Kennedy v. Khrushchev*, p. 101.

37. Editorial Note 84, *Foreign Relations of the United States* [FRUS], *1961–1963, Vol. X, Cuba 1961–1962* (Washington: United States Government Printing Office, 1997), p. 191.

38. Horne, *Macmillan, 1957–1986*, p. 300.

39. *The Guardian*, 17 April 1961, p. 8.

40. *The Guardian*, 22 April 1961, p. 6.

41. Fursenko and Naftali, '*One Hell of a Gamble*', p. 102.

42. Memorandum from the President's Special Assistant (Schlesinger) to President Kennedy, 3 May 1961, *FRUS, 1961–1963, Vol. X*, p. 425.

43. Ibid., p. 426; also quoted in Williams, *Hugh Gaitskell*, p. 685.

44. Ibid.

45. Williams, *Hugh Gaitskell*, p. 685.

46. Ibid.

47. *HC Deb.* vol. 638, 18 April 1961, col. 972. Washington was still denying involvement at this stage.

48. Memorandum from the President's Special Assistant (Schlesinger) to President Kennedy, 3 May 1961, *FRUS, 1961–1963, Vol. X*, p. 426.
49. PRO: FO 371/168421, Air Chief Marshal Sir John Slessor, Speech to the English-Speaking Union, Spring 1963.
50. Correspondence, Lord Healey, 30 August 1993; for Healey's view on the missiles see Chapter Five.
51. Lebow and Stein, *We All Lost the Cold War*, pp. 44–7, 70–2. For account of the summit, see Beschloss, *Kennedy v. Khrushchev*, pp. 182–236 and Fursenko and Naftali, '*One Hell of a Gamble*', pp. 101–31.
52. L. Chang and P. Kornbluh, *The Cuban Missile Crisis, 1962 – A National Security Archive Documents Reader* (New York: The New Press, 1992), p. 4. For Mongoose planning documents, see Chang and Kornbluh, ibid., pp. 20–47, 52–3. For discussion, see Garthoff, *Reflections*, pp. 8–9, 32–3, 122–3, Fursenko and Naftali, '*One Hell of a Gamble*', pp. 146–8, 156–8, Blight and Kornbluh, *Politics of Illusion*, pp. 107–32.
53. Beschloss, *Kennedy v. Khrushchev*, pp. 135–9.
54. PRO: PREM 11/3689, Record of a Conversation After Dinner at 1 Carlton Gardens on June 24, 1962.
55. PRO: FO 371/164507, Godber to Home, COCOM, 19 February 1962; F.C. Mason, COCOM Strategic Controls, 21 February 1962.
56. PRO: FO 371/164507, Macmillan to Home, PM's Pers. Min. M. 39/62, 14 February 1962.
57. PRO: PREM 11/3689, Trade with Cuba, Home to Erroll, PS/62/52, 7 June 1962.
58. Ibid.
59. PRO: PREM 11/3689, Erroll to Home, 8 June 1962.
60. Ibid.
61. Comment on ibid., 8 June 1962.
62. PRO: PREM 11/3689, P. Mason, Tel. 97, 13 June 1962.
63. PRO: PREM 11/3689, Home to Erroll, Trade with Cuba, FS/62/56, 15 June 1962.
64. Ibid.
65. PRO: PREM 11/3689, NATO discussions on Cuba, memo. by Erroll, June 1962.
66. PRO: PREM 11/3689, Record of a Conversation After Dinner at 1 Carlton Gardens on June 24, 1962.
67. Ibid.
68. Ibid.
69. PRO: PREM 11/3689, Record of a Meeting at the Foreign Office at 11 a.m. on June 25, 1962.
70. Ibid.
71. PRO: CAB 128/36, C.C. (62) 42nd Concs., 26 June 1962.
72. PRO: FO 371/162373, P. Mason, Tel. 132, 5 September 1962.
73. Bowles to Bruce, State Dept. Tel. 5335, 13 May 1961 (NSA: CMC), Doc. 00084.
74. Marine Corps Emergency Actions Center, Summary of Items of Significant Interest, 9–10 October 1962, (NSA: CMC), Doc. 00571. See 'Britain "gave US use of Bahamas air base" in Cuba missile

crisis', *The Guardian*, 23 December 1992. I am grateful to Maurice Frankel to drawing my attention to this information.

75. Garthoff, *Reflections*, p. 31.

76. PRO: FO 371/162373, R.M.K. Slater, Cuba, memo. to PS/Foreign Sec., AK1193/24, 13 September 1962. This assessment of CIA's links with Alpha 66 appears to be correct, see Blight and Kornbluh, *Politics of Illusion*, p. 128, 130–1.

77. E. Grove, *Vanguard to Trident, British Naval Policy since World War II* (Bodley Head, 1987), p. 303.

78. PRO: FO 371/162377, FO to Washington, Tel. 7474, 24 October 1962.

79. *New York Times*, 28 April 1966. I am grateful to Tom Paterson for this information.

80. T.G. Paterson (Ed.), *Kennedy's Quest for Victory: American Foreign Policy, 1961–1963* (OUP, 1989), p. 138.

81. PRO: CAB 134/2153, L.A.C. (62) 16, The Cuban Problem, note by Foreign Office for the Inter-departmental Committee on Latin America and the Caribbean, 12 December 1962.

82. PRO: FO 371/162374, Iain Sutherland to Tony Parsons, AK1201/17/G, 14 August 1962; see also PRO, FO 371/162374, Minute by I.J.M. Sutherland, 12 September 1962, AK1201/20/G. The Joint Intelligence Bureau's (JIB) advice to the Head of Chancery at the embassy in May 1962, on photographing military convoys, and the statement that the chancery was the JIB's only source in Cuba, may indicate that SIS did not maintain a station in Havana at this time, PRO: FO 371/162374, G.R. Way to Head of Chancery, Havana, 7 May 1962. According to Nigel West in his 'documentary novel' on the crisis, SIS lost most of its local 'assets' when Shell was nationalised, *Cuban Bluff* (New York: Crown, 1991), p. 78.

83. PRO: FO 371/162374, Sutherland to Parsons, AK1201/18/G, 28 August 1962; PRO: FO 371/162374, I.J.M. Sutherland, minute, 12 September 1962, AK1201/20/G.

84. PRO: FO 371/162374, Iain Sutherland to Tony Parsons, AK1201/17/G, 14 August 1962.

85. PRO: FO 371/162373, Ormsby-Gore, Tel. 2237, 6 September 1962.

86. PRO: FO 371/162373, R.M.K. Slater, Cuba, memo. to PS/Foreign Sec., AK1193/24, 13 September 1962.

87. PRO: FO 371/162373, Ormsby-Gore, Tel. 2237, 6 September 1962.

88. PRO: PREM 11/3689, J.C. Thomas to de Zulueta, Shipping to Cuba, 27 September 1962.

89. Ibid.

90. PRO: FO 371/162373, R.M.K. Slater, Cuba, memo. to PS/Foreign Sec., AK1193/24, 13 September 1962.

91. PRO: PREM 11/3689, Home to Macmillan, Tel. 1461, PM's Pers. Tel. T.48A/62, 1 October 1962.

92. Ibid.

93. PRO: PREM 11/3689, Macmillan to Home [at the UN], Tel. 3423, PM's Pers. Tel. T.480/62, 1 October 1962.

94. PRO: CAB 128/36. C.C. (62) 59th Concs., 9 October 1962.

95. PRO: PREM 11/3689, Ormsby-Gore, Tel. 2465, 2 October 1962.
96. PRO: PREM 11/3689, FO to Washington, Tel. 6952, 5 October 1962. After the war of 1812, the British and American governments negotiated the Anglo-American Convention of Commerce, D.P. O'Connell, *The International Law of the Sea, Vol. I* (OUP, 1982), pp. 133–4, 139, 140, 513–14. The American *casus belli* in 1812 was freedom of the seas.
97. PRO: PREM 11/3689, Ormsby-Gore, Tel. 2499, 5 October 1962. No such ridicule, of course, attached itself to the unilateral declarations of an American President in 1823.
98. PRO: FO 371/162391, Ormsby-Gore, Tel. 2751, 1 November 1962.
99. PRO: PREM 11/3689, Ormsby-Gore, Tel. 2553, 11 October 1962.
100. PRO: PREM 11/3689, J.C. Thomas to de Zulueta, Shipping to Cuba, 27 September 1962. A further three tankers were in ballast, carrying molasses or sugar to the UK.
101. PRO: PREM 11/3689, Ormsby-Gore, Tel. 2623, 20 October 1962.
102. Ibid.
103. Ibid.
104. Ibid.
105. PRO: FO 371/162347, H.S. Marchant to N.J.A. Cheetham, AK1051/11, 22 October 1962.
106. Ibid.
107. Ibid.
108. PRO: FO 371/162347, Cuba, memo. by Joseph Godber, AK 1051/1, 27 September 1962.
109. Garthoff, *Reflections*, p. 60.
110. For discussion of Soviet decision-making, see Lebow and Stein, *We All Lost the Cold War*, pp. 19–93; Garthoff, *Reflections*, pp. 6–42; and Fursenko and Naftali, '*One Hell of a Gamble*', pp. 166–83.
111. For Bolshakov's role, see Fursenko and Naftali, '*One Hell of a Gamble*', pp. 109–114, et seq; see also Beschloss, *Kennedy v. Khrushchev*, pp. 152–7, et seq.
112. Bolshakov's role in deceiving Kennedy also became known to London, PRO: FO 371/162404, Ormsby-Gore to Caccia, AK 1261/586, 7 November 1962; FO 371/162403, Ormsby-Gore to Caccia, 9 November 1962, AK1216/571.
113. A. Dobrynin, *In Confidence: Moscow's Ambassador to America's Six Cold War Presidents (1962–1986)* (New York: Times Books, 1995), p. 74, et seq; Fursenko and Naftali, '*One Hell of a Gamble*', p. 231.
114. May and Zelikow, *The Kennedy Tapes*, pp. 168–9. Kennedy's anger at Gromyko's behaviour was viewed sympathetically within the Foreign Office. Sir Harold Caccia, opined that 'Gromyko failed to live up to Sir Harold Nicholson's injunction that truthfulness as observed by a diplomatist should include "a constant anxiety to avoid, even inadvertently, leaving a false impression"', PRO: FO 371/162401, Caccia to Home, 31 October 1962. Sir Frank Roberts, however, was 'not quite sure that even our own records is 100 per cent clean. Soviet behaviour was of course deceitful but no one here ever suggested to me, or so far as I know to the Americans,

that there were no long-range Soviet missiles involved in this operation', PRO: FO 371/162405, Roberts to Caccia, AK1261/611, 8 November 1962. Roberts also alluded to the long tradition of deception in Russian foreign policy dating back to Peter the Great. Eisenhower's initial denials concerning U-2 flights over the USSR and Kennedy administration statements over the Bay of Pigs invasion, were examples of American disregard for the injunctions of Sir Harold Nicholson. Kennedy himself, was less prosaic, referring to Mr Gromyko as that 'lying bastard', Brugioni, *Eyeball to Eyeball*, p. 287.

115. A.I. Gribkov and W.Y. Smith, *Operation Anadyr: US and Soviet Generals Recount the Cuban Missile Crisis* (Chicago: Edition Q, 1994), pp. 45–6; Fursenko and Naftali, *'One Hell of a Gamble'*, pp. 184–215.
116. PRO: FO 371/162405, FO Minute, A.D. Parsons, 9 November 1962.
117. PRO: FO 371/162777, Sir P. Dixon, Tel. 348, 24 October 1962.
118. P. Nitze, *From Hiroshima to Glasnost: At the Center of Decision* (New York: Grove Weidenfeld, 1989), p. 214.
119. For details of the U-2 missions see Brugioni, *Eyeball to Eyeball*, passim.
120. Nunnerley, *President Kennedy*, p. 78.
121. PRO: FO 371/162408, Marchant to Home, AK1261/667, 10 November 1962.
122. JFKL: Oral History Interview, Henry Brandon, 23 February 1970. In his memoir, Brandon quotes the anonymous Cuban official as stating that the missiles, manned by Russians, could 'hit the United States and not only Florida', Brandon, *Special Relationships*, pp. 171–2.
123. PRO: FO 371/162408, Marchant to Home, AK1261/667, 10 November 1962.
124. John McCone, Memo. for the President, 28 February 1963, in M.S. McAuliffe (Ed.), *CIA Documents on the Cuban Missile Crisis 1962* (Washington: CIA, 1992), p. 373.
125. PRO: FO 371/162408, Marchant to Home, AK1261/667, 10 November 1962.
126. Brandon, *Special Relationships*, p. 172.
127. For example, R. Hathaway, *Great Britain and the United States: Special Relations since World War II* (Boston: Twayne, 1990), pp. 50–73; J. Dickie, *'Special' No More – Anglo-American Relations: Rhetoric and Reality* (Weidenfeld and Nicolson, 1994), pp. 105–32.
128. PRO: PREM 11/3689, Macmillan to Home, Tel. 3423, PM's Pers. Tel. T480/62, 1 October 1962.
129. PRO: FO 371/162347, H.S. Marchant to N.J.A. Cheetham, AK1051/11, 22 October 1962.
130. Hennessy and Lambie, *The Fractured Blockade*.

3 Discovery and Blockade: Informing or Consulting?

1. For details of the discovery and identification of the missile bases, see Brugioni, *Eyeball to Eyeball*, pp. 120–217.
2. May and Zelikow, *The Kennedy Papers*, p. 54.

3. Ibid., p. 56.
4. Ibid., p. 66.
5. R.F. Kennedy, *13 Days, The Cuban Missile Crisis 1962* (Pan, 1969), p. 51.
6. *HC Deb.* vol. 664, 25 October 1962, col. 1057.
7. PRO: FO 371/168421, Air Chief Marshal Sir John Slessor, Speech to the English-Speaking Union, Spring 1963.
8. See Chapter One.
9. PRO: PREM 11/3689, Macmillan to Home [at the UN], Tel. 3423, PM's Pers. Tel. T.480/62, 1 October 1962.
10. Beschloss, *Kennedy v. Khrushchev*, pp. 105–6, 121, 144–5.
11. PRO: PREM 11/3689, Home to Macmillan, Tel. 1461, PM's Pers. Tel. T.48A/62, 1 October 1962.
12. May and Zelikow, *The Kennedy Papers*, p. 61.
13. Ibid., p. 175.
14. Kennedy to Macmillan, 22 October 1962, in Macmillan, *End of the Day*, pp. 182–3.
15. Dickie, *'Special' No More*, pp. 108–9.
16. A receptionist at CIA headquarters was overheard speculating about the numbers of 'methodists' visiting the agency. Brugioni, *Eyeball to Eyeball*, p. 219; for accounts of the conference see Abel, *Missiles of October*, pp. 64, 71–2; Dickie, *'Special' No More*, pp. 105–9; Brugioni, *Eyeball to Eyeball*, pp. 219–20, 327–8, 584–5 n.; see also R. Deacon, *'C': A Biography of Sir Maurice Oldfield* (Futura, 1984), p. 135.
17. Dickie, *'Special' No More*, p. 105.
18. Central Intelligence Agency (CIA): Chester Cooper, Memorandum for the Record, 29 October 1962, quoted in S. Kent, 'The Cuban Missile Crisis of 1962: Presenting the Photographic Evidence Abroad', *Studies in Intelligence* Vol. 10, No. 2 (Spring, 1972), p. 24.
19. Deacon, *'C': A Biography*, p. 135.
20. Abel, *Missiles of October*, pp. 64, 81; Nunnerley, *President Kennedy*, pp. 77–8.
21. Abel, *Missiles of October*, p. 81.
22. *The Listener*, 30 January 1969, p. 143.
23. May and Zelikow, *The Kennedy Papers*, pp. 396–7.
24. PRO: FO 371/162401, Ormsby-Gore to Home, Air Bag 185, 9 November 1962.
25. Macmillan, *End of the Day*, p. 180. Macmillan suggests that the source for this was the President who had spoken to Ormsby-Gore in guarded terms.
26. PRO: PREM 11/3689, Ormsby-Gore, Tel. 2624, 20 October 1962. Ormsby-Gore explained that Sir Hugh Stephenson would provide the Foreign Secretary with a full report on his return.
27. The British were told on 22 October that they had been identified in Cuba in 'early October', PRO: PREM 11/3689, Top Secret Document delivered by the US Ambassador, 22 October 1962; see also Brugioni, *Eyeball to Eyeball*, pp. 172–5; May and Zelikow, *The Kennedy Papers*, p. 70 n.
28. Franklin Sieverts, The Cuban Missile Crisis, 1962, State Depart-

ment History, August 1963, p. 78 (NSA: CMC), Doc. 03154. This
same account states that Kennedy briefed Macmillan on the phone
later that evening. No other evidence supports this suggestion,
and as Macmillan was at Chequers on Saturday, which lacked a
secure telephone facility, it seems unlikely.

29. PRO: PREM 11/3689, Ormsby-Gore to Macmillan, Tel. 2636, PM's
    Pers. Tel. T.495/62, 22 October 1962, quoted *in extenso* in Macmillan,
    End of the Day, pp. 190–4.
30. Ibid.
31. Ibid.
32. Ibid. The Commander of the US Tactical Air Force, General
    Sweeney, had told the President earlier that morning that, at best,
    he could destroy 90 per cent of known missiles (which were esti-
    mated to be some 60 per cent of those on the island), May and
    Zelikow, *The Kennedy Papers*, p. 206.
33. Schlesinger, *A Thousand Days*, p. 699.
34. Abel, *Missiles of October*, p. 100; Ormsby-Gore's own recollection,
    that he was presented with three options – invasion, blockade and
    political action – is also misleading, *The Listener*, 30 January 1969,
    p. 143.
35. PRO: PREM 11/3689, Ormsby-Gore to Macmillan, Tel. 2636, PM's
    Pers. Tel. T.495/62, 22 October 1962, quoted *in extenso* in Macmillan,
    End of the Day, pp. 190–4.
36. Ibid.
37. Ibid.
38. See White, *The Cuban Missile Crisis*, pp. 115–34; May and Zelikow,
    The Kennedy Papers, pp. 47–117.
39. PRO: PREM 11/3689, Ormsby-Gore to Macmillan, Tel. 2636, PM's
    Pers. Tel. T.495/62, 22 October 1962, quoted *in extenso* in Macmillan,
    End of the Day, pp. 190–4.
40. Ibid.
41. Ibid.
42. PRO: PREM 11/3689, Ormsby-Gore to Macmillan, Tel. 2630, PM's
    Pers. Tel. T.487/62, 21 October 1962, reproduced *in extenso* in
    Macmillan, *End of the Day*, p. 182.
43. Macmillan, *End of the Day*, pp. 182–3.
44. Ibid.
45. Ibid.
46. Ibid.
47. Macmillan, *End of the Day*, p. 184.
48. PRO: PREM 11/3689, Timothy Bligh, Note, 22 October 1962.
49. Macmillan, *End of the Day*, pp. 187, 189, 190.
50. PRO: PREM 11/3689, Ormsby-Gore to Macmillan, Tel. 2650, PM's
    Pers. Tel. T.505/62, 23 October 1962. Macmillan's account makes
    no mention of this second telegram, *End of the Day*, pp. 190–220,
    and in contrast to Ormsby-Gore's first telegram (Tel. 2636), the Cabinet
    were not briefed on the ambassador's highly confidential report.
51. PRO: PREM 11/3689, Macmillan to Ormsby-Gore Tel. 7395, PM's
    Pers. Tel. T.493/62, 22 October 1962.

52. PRO: PREM 11/3689, Ormsby-Gore to Macmillan Tel. 2650, PM's Pers. Tel. T.505/62, 23 October 1962.
53. Ibid.
54. Ibid.
55. Ibid.
56. Abel, *Missiles of October*, pp. 103–4. For details of the various briefings, see CIA: Kent, 'The Cuban Missile Crisis of 1962'. Bruce was armed with a gun to ensure that Cooper was provided with an armed escort, JFKL: Oral History Interview, Chester Cooper, 16 May 1966.
57. For Macmillan's account see *End of the Day*, pp. 184–5; for the official minute of the meeting, see PRO: PREM 11/3689, P. de Zulueta to A.C.I. Samuel, PS/Foreign Sec., 22 October 1962.
58. JFKL: Bruce to Rusk, Tel. 1656, 22 October 1962, NSF: CO: Cuba, Cables 10/22/26, Box 40.
59. Macmillan, *End of the Day*, p. 186.
60. CIA: Kent, 'The Cuban Missile Crisis of 1962', pp. 22–3.
61. Brugioni, *Eyeball to Eyeball*, p. 328.
62. CIA: Kent, 'The Cuban Missile Crisis of 1962', p. 23; see also C.L. Cooper, *The Lion's Last Roar: Suez, 1956* (Harper and Row, 1978), p. 260.
63. Brugioni, *Eyeball to Eyeball*, p. 328.
64. JFKL: Bruce to Rusk, Tel. 1656, 22 October 1962, NSF: CO: Cuba, Cables 10/22/26, Box 40.
65. *Observer*, 28 October 1962.
66. CIA: Kent, 'The Cuban Missile Crisis of 1962', p. 23.
67. Brugioni, *Eyeball to Eyeball*, p. 329.
68. JFKL: Bruce to Rusk, Tel. 1656, 22 October 1962, NSF: CO: Cuba, Cables 10/22/26, Box 40.
69. PRO: PREM 11/3689, Macmillan to Ormsby-Gore, Tel. 7395, PM's Pers. Tel. T.493/62, 22 October 1962.
70. Interview, BBC Radio *Today* programme, 1 January 1993.
71. Macmillan, *End of the Day*, p. 187.
72. Ibid.
73. Ibid., p. 190.
74. HMD, 22 October 1962, quoted in Macmillan, *End of the Day*, p. 187.
75. PRO: PREM 11/3689, Macmillan to Kennedy, Tel. 7396, PM's Pers. Tel. T.492/62, 22 October 1962 – quoted *in extenso* in Macmillan, *End of the Day*, pp. 188–9; see also May and Zelikow, *The Kennedy Papers*, pp. 268–9.
76. Ibid.
77. Ibid.
78. Ibid.
79. Lyon to Rusk, 22 October 1962, *FRUS, 1961–1963 Vol. XI, Cuban Missile Crisis and Aftermath* (Washington: United States Government Printing Office, 1996), p. 166.
80. *The Daily Mail*, 23 October 1962.
81. *The Guardian*, 23 October 1962.
82. Quoted in Nunnerley, *President Kennedy*, p. 72.

83. PRO: PREM 11/3689, Macmillan to Ormsby-Gore, Tel. 7410, PM's Pers. Tel. T.497/62, 23 October 1962.
84. HMD, 4 November 1962, quoted in Macmillan, *End of the Day*, p. 219.
85. *HC Deb.*, vol. 666, 30 October 1962, col. 36.
86. CIA: Kent, 'The Cuban Missile Crisis of 1962', p. 24.
87. Ibid.
88. Minutes of the 507th Mtg. of the NSC, 22 October 1962, *FRUS, 1961–1963, Vol. XI, Cuban Missile Crisis and Aftermath* (Washington: United States Government Printing Office, 1996), p. 152.
89. Ibid.
90. May and Zelikow, *The Kennedy Papers*, pp. 268–9.
91. For discussion of how far domestic politics influenced Kennedy's decisions, see T.G. Paterson and W.J. Brophy, 'October Missiles and November Elections: The Cuban Missile Crisis and American Politics, 1962', *Journal of American History*, Vol. 73 (June 1986), and R.N. Lebow, 'The Traditional and Revisionist Interpretations Reevaluated: Why was Cuba a Crisis?' in Nathan, *The Cuban Missile Crisis Revisited*.
92. PRO: PREM 11/3689, Kennedy to Macmillan, PM's Pers. Tel. T.494/62, 22 October 1962; May and Zelikow, pp. 282–3.
93. Ibid.
94. Ibid.
95. PRO: FO 371/162401 Ormsby-Gore to Home, Air Bag 185, 9 November 1962.
96. PRO: FO 371/166970, Evelyn Shuckburgh, Cuba and Anglo-American Consultation, 6 November 1962; reproduced in J. Baylis (Ed.), *Anglo-American Relations since 1939* (Manchester University Press [MUP], 1997). Shukburgh chaired an ad hoc committee after the crisis, tasked with evaluating the crisis.
97. For discussion of Macmillan and Suez, see A. Horne, *Macmillan, 1894–1956: Volume I of The Official Biography* (Macmillan, 1988), pp. 394–447.
98. Macmillan, *End of the Day*, p. 187.
99. HMD, 22 October 1962, quoted in ibid.
100. PRO: PREM 11/3689, Record of a Conversation between the Prime Minister and President Kennedy at 12.30 am on Tuesday, 23 October 1962; May and Zelikow, *The Kennedy Papers*, pp. 284–5. The transcripts of these conversations were then forwarded to Ormsby-Gore, with instructions that they be destroyed when he had read them, PRO: PREM 11/3689, de Zulueta to Ormsby-Gore, 23 October 1962.
101. Record of Conversation, 23 October, ibid.; May and Zelikow, *The Kennedy Papers*, p. 287.
102. PRO: PREM 11/3689, de Zulueta to Ormsby-Gore, 23 October 1962.

4 Converging Perspectives and Divergent Views

1. *HC Deb.*, vol. 666, 30 October 1962, col. 19.
2. John Rankin, *HC deb.*, vol. 666, 30 October 1962, col. 81.
3. *The Guardian*, 26 October 1962.
4. *New Statesman*, 26 October 1962.
5. HMD, 4 November 1962, quoted in Macmillan, *End of the Day*, p. 220.
6. B. Brodie, *War and Politics* (Cassell, 1973), p. 431.
7. JFKL: Minute, [of Amb. mtg.], 23 October 1962, NSF: RS: NATO Weapons, Cables, Turkey, Box 226; see also Franklin Sieverts, *The Cuban Missile Crisis, 1962*, State Department History, August 1963, p. 125 (NSA: CMC), Doc. 03154.
8. CIA: Kent, 'The Cuban Missile Crisis of 1962', p. 20.
9. The North Atlantic Treaty, Washington, April 1949, *The North Atlantic Treaty Organisation* (NATO Information Service 1983 edn), p. 264.
10. See Chapter Eight.
11. May and Zelikow, *The Kennedy Papers*, p. 279.
12. For Kennedy's approach to NATO strategy, see J.E. Stromseth, *The Origins of Flexible Response: NATO's Debate Over Strategy in the 1960s* (Macmillan, 1988) and D.N. Schwartz. *NATO's Nuclear Dilemmas* (Washington: The Brookings Institution, 1983); for the development of American national policy under Kennedy, see F. Kaplan, *The Wizards of Armageddon* (Stanford: Stanford University Press, 1991) and D. Ball, *Politics and Force Levels* (University of California Press, 1980).
13. PRO: PREM 11/3689, P. Mason Tel. 163, 23 October 1962.
14. PRO: PREM 11/3690, Ormsby-Gore, Tel. 2674, 24 October 1962.
15. Ibid. Similarly, Acheson told the NAC that Kennedy's choice of the quarantine reflected anxiety 'to avoid any action which might have brought drastic Soviet retaliation on America's allies', PRO: PREM 11/3689, P. Mason, Tel. 163, 22 October 1962.
16. Garthoff, *Reflections*, p. 21.
17. Lebow and Stein, *We All Lost the Cold War*, p. 27.
18. N. Khrushchev (edited/translated by S. Talbott), *Khrushchev Remembers* (London: Andre Deutsch, 1971), pp. 488–505; N. Khrushchev, (ed./ trans. by J.L. Schecter and V.V. Luchkov), *Khrushchev Remembers: The Glasnost Tapes* (Little Brown, and Co., 1990), pp. 170–83.
19. Lebow and Stein, *We All Lost the Cold War*, pp. 42–50, 90–1.
20. A JIC report, not yet declassified, was produced in December – PRO: DEFE 4/142, Soviet Motives in Cuba, JIC (62) 101, 18 December 1962, discussed at COS (62) 81st.
21. PRO: FO 371/162398, The Soviet Union and Cuba, FO to Certain HM Reps., Tel. 174 Intel, 2 November 1962.
22. The photographs were evaluated at the Joint Air Reconnaissance Intelligence Centre (JARIC) at Brampton, Brugioni, *Eyeball to Eyeball*, p. 380.
23. PRO: CAB 129/111, C. (62) 166, Cuba: Threat Posed by Soviet

Missiles, 26 October 1962, covering The Threat Posed by Soviet Missiles in Cuba, JIC (62) 93 (Final), 26 October 1962. On 18 October, Kennedy was told that further analysis of the photographs revealed IRBM installations under construction, May and Zelikow, *The Kennedy Papers*, p. 122.

24. JIC (62) 93 (Final), ibid.
25. Ibid.
26. Ibid. The Americans were right. Soviet IRBMs were being deployed, though none of the missiles reached Cuba, see Fursenko and Naftali, '*One Hell of a Gamble*', pp. 188, 230, 247; Gribkov and Smith, *Operation Anadyr*, pp. 13, 19, 26, 45, 62–3.
27. PRO: CAB 129/111, C. (62) 166, Cuba: Threat Posed by Soviet Missiles, 26 October 1962, covering The Threat Posed by Soviet Missiles in Cuba, JIC (62) 93 (Final), 26 October 1962. Initially, the US intelligence community was unsure whether the missiles were SS-3s or SS-4s; see below, Chapter Seven and Brugioni, *Eyeball to Eyeball*, pp. 199–217.
28. PRO: CAB 128/36, C.C. (62) 61st Concs., 23 October 1962.
29. JFKL: Bruce to Rusk, State Dept. Tel. 1696, 26 October 1962, NSF: CO: Cuba, Cables, 10/26/62, Part 1 Box 41. According to Sir Nicholas Henderson, the head of the FO Northern Dept., R.H. Mason, chaired the JIC sub-committee which did most of the work of the JIC, conversation with author, 29 November 1994.
30. JFKL: Bruce to Rusk, State Dept. Tel. 1696, 26 October 1962, NSF: CO: Cuba, Cables 10/26/62, Part 1 Box 41.
31. PRO: FO 371/162398, The Soviet Union and Cuba, FO to Certain HM Reps., Tel. 174 Intel, 2 November 1962.
32. PRO: FO 371/162395, Evelyn Shuckburgh, Notes for the Lord Privy Seal, 30 October 1962.
33. May and Zelikow, *The Kennedy Tapes*, p. 89. For analysis of the significance of the missiles, see Garthoff, 'The Military Significance of Soviet Military Bases in Cuba', 27 October 1962, Garthoff, *Reflections*, pp. 202–11.
34. PRO: PREM 11/3689, Ormsby-Gore to Macmillan, Tel. 2636, PM's Pers. Tel. T.495/62, 22 October 1962, quoted *in extenso* in Macmillan, *End of the Day*, pp. 190–4.
35. For details of the Cuban Missile Early Warning System (CMEWS) see Sagan, *Limits of Safety*, pp. 122–34.
36. Ibid., pp. 130–1.
37. B. Lovell, *Astronomer by Chance* (Basic Books, 1990), pp. 321–2.
38. Brugioni, *Eyeball to Eyeball*, p. 365.
39. PRO: PREM 11/3689, P. Mason, Tel. 163, 23 October 1962.
40. JFKL: Bruce to Rusk, State Dept. Tel. 1696, 26 October 1962, NSF: CO: Cuba, Cables, 10/26/62, Part 1 Box 41.
41. CIA: Khrushchev's Cuban Venture in Retrospective, Ray Cline to McGeorge Bundy, 7 December 1962.
42. PRO: PREM 11/3690, Ormsby-Gore, Tel. 2674, 24 October 1962.
43. Ibid.
44. JFKL: State Dept. Policy telegram, 24 October 1962.

45. Ibid.
46. PRO: FO 371/162398, The Soviet Union and Cuba, FO to Certain HM Reps., Tel. 174 Intel, 2 November 1962.
47. PRO: PREM 11/3691, Roberts, Tel. 2077, 28 October 1962.
48. PRO: FO 371/162400, Roberts, Tel. 2202, 8 November 1962.
49. PRO: FO 371/162398, The Soviet Union and Cuba, FO to Certain HM Reps., Tel. 174 Intel, 2 November 1962.
50. Lebow and Stein, *We All Lost the Cold War*, p. 62.
51. Macmillan, *End of the Day*, p. 194. The American K-9 secure speech link was established in 1960. It was augmented by a teletype facility, which during the crisis operated between the White House and Admiralty House. In November, a British speech link, TWILIGHT, was installed, and used when Kennedy and Macmillan discussed the prolongation of the crisis; see Twigge and Scott, *Fail Deadly?*, pp. 350–1.
52. PRO: PREM 11/3689, Home's speech to the National Committee of the International Chamber of Commerce, 23 October 1962, FO to Certain HM Reps., Tel. 421 Guidance, 24 October 1962.
53. For discussion, see Boyle 'British Government's View', pp. 32–4.
54. Chayes, *The Cuban Missile Crisis*, p. 49.
55. 507th NSC mtg., *FRUS, Vol. XI 1961–1963*, p. 152. Abram Chayes notes Robert Kennedy's initial view, in contrast, was that OAS action was 'political not legal', Chayes, *Cuban Missile Crisis*, p. 16.
56. May and Zelikow, *The Kennedy Tapes*, pp. 256–7, 266, 269, 272.
57. PRO: PREM 11/3689, Ormsby-Gore, Tel. 2646, 22 October 1962.
58. PRO: CAB 128/36, C.C. (62) 61st Concs., 23 October 1962.
59. PRO: CAB 129/111, Cuba, Memo. by the Lord Chancellor, C. (62) 170, 25 October 1962. It was shown to Macmillan on 24 October.
60. Ibid.
61. Ibid.
62. Ibid.
63. PRO: FO 371/162388, Hailsham to Dilhorne, 25 October 1962. After the crisis, American legal experts generally endorsed the US government's interpretation of international law, see *The American Journal of International Law*, Vol. LVII, No. 3 (July 1963), pp. 515–604.
64. Correspondence, Lord Hailsham, 23 August 1994.
65. Chayes, *Cuban Missile Crisis*, p. 16.
66. PRO: PREM 11/3689, FO to Dean, Tel. 3874, 23 October 1962.
67. Chayes, *Cuban Missile Crisis*, pp. 14–15 n.
68. PRO: PREM 11/3689, FO to Dean, Tel. 3874, 23 October 1962.
69. *HC Deb*. vol. 664, 25 October 1962, col. 1060.
70. PRO: PREM 11/3690, Home to Macmillan, PM/62/140, 27 October 1962.
71. PRO: CAB 128/36, C.C. (62) 61st Concs., 23 October 1962.
72. PRO: FO 371/162377, FO to Ormsby-Gore, Tel. 7461, 24 October 1962.
73. PRO: PREM 11/3690, FO to Washington, Tel. 7488, 25 October 1962.

74. Ibid.
75. PRO: FO 371/162380, Ormsby-Gore, Tel. 2682, 25 October 1962; an *aide memoire* based on Tel. 7488 was handed to the State Department. The American response was that the quarantine was consistent with the principles of international law and the UN Charter, PRO: FO 371/162393, Ormsby-Gore, Tel. 2767, 2 November 1962.
76. PRO: FO 371/162388, Dilhorne to Home, AK1261/275, Cuba, 26 October 1962.
77. PRO: FO 371/162388, FO Minute, Francis Vallat, AK1261/275, 29 October 1962.
78. Ibid.
79. PRO: PREM 11/3690, comment on Home to Macmillan, PM/62/140, 28 October 1962.
80. PRO: PREM 11/3690, FO to Washington, Tel. 7488, 25 October 1962.
81. Ibid.
82. Ibid.
83. PRO: FO 371/162380, Ormsby-Gore, Tel. 2682, 25 October 1962.
84. May and Zelikow, *The Kennedy Tapes*, p. 446 n.
85. PRO: CAB 128/36, C.C. (62) 61st Concs., 23 October 1962.
86. HMD, 22 October 1962 quoted in Macmillan, *End of the Day*, p. 188.
87. PRO: PREM 11/3690, FO to Washington, Tel. 7418, 23 October 1962.
88. JFKL: Minute, [of Amb. mtg.], 23 October 1962, NSF: RS: NATO Weapons, Cables, Turkey, Box 226.
89. PRO: PREM 11/3689, Ormsby-Gore to Macmillan, Tel. 2650, PM's Pers. Tel. T.505/62, 23 October 1962.
90. PRO: PREM 11/3690, Macmillan to Home, 26 October 1962, PM's Pers. Minute M. 295/62.

5   Westminster and Hyde Park: British Politics and the Crisis

1. See Williams, *Hugh Gaitskell*, pp. 574–653; B. Brivati, *Hugh Gaitskell* (Richard Cohen, 1996), pp. 349–75.
2. Ibid.; see also D. Healey, *The Time of My Life* (Michael Joseph, 1989), pp. 241–2.
3. Williams, *Hugh Gaitskell*, p. 689.
4. Ibid.
5. Horne, *Macmillan, 1957–1986*, p. 332.
6. See Clark, *Nuclear Diplomacy* and J. Baylis, *Ambiguity and Deterrence*; for analysis of intelligence relations see R. Aldrich, 'British Intelligence and the Anglo-American "Special Relationship" during the Cold War', *Review of International Studies* Vol. 24, No. 3 (Autumn, 1998).
7. Horne, *Macmillan, 1957–1986*, pp. 332–59.
8. *New Statesman*, 26 October 1962, p. 554.
9. For analysis of the anti-nuclear movement during the crisis, see Taylor, *Against the Bomb*, pp. 88–94.
10. JFKL: Hilsman to Rusk, Western European Reactions to the Cuban

Situation (Through October 27, 1962), 28 October 1962; see also Francis Williams, 'Fleet Street and the Crisis', *New Statesman*, 26 October 1962, p. 557.

11. JFKL: Hilsman to Rusk, Western European Reactions to the Cuban Situation (Through October 27, 1962), 28 October 1962.

12. Ibid. Thus nearly one in ten British people appear to have believed that, while American action was not justified, it should still be supported.

13. Minutes of the 507th Mtg. of the NSC, 22 October 1962, *FRUS, 1961–1963 Vol. XI, Cuban Missile Crisis and Aftermath* (Washington: United States Government Printing Office, 1996), p. 153.

14. HMD, 22 October 1962, quoted in Macmillan, *End of the Day*, p. 190.

15. PRO: CAB 128/36, C.C. (62) 61st Concs, 23 October 1962.

16. HMD, 23 October 1962, quoted in Macmillan, *End of the Day*, p. 195.

17. PRO: PREM 11/3689, Ormsby-Gore to Macmillan, Tel. 2636, PM's Pers. Tel. T.495/62, 22 October 1962, quoted *in extenso* in Macmillan, *End of the Day*, pp. 190–4.

18. *New Statesman*, 26 October 1962, p. 554.

19. HMD, 23 October 1962, quoted in Macmillan, *End of the Day*, p. 195.

20. PRO: PREM 11/3689, Record of a meeting held at Admiralty House at 5 pm on Tuesday, October 23, 1962.

21. PRO: PREM 11/3690, Record of telephone message between the Prime Minister and President Kennedy, 24/10/62; May and Zelikow, *The Kennedy Tapes*, p. 389; see also Macmillan, *End of the Day*, p. 203.

22. PRO: PREM 11/3689, Record of a meeting held at Admiralty House at 5 pm on Tuesday, October 23, 1962.

23. PRO: CAB 128/36, C.C. (62) 62nd Concs., 25 October 1962.

24. CIA: Kent, 'The Cuban Missile Crisis of 1962'; David Bruce's Diaries, 23 October 1962 (NSA: CMC), Doc. 01623; see also A. Roosevelt, *For Lust of Knowing, Memoirs of an Intelligence Officer* (Weidenfeld and Nicolson, 1988), p. 469.

25. CIA: Kent, 'The Cuban Crisis of 1962', p. 24.

26. CIA: Chester Cooper, Memorandum for the Record, 29 October 1962, quoted in Kent, ibid., p. 23.

27. JFKL: Oral History Interview, Chester Cooper, 16 May 1966.

28. *HC Deb.* vol. 664, 25 October 1962, col. 1057; the State Department described Gaitskell as 'unusually restrained', JFKL: Hilsman to Rusk, Western European Reactions to the Cuban Situation (Through October 27, 1962), 28 October 1962.

29. CIA: Chester Cooper, Memorandum for the Record, 29 October 1962, quoted in Kent, 'The Cuban Missile Crisis of 1962', pp. 23–4.

30. Roosevelt, *Lust of Knowing*, p. 469.

31. Ibid.

32. CIA: Kent, 'The Cuban Missile Crisis of 1962', p. 24. Brugioni asserts that Kent briefed Gaitskell and Brown, Brugioni, *Eyeball to*

Eyeball, pp. 329–30. His claim that 'the usually ebullient George Brown had no comment that was remembered by Kent', p. 329, is belied by Kent's account.

33. JFKL: CIA Memorandum, The Crisis USSR/Cuba, 24 October 1962, NSF, Exec. Mtgs. 1–5, 10/23/62 – 10/25/62, Box 315.
34. JFKL: Bruce to Rusk, Tel. 1699, 26 October 1962.
35. National Museum of Labour History (NMLH): Statement by the NEC, 24 October 1962. The draft statement prepared for the NEC by the international secretariat was much more critical of the Americans: 'the Labour Party cannot support the actions of the United States Government in taking the law into its own hands and imposing a blockade on Cuba. Interference with the freedom of a state to control its own territorial waters is an act contrary to accepted principles of international law. Attacks on the shipping of other nations on the high seas will lead almost inevitably to retaliation . . . We regret that this drastic decision was taken by the United States Government in advance of the meeting of the United Nations Security Council. The United Nations exists to deal with threats to the peace. Its authority must not be undermined. . . .', NMLH: Draft Statement on Cuba.
36. JFKL: Bruce to Rusk, Tel. 1699, 26 October 1962.
37. Ibid.
38. NMLH: Statement by the General Council of the TUC, 24 October 1962.
39. NMLH: Statement by the NEC, 24 October 1962.
40. PRO: PREM 11/3690, Record of telephone message between the Prime Minister and President Kennedy, 24/10/62; May and Zelikow, *The Kennedy Tapes*, p. 386; see also Macmillan, *End of the Day*, p. 200.
41. JFKL: Bruce to Rusk, Tel. 1699, 26 October 1962.
42. David Bruce's Diaries, 25 October 1962 (NSA: CMC), Doc. 01623.
43. Ibid.
44. Ibid.
45. NMLH: Statement by the NEC, 24 October 1962.
46. Ibid.
47. *HC Deb.*, vol. 664, 25 October 1962, cols. 1056–9.
48. PRO: PREM 11/3690, Dilhorne to Macmillan, 25 October 1962.
49. Ibid.
50. Ibid.
51. JFKL: Hilsman to Rusk, Western European Reactions to the Cuban Situation (Through October 27, 1962), 28 October 1962.
52. NMLH: Overseas Dept., Resolutions from CLPs, Ov/1962–3/15.
53. Ibid.
54. Ibid.
55. David Bruce's Diaries, 23 October 1962 (NSA: CMC), Doc. 01623.
56. May and Zelikow, *The Kennedy Tapes*, p. 333.
57. David Bruce's Diaries, 24 October 1962 (NSA: CMC), Doc. 01623.
58. Ibid.
59. Ibid.

60. Taylor, *Against the Bomb*, p. 89.
61. *Peace News*, 26 October 1962, quoted in Taylor, *Against the Bomb*, p. 89.
62. Taylor, *Against the Bomb*, p. 90.
63. Russell, *Unarmed Victory*, p. 29.
64. C. Driver, *The Disarmers* (Hodder and Stoughton, 1964), p. 120.
65. Russell, *Unarmed Victory*, p. 31.
66. Ibid., pp. 31–2.
67. Kennedy, *13 Days*, p. 75; Russell, *Unarmed Victory*, p. 45. Russell later felt he should have couched his telegram to Kennedy 'more gently', B. Russell, *The Autobiography of Bertrand Russell, 1944–1967, Volume III* (George Allen and Unwin, 1969), p. 125.
68. Brugioni, *Eyeball to Eyeball*, p. 405. Brugioni also makes the rather absurd claim that 'to a degree Lord Russell reflected the official British government view on the Cuban crisis', ibid., p. 407.
69. R.W. Clark, *The Life of Bertrand Russell* (Jonathan Cape, 1975), p. 600.
70. For Khrushchev's telegram see Russell, *Unarmed Victory*, pp. 36–9.
71. PRO: FO 371/162389, FO. Minute, R.H. Mason, AK1261/293, 25 October 1962.
72. HMD, 25 October 1962, quoted in Macmillan, *End of the Day*, p. 205.
73. PRO: PREM 11/3690, Record of telephone message between the Prime Minister and President Kennedy, 24/10/62; May and Zelikow, *The Kennedy Tapes*, p. 386; see also Macmillan, *End of the Day*, pp. 200–1.
74. Ibid., p. 205.
75. JFKL: Hilsman to Rusk, Western European Reactions to the Cuban Situation (Through October 27, 1962), 28 October 1962.
76. Ibid. The Cabinet minute erroneously refers to the conversation having taken place on the evening of 23 October.
77. PRO: CAB 128/36, C.C. (62) 62nd Concs., 25 October 1962.
78. Ibid.
79. Quoted in Williams, *Hugh Gaitskell*, p. 693.
80. Ibid., p. 694.
81. Ibid. Gaitskell was nevertheless adamant about the need for negotiations to settle the dispute.
82. PRO: PREM 11/3691, Record of a Conversation Between the Foreign Secretary and Soviet *Chargé d'Affaires* on 25 October 1962, Home to Roberts, Tel. 235, 29 October 1962.
83. *Labour Party Conference Report 1962* (Labour Party, 1963).
84. Taylor, *Against the Bomb*, pp. 91–5.

6 Diplomatic Initiatives and Devious Approaches

1. T.C. Sorenson, *Kennedy* (Hodder and Stoughton, 1965), p. 559; for discussion of Ormsby-Gore's relationship with Kennedy, see Nunnerley, *President Kennedy*, pp. 39–48. Horne recounts that at the height of the crisis, arrangements were made for Ormsby-Gore's

family to be evacuated to the Presidential nuclear fall-out shelter in the Appalachians; Horne, *Macmillan*, 1957–1986, p. 368.

2. Beschloss, *Kennedy v. Khrushchev*, p. 249.
3. PRO: FO 371/162401, Ormsby-Gore to Home, Air Bag 185, 9 November 1962.
4. JFKL: Oral History Interview, David Bruce, 1964.
5. Nunnerley, *President Kennedy*, p. 45.
6. For example, Beschloss, *Kennedy v. Khrushchev*, pp. 493–4.
7. PRO: FO 371/162378, FO to Ormsby-Gore, Tel. 7457, 24 October 1962.
8. Ibid.
9. May and Zelikow, *The Kennedy Papers*, pp. 55, 82–3.
10. PRO: PREM 11/3690, Ormsby-Gore, Tel. 2667, 24 October 1962. Home duly concurred. PRO: PREM 11/3690, FO to Washington, Tel. 7554, 26 October 1962.
11. PRO: PREM 11/3689, Ormsby-Gore to Macmillan, Tel. 2650, PM's Pers. Tel. T.505/62, 23 October 1962.
12. Ibid.
13. Ibid.
14. Home cabled Ormsby-Gore: 'You have unique opportunities of access to the President and it is a great comfort to us to feel that you can see him at any time and let him know our thinking', PRO: PREM 11/3690, Home to Ormsby-Gore, Tel. 7460, 24 October 1962.
15. PRO: PREM 11/3689, Ormsby-Gore to Macmillan, Tel. 2650, PM's Pers. Tel. T.505/62, 23 October 1962.
16. PRO: FO 371/162378, FO to Ormsby-Gore, Tel. 7457, 24 October 1962.
17. Ibid.
18. PRO: PREM 11/3690, Ormsby-Gore, Tel. 2667, 24 October 1962; Brugioni, *Eyeball to Eyeball*, p. 403.
19. PRO: FO 371/162378, FO to Ormsby-Gore, Tel. 7457, 24 October 1962.
20. JFKL: McGeorge Bundy, Memorandum for the President, 24 October 1962, NSF: CO: Cuba, General, Macmillan Telephone Conversations 10/62–11/62, Box 37.
21. Ibid. When Ormsby-Gore learned that the Soviet ships had stopped he remarked to his Head of Chancery, Denis Greenhill: 'Thank God, they've turned back, just before the Prime Minister gave way', Denis Greenhill, *More by Accident* (Wilton 65, 1992), p. 103.
22. PRO: PREM 11/3689, Roberts, Tel. 1810, 19 September 1962.
23. Beschloss, *Kennedy v. Khrushchev*, p. 496. Ormsby-Gore was later briefed on this meeting, PRO: PREM 11/3691, Ormsby-Gore, Tel. 2735, 30 October 1962.
24. Kennedy, *13 Days*, p. 69. Commenting on how the President behaved during the crisis, Ormsby-Gore was clear that the 'period of most acute tension was during Tuesday night and Wednesday morning when the President assumed that contact would shortly be made between Soviet and American ships. . . . Once it was known

that the Communist bloc ships were turning back and the surprisingly mild reactions from Moscow had been gauged the President was visibly relieved of a great burden. It is true that by Friday night he was becoming impatient and even angry . . . but it was something very different from the grim subdued mood he was in earlier in the week', PRO: FO 371/162401, Ormsby-Gore to Home, Air Bag 185, 9 November 1962.

25. Kennedy, *13 Days*, p. 73; May and Zelikow, *The Kennedy Papers*, pp. 347–66. For details of the blockade, see J. Bouchard, *Command in Crisis: Four Case Studies* (New York: Colombia University Press, 1991), pp. 87–137.
26. Chang and Kornbluh, *The Cuban Missile Crisis, 1962*, pp. 370–1.
27. PRO: PREM 11/3690, Record of telephone message between the Prime Minister and President Kennedy, 24/10/62; May and Zelikow, *The Kennedy Tapes*, p. 384; see also Macmillan, *End of the Day*, pp. 198–203.
28. Record of telephone message, 24 October, ibid.; May and Zelikow, *The Kennedy Tapes*, p. 385; Macmillan, *End of the Day*, p. 199.
29. Ibid.
30. Record of telephone message, 24 October, ibid.; May and Zelikow, *The Kennedy Tapes*, p. 386; Macmillan, *End of the Day*, p. 200.
31. PRO: PREM 11/3690, de Zulueta to Bundy, T.505/62, 25 October 1962; quoted *in extenso*, Macmillan, *End of the Day*, p. 204; May and Zelikow, *The Kennedy Papers*, pp. 393–4.
32. Horne, *Macmillan, 1957–1986*, p. 368; Horne later concludes that if the $64 000 question was not consultation, 'it was something very close to it', ibid., p. 372.
33. PRO: PREM 11/3690, de Zulueta to Bundy, T.505/62, 25 October 1962; Macmillan, *End of the Day*, p. 204; May and Zelikow, *The Kennedy Papers*, p. 394.
34. Ibid.
35. *HC Deb.* vol. 664, 25 October 1962, col. 1058.
36. *The Daily Telegraph*, 23 October 1962.
37. *The Daily Herald*, 23 October 1962.
38. JFKL: CIA Memorandum, The Crisis USSR/Cuba, 24 October 1962, NSF, Exec. Mtgs. 1–5, 10/23/62 – 10/25/62, Box 315.
39. D. Owen, *The Politics of Defence* (Jonathan Cape, 1972), p. 41.
40. PRO: PREM 11/3689, Macmillan to Kennedy, Tel. 7396, PM's Pers. Tel. T.492/62, 22 October 1962 – quoted *in extenso* in Macmillan, *End of the Day*, pp. 188–9; see also May and Zelikow, *The Kennedy Papers*, pp. 268–9.
41. In the words of the British Ambassador in New York, 'the UN provided an outlet for passions, a forum for reflection and a framework for compromise', PRO: FO 371/162409, Dean to Home, Despatch No. 28, AK 1261/558, 9 November 1962.
42. PRO: PREM 11/3690, Dean, Tel. 1741, 24 October 1962.
43. PRO: PREM 11/3690, Record of telephone message between the Prime Minister and President Kennedy, 24/10/62; May and Zelikow, *The Kennedy Tapes*, p. 388.

44. PRO: PREM 11/3690, Dean, Tel. 1723, 24 October 1962.
45. Ibid.
46. Ibid.
47. Ibid.
48. Macmillan, *End of the Day*, pp. 213–14.
49. *Lord Denning's Report*, Cmnd 2512, September 1963.
50. Y. Ivanov (with G. Sokolov), *The Naked Spy* (Blake, 1992).
51. P. Knightley and C. Kennedy, *An Affair of State: The Profumo Scandal and the Framing of Stephen Ward* (Jonathan Cape, 1987) and A. Summers and S. Dorril, *Honeytrap: The Secret Worlds of Stephen Ward* (Weidenfeld and Nicolson, 1987).
52. See Chapter Two.
53. Beschloss, *Kennedy v. Khrushchev*, pp. 425–6, 500, 514, 559–60; Fursenko and Naftali, '*One Hell of a Gamble*', p. 184, et seq; see also Chapter Two.
54. See Chapter Nine.
55. Ivanov, *Naked Spy*, p. vii.
56. Ibid., p. 148.
57. Ibid.
58. PRO: PREM 11/4368, Stephen Ward to Harold Wilson, 1 November 1962; also quoted in Knightley and Kennedy, *Affair of State*, p. 126.
59. PRO: PREM 11/4368, Record of conversation at Admiralty House, 27 March 1963. This is a verbatim account, in contrast to the normal Whitehall minute taking, suggesting that a transcript, and therefore a recording, was made of the meeting between the Prime Minister and the Leader of the Opposition. A similar record exists of the meeting between Ward and Macmillan's private secretary, also attended by a senior MI5 officer, PRO: PREM 11/4368, Record of conversation between Dr Stephen Ward and Mr Bligh and Admiralty House, 9 pm, 7 May 1963.
60. PRO: PREM 11/4368, George Wigg, Note of a meeting between Wigg and Stephen Ward, 26 March 1963.
61. PRO: PREM 11/4368, Record of conversation at Admiralty House, 27 March 1963.
62. *HC Deb.*, vol. 679, 17 June, 1963, col. 69.
63. *Lord Denning's Report*, para 41. Denning described Nicholson as 'a most loyal Englishman', para. 40.
64. PRO: PREM 11/3690, Caccia to Roberts, Tel. 2706, 24 October 1962.
65. PRO: PREM 11/3690, Roberts to Caccia, Tel. 1039, 25 October 1962.
66. Sir Frank Roberts, interview with author, 6 December 1994.
67. *Lord Denning's Report*, para. 13.
68. Ibid., para. 251.
69. N. West, *A Matter of Trust, M.I.5 1945–72* (Coronet, 1983), p. 117; C. Pincher, *Their Trade is Treachery* (Sidgwick and Jackson, 1981), p. 81.
70. Ivanov, *Naked Spy*, pp. 25–6. Ivanov was identified as a GRU officer in the book published posthumously under Penkovsky's name,

O. Penkovskiy, *The Penkovskiy Papers* (New York: Doubleday, 1965), pp. 311–12.

71. PRO: PREM 11/3690, Roberts to Caccia, Tel. 1039, 25 October 1962.
72. Ibid.
73. *HC Deb.*, vol. 679, 17 June 1963, cols. 69–70.
74. PRO: PREM 11/3691, Record of a Conversation Between the Foreign Secretary and Soviet *Chargé d'Affaires* on 25 October 1962. Home to Roberts, Tel. 235, 29 October 1962.
75. PRO: FO 371/162379, Draft Record of a Conversation between the Secretary of State and the Polish Ambassador on October 24, 1962, AK1261/98, 26 October 1962.
76. PRO: PREM 11/3691, Record of a Conversation Between the Foreign Secretary and Soviet *Chargé d'Affaires* on 25 October 1962. Home to Roberts, Tel. 235, 29 October 1962.
77. PRO: CAB 128/36, C.C. (62) 62nd Concs., 25 October 1962.
78. Bruce to Rusk, Tel. 1688, 25 October 1962 (NSA: CMC), Doc. 01371.
79. PRO: FO 371/162381, Ormsby-Gore, Tel. 2686, 26 October 1962; a summary of the meeting was forwarded from London, PRO: PREM 11/3691, FO to Washington, Tel. 7558, 26 October 1962.
80. *HC Deb.* vol. 679, 17 June 1963, col. 70. Arran's account of this meeting was sent to the Foreign Secretary and the PM's office, PRO: PREM 11/4494, Arran to de Zulueta, 1 November 1962, covering memo. dated 31 October 1962. It was passed to Macmillan on 3 November.
81. *HC Deb.*, vol. 679, 17 June 1963, col. 70.
82. PRO: PREM 11/4370, *Pravda*, 17 June 1963, quoted in Trevelyan to FO, Tel. 1222, 17 June 1963.
83. PRO: PREM 11/4494, Arran to de Zulueta, 1 November 1962, covering memo. dated 31 October 1962.
84. Ivanov, *Naked Spy*, p. 149.
85. PRO: PREM 11/3691, FO to Washington, Tel. 7574, 27 October 1962.
86. PRO: PREM 11/3690, Caccia to Roberts, Tel. 2706, 24 October 1962.
87. PRO: PREM 11/3689, Ormsby-Gore to Macmillan, Tel. 2636, PM's Pers. Tel. T.495/62, 22 October 1962, quoted *in extenso* in Macmillan, *End of the Day*, pp. 190–4; PREM 11/3689, P. Mason, Tel. 163, 23 October 1962.
88. Fursenko and Naftali, '*One Hell of a Gamble*', pp. 217, 247; Gribkov and Smith, *Operation Anadyr*, pp. 45–6, 62–3.
89. PRO: PREM 11/3690, Caccia to Roberts, Tel. 2706, 24 October 1962.
90. The corresponding British estimates of these missile ranges were 650 nm and 1100 nm, see Chapter Four.
91. PRO: PREM 11/4494, Arran to de Zulueta, 1 November 1962, covering memo. dated 31 October 1962.
92. Beschloss, *Kennedy v. Khrushchev*, p. 500; Fursenko and Naftali, '*One Hell of a Gamble*', p. 249.

93. PRO: PREM 11/3690, Ormsby-Gore to Macmillan, Tel. 2662, 24 October 1962, PM's Pers. Tel. T.503/62; see also Memo. from Attorney General Kennedy to President Kennedy, 24 October 1962, *FRUS, 1961–1963, Vol. XI*, p. 176.

94. PRO: PREM 11/3690, Ormsby-Gore, Tel. 2697, 26 October 1962. According to Garthoff, however, Zorin had been given instructions to deny the presence of the missiles, Garthoff, *Reflections*, p. 79 n. 131.

95. PRO: PREM 11/3690, Ormsby-Gore, Tel. 2697, 26 October 1962.

96. Garthoff, *Reflections*, p. 79.

97. PRO: PREM 11/3691, Ormsby-Gore, Tel. 2735, 30 October 1962; Beschloss, *Kennedy v. Khrushchev*, p. 496.

98. PRO: PREM 11/3691, Ormsby-Gore, Tel. 2735, 30 October 1962.

99. Knightley and Kennedy, *Affair of State*, p. 109; for a different account, see Summers and Dorril, *Honeytrap*, p. 132.

100. PRO: PREM 11/3691, Record of a Conversation Between the Foreign Secretary and Soviet *Chargé d'Affaires* on 25 October 1962, Home to Roberts, Tel. 235, 29 October 1962.

101. PRO: PREM 11/3690, Caccia to Roberts, Tel. 2706, 24 October 1962.

102. PRO: PREM 11/3691, Record of a Conversation Between the Foreign Secretary and Soviet *Chargé d'Affaires* on 25 October 1962, Home to Roberts, Tel. 235, 29 October 1962. By way of contrast Loginov made reference to rockets in Japan directed against the USSR.

103. The CIA eventually identified 36 MRBM launchers and later counted 42 missiles; it has now emerged that six of these were dummy or training missiles, Fursenko and Naftali, 'One Hell of a Gamble', p. 216; Gribkov and Smith, *Operation Anadyr*, p. 73.

104. PRO: Home to Roberts, Tel. 235, 29 October 1962.

105. PRO: PREM 11/3690, Caccia to Roberts, Tel. 2706, 24 October 1962.

106. Abel, *Missiles of October*, p. 155.

107. *HC Deb.*, vol. 679, 17 June 1963, col. 70.

108. Abel, *Missiles of October*, p. 155.

7 Ormsby-Gore and Penkovsky: British Contributions?

1. See Chapter One.

2. Kennedy, *13 Days*, pp. 68–9; Schlesinger, *A Thousand Days*, p. 699; Macmillan, *End of the Day*, p. 197; Horne, *Macmillan, 1957–1986*, p. 369; Nunnerley, *President Kennedy*, pp. 84–5.

3. Schlesinger, *A Thousand Days*, p. 699.

4. G.T. Allison, *Essence of Decision, Explaining the Cuban Missile Crisis* (Boston: Little, Brown and Co., 1971), pp. 129–30.

5. D. Caldwell, 'A Research Note on the Quarantine of Cuba, October, 1962', *International Studies Quarterly*, Vol. 22, No. 4, (December 1978).

6. PRO: PREM 11/3689, Ormsby-Gore, Tel. 2646, 22 October 1962.

7. PRO: FO 371/162375, Ormsby-Gore, Tel. 2655, 23 October 1962.
8. PRO: PREM 11/3690, Ormsby-Gore, Tel. 2664, 24 October 1962.
9. Ibid. Horne states that Ormsby-Gore made the proposal at the National Security Council on 23 October, *Macmillan, 1957–1986*, p. 369. In fact, the NSC met on 22 October and did not meet again until January 1963. Neither then, nor at any ExComm meeting, is there a record of Ormsby-Gore's presence. *FRUS, Vol XI 1961–1963*, pp. 152–6, et seq; May and Zelikow, *The Kennedy Tapes*, passim.
10. Bouchard, *Command in Crisis*, p. 111. Caldwell notes, however, Soviet supplied Il-28 and MIG-17 aircraft had combat ranges in excess of 500 miles, Caldwell, 'A Research Note', p. 628.
11. May and Zelikow, *The Kennedy Tapes*, p. 295.
12. Ibid., p. 328.
13. Schlesinger, *Thousand Days*, p. 699.
14. See R. Medvedev, *All Stalin's Men* (New York: Doubleday, 1985), p. 52; Blight and Welch, *On the Brink*, p. 306.
15. See Chapter Six.
16. Fursenko and Naftali, *'One Hell of a Gamble'* pp. 247–8; four of these were transporting the IRBMs, the fifth, which reached Cuba before the blockade came into effect, was carrying nuclear warheads for the IRBMs and for land-based cruise missiles.
17. Ibid.
18. May and Zelikow, *The Kennedy Tapes*, pp. 348, 683.
19. Ibid., p. 361; a second ship, which the Americans believed was also carrying offensive materials, the *Gagarin*, was 30 to 50 miles behind the *Kimovsk*, ibid., p. 353.
20. Ibid., p. 361.
21. CIA: Chester Cooper, Release of Pictures to Press, Annex to Memo. for the Record, 29 October 1962, quoted in Kent, 'The Cuban Missile Crisis of 1962', p. 26.
22. H. Evans, *Downing Street Diary: The Macmillan Years 1957–1963* (Hodder and Stoughton, 1981), p. 224.
23. May and Zelikow, *The Kennedy Tapes*, p. 126.
24. PRO: PREM 11/3690, Ormsby-Gore, Tel. 2662, PM's Pers. Tel. T.503/62, 24 October 1962; quoted *in extenso*, Macmillan, *End of the Day*, p. 197; the issue had been discussed in ExComm that morning, May and Zelikow, *The Kennedy Tapes*, pp. 303–4, et seq.
25. Horne, *Macmillan 1957–1986*, p. 369; see also Abel, *Missiles of October*, p. 129; Nunnerley, *President Kennedy*, pp. 85–6; and Sorenson, *Kennedy*, p. 706.
26. PRO; PREM 11/3689, Macmillan to Ormsby-Gore, Tel. 7410, PM's Pers. Tel. T.497/62, 23 October 1962.
27. Ibid.
28. For an account, see S. Marlow, *Personality and policy-making: the case of the Cuban missile crisis* (MPhil thesis, University of Keele, 1996), pp. 122–8.
29. Brugioni, *Eyeball to Eyeball*, p. 390.
30. Oral History Interview, Roger Hilsman, 26 January 1970, (NSA: CMC), Doc. 03251.

31. PRO: FO 371/162401, Ormsby-Gore to Home, Air Bag 185, 9 November 1962. David Bruce's biographer also credits the ambassador with releasing the photographs to the BBC without authorisation, Nelson D. Lankford, *The Last American Aristocrat, the Biography of David K.E. Bruce, 1898–1977* (Little, Brown and Co., 1996), p. 308.

32. Brugioni, *Eyeball to Eyeball*, pp. 389–90. There is no record in Macmillan's account or his dairies, or in the PRO files, of any conversation between Kennedy and Macmillan on the evening of 23 October. Macmillan did phone Bruce at 1 am on 23 October, after he had spoken to the President, David Bruce's Diaries, 25 October 1962, (NSA: CMC), Doc. 01623. The publication of the photographs was not discussed by the Prime Minister and the President in their first conversation, which was, in any case, *before* Ormsby-Gore had dined at the White House, PRO: PREM 11/3689, Record of a Conversation between the Prime Minister and President Kennedy at 12.30 am on Tuesday, 23 October 1962; May and Zelikow, *The Kennedy Papers*, pp. 283–7.

33. CIA: Chester Cooper, Release of Pictures to Press, Annex to Memo. for the Record, 29 October 1962, quoted in Kent, 'The Cuban Missile Crisis of 1962', p. 26.

34. Ibid., p. 27.

35. JFKL: Bruce to Forrestal, Tel. 1670, 24 October 1962, NSF: CO: Cuba, General 10/24/62-10/25/62, Box 36.

36. CIA: Chester Cooper, Release of Pictures to Press, Annex to Memo. for the Record, 29 October 1962, quoted in Kent, 'The Cuban Missile Crisis of 1962', p. 26.

37. JFKL: Oral History Interview, Chester Cooper, 16 May 1966.

38. JFKL, Forrestal to Bruce, CAP 5501-62, 23 October 1962, NSF: CO: Cuba, General, 10/24/62-10/25/62, Box 36.

39. JFKL: Oral History Interview, Chester Cooper, 16 May 1966.

40. Brugioni, *Eyeball to Eyeball*, p. 389.

41. JFKL: Hilsman to Rusk, Western European Reactions to the Cuban Situation (Through October 27, 1962), 28 October 1962.

42. Kennedy, *13 Days*, p. 28.

43. CIA: Kent, 'The Cuban Missile Crisis of 1962', p. 42.

44. Horne, *Macmillan, 1957–1986*, p. 369.

45. For details of the operation, see J.L. Schecter and P.S. Deriabin, *The Spy Who Saved the World* (New York: Charles Scribner's Sons, 1992). The first information Penkovsky passed to the West, in August 1960, was to establish his *bona fides*. He was subsequently run as an agent or 'defector in place', in a joint SIS–CIA operation from April 1961 until his arrest in (probably) October 1962.

46. Ibid., p. 104.

47. C. Andrew, *Secret Service: The Making of the British Intelligence Community* (Sceptre, 1986), pp. 691–2; A. Verrier, *Through the Looking Glass – British Foreign Policy in an Age of Illusions* (Jonathan Cape, 1983), p. 193; G. Brook-Shepherd, *The Storm Birds – Soviet Postwar Defectors* (Weidenfeld and Nicolson, 1988), p. 135; for a recent well-informed account, see also C. Andrew, *For the President's*

Eyes Only: Secret Intellegence and the American Presidency From Washington to Bush (HarperCollins, 1995), pp. 267–71, 273, 274, 290.
48. Schecter and Deriabin, *Spy Who Saved the World*, p. 3.
49. Allyn, Blight and Welch, *Back to the Brink*, p. 40.
50. Bundy, *Danger and Survival*, pp. 391–462.
51. Garthoff, *Reflections* p. 63.
52. Schecter and Deriabin, *Spy Who Saved the World*, pp. 204–5; T. Mangold, *Cold Warrior – James Jesus Angleton: The CIA's Master Spy Hunter* (New York: Simon and Schuster, 1991), pp. 77–8.
53. P. Wright (with P. Greengrass), *Spycatcher* (Richmond, Victoria, Australia: Heinemann, 1987), pp. 204–12.
54. For example, Pincher, *Their Trade*, pp. 183–9.
55. Knightley and Kennedy, *An Affair of State*, pp. 107–8.
56. G. Wynne, *The Man From Moscow* (Hutchinson, 1967) and *The Man From Odessa* (Robert Hale, 1981); for criticism of these accounts, see Nigel West, *Seven Spies Who Changed the World* (Mandarin, 1992), pp. 178–212. Details of SIS and CIA operations are provided in Schecter and Deriabin, *Spy Who Saved the World*, passim.
57. Interviews with Peter Hennessy, 1994, quoted in G. Smith, *Britain and the Cuban missile crisis*, (BA dissertation, University of London, 1994), p. 6.
58. Horne, *Macmillam, 1957–1986*, p. 370; this view was also shared by the London CIA Station Chief, Archie Roosevelt, Horne, ibid.
59. Henderson, conversation with author, Roberts, interview with author. Richard Deacon claims that Maurice Oldfield played a personal role in persuading Kennedy of the value of Penkovsky's intelligence, *'C': A Biography*, pp. 133–4, 136.
60. McAuliffe, *CIA Documents*. Material from Penkovsky's briefings was circulated through the 'special information handling channel', codenamed CHICKADEE; documentary material was circulated under IRONBARK, ibid., xiii, xiv. A different system was apparently adopted by the British apparently to distinguish information on the Soviet intelligence services (RUPEE) and material on Soviet military capabilities (ARNIKA), respectively, N. West, *The Friends: Britain's Post-War Secret Intelligence Operations* (Coronet Books, 1990), pp. 173, 182–3; Wright, *Spycatcher*, pp. 208–9.
61. Pincher, *Their Trade*, p. 184.
62. Wright *Spycatcher*, p. 204.
63. Mtg. No. 1 (London), 20 April 1961, para. 110, in National Security Archive, *The Soviet Estimate: US Analysis of the Soviet Union 1947–1991*, Microfiche Collection (Washington: Chadwyck-Healey, 1995) [hereafter NSA: Sov.Est.], Doc. 00286; see also Schecter and Deriabin, *Spy Who Saved the World*, p. 81.
64. Fursenko and Naftali, *'One Hell of a Gamble'*, p. 52.
65. Ibid., p. 70.
66. Lebow and Stein, *We All Lost the Cold War*, pp. 72–7; Garthoff, *Reflections*, pp. 6–42; Fursenko and Naftali, *'One Hell of a Gamble'*, pp. 166–83.
67. Fursenko and Naftali, ibid., pp. 210, 211–12.

68. Allyn, Blight and Welch, *Back to the Brink*, p. 101.
69. Schecter and Deriabin, *Spy Who Saved the World*, p. 328.
70. Mtg. 1, 20 April 1961, paras. 40–1; see also Schecter and Deriabin, *Spy Who Saved the World*, p. 68. The R-11 was a 150 km 'operational-tactical missile'; the ground forces version, NATO designation, SS-1, became known as the SCUD, David Holloway, *Stalin and the Bomb: The Soviet Union and Atomic Energy 1939–56* (Yale University Press, 1994), p. 324.
71. Mtg. 1, 20 April 1961, para. 42; Schecter and Deriabin, *Spy Who Saved the World*, p. 68.
72. Mtg. 1, 20 April 1961, paras. 101–2; Mtg. No. 4 at Leeds, 23 April 1962, para. 36 (NSA: Sov.Est.), Doc. 00288; Mtg. 12, London, 1 May 1961, paras. 19, 25, 62 (NSA: Sov.Est.), Doc. 00295; see also Schecter and Deriabin, *Spy Who Saved the World*, pp. 149–50.
73. For discussion of US intelligence and the crisis, see C. C. Cogan, 'A surprise, surprise et demie: le role du renseignement', in Vaisse, *L'Europe et la Crise de Cuba*; P. Usowski, 'John McCone and the Cuban Crisis: A Persistent Approach to the Intelligence–Policy Relationship', *International Journal of Intelligence and Counter Intelligence*, (Winter 1988); and D. Welch, 'Intelligence Assessment in the Cuban Missile Crisis', *Queen's Quarterly*, Vol. 100, No. 2 (Summer 1993).
74. PRO: FO 371/162374, I.J.M. Sutherland, minute, 12 September 1962, AK1201/20/G.
75. Peter Wright makes the highly erroneous assertion that, when Gary Powers' U-2 was shot down in May 1960, the West lacked any photo-reconnaissance capabilities, 'until the launch of the first satellite toward the end of 1962', Wright, *Spycatcher*, p. 210. For details of the US' first satellite programme, see K.C. Ruffner (Ed.), *CORONA: America's First Satellite Program* (Washington: Central Intelligence Agency, 1995)
76. Horne, *Macmillan, 1957–1986*, pp. 369–70; Brook-Shepherd, *Storm Birds*, pp. 136–7; Verrier, *Through the Looking Glass*, pp. 193–243; Wright, *Spycatcher*, p. 204.
77. For description of the NIE process, see Donald P. Steury (Ed.), *Intentions and Capabilities: Estimates on Soviet Strategic Forces, 1950–1983* (Washington DC: CIA, 1996), pp. xi–xix; for key NIEs, see pp. 55–138.
78. Schecter and Deriabin, *Spy Who Saved the World*, p. 374.
79. For differing evaluations of Penkovsky's intelligence, see Ball, *Politics and Force Levels*, pp. 100–4; L. Freedman, *US Intelligence and the Soviet Strategic Threat* (Macmillan, 1986), pp. 73–4; J. Prados, *The Soviet Estimate* (Princeton: Princeton University Press, 1982), pp. 116–18; Lebow and Stein, *We All Lost the Cold War*, pp. 35–8; and Schecter and Deriabin, *Spy Who Saved the World*, pp. 271–82.
80. Schecter and Deriabin, *Spy Who Saved the World*, ibid.
81. NIE 11-8-61 Soviet Capabilities for Long Range Attack, 7 June 1961, Steury, *Intentions and Capabilities*, pp. 115–19.
82. CIA: Jack Maury, Memorandum for the Record, Conversation with

Messrs. Ed Proctor and Jack Smith Re Use of CHICKADEE Material in NIE 11-8-61, 7 June 1961.
83. Schecter and Deriabin *Spy Who Saved the World*, pp. 276–8.
84. NIE-11-8-61 contained various dissenting 'footnotes', mostly by Army and Navy Intelligence, effectively undermining the agreed position of the intelligence community, Steury, *Intentions and Capabilities*, pp. 115–19.
85. NIE 11-8/1-61 Strength and Deployment of Soviet Long Range Ballistic Missile Forces, 21 September 1961, Ruffner, CORONA, pp. 127–55.
86. Ibid.
87. For example, Bundy, *Danger and Survival*; D. Rusk, R. McNamara, G. Ball, R. Gilpatrick, T. Sorenson and M. Bundy, 'The Lessons of the Cuban Missile Crisis', *Time*, 27 September 1982, pp. 85–6; Lebow and Stein, *We All Lost the Cold War*. For the argument that US nuclear superiority deterred any response from the Soviets, see Nitze, *From Hiroshima to Glasnost*, p. 227.
88. F. Roberts, *Dealing with Dictators: The Destruction and Revival of Europe 1930–1970*, (Weidenfeld and Nicolson, 1991), pp. 220–1.
89. See Lebow and Stein, *We All Lost the Cold War*, pp. 36–8.
90. May and Zelikow, *The Kennedy Tapes*, pp. 81–2; see also Brugioni, *Eyeball to Eyeball*, p. 199. For details of the NPIC's work during the crisis see ibid., p. 190, et seq.
91. May and Zelikow, *The Kennedy Tapes*, p. 48.
92. CIA Memorandum, Probable Soviet MRBM Sites in Cuba, 16 October 1962, McAuliffe, *CIA Documents*, pp. 140–2; Cline: Memo. for the Record: Notification of NSC Officials of Intelligence on Missile Bases in Cuba, 27 October 1962, ibid., p. 150.
93. Albert Wheelon, Memo. for Chairman, US Intelligence Board, Evaluation of Offensive Missile Threat in Cuba, 17 October 1962, McAuliffe, ibid., p. 176; see also Joint Evaluation of Soviet Missile Threat in Cuba, 18 October 1962, McAuliffe, ibid., pp. 187–191. The CIA knew, presumably assisted by Penkovsky's material, that the SS-3 was a liquid-fuelled missile requiring radar guidance. The SS-4 had inertial guidance and storable propellant; the absence of fuel tankers and radar equipment was an indicator that the SS-4 was being deployed, see May and Zelikow, *The Kennedy Tapes*, p. 78. The 73 feet long SS-4 compared with the 68 feet long SS-3, and positive confirmation that some SS-4s were present was made on this basis by 17 October, Wheelon, memo for Chairman; for discussion of length, see also May and Zelikow, ibid., *The Kennedy Tapes*, pp. 48–9.
94. Annex: Strategic Considerations, CIA Memo., Probable MRBM Sites in Cuba, 16 October 1962, McAuliffe, ibid., p. 143.
95. May and Zelikow, *The Kennedy Tapes*, p. 338.
96. Ibid., p. 57.
97. Ibid., p. 59.
98. Memorandum of Meeting attended in Secretary Ball's Conference Room, 17 October 1962, McAuliffe, *CIA Documents*, p. 160.

99. Schecter and Deriabin, *Spy Who Saved the World*, pp. 334–5.
100. Ibid., p. 334.
101. Ibid., p. 335.
102. May and Zelikow, *The Kennedy Tapes*, p. 173; see also Joint Evaluation of Soviet Missile Threat in Cuba, 19 October 1962, McAuliffe, *CIA Documents*, pp. 203–8.
103. Lebow and Stein, *We All Lost the Cold War*, p. 107.
104. Ibid., p. 428, 82 n.
105. Quoted in Schecter and Deriabin, *Spy Who Saved the World*, pp. 393–4.
106. Schecter and Deriabin, ibid., p. 194.

8   Thor and Vulcan: British Gods of War

1. S. Zuckerman, *Monkeys, Men and Missiles* (Collins, 1988), p. 303.
2. McNamara, *Blundering into Disaster*, p. 8; see Appendix; see also Garthoff, *Reflections*, p. 208.
3. For discussion of the risk of nuclear war in 1962, see J.G. Blight and D.A. Welch, 'Risking "The Destruction of Nations": Lessons of the Cuban Missile Crisis for New and Aspiring Nuclear States', *Security Studies*, Vol. 4, No. 4 (Summer 1995) and Trachtenberg "The Influence of Nuclear Weapons' and *History and Strategy*; see also Bundy, *Danger and Survival*, pp. 445–58; for discussion of the role of nuclear weapons in the crisis, see E. Herring, *Danger and Opportunity* (MUP, 1995), pp. 149–73.
4. Sagan, *Limits of Safety*, p. 151.
5. B.G. Blair, *The Logic of Accidental Nuclear War*, (The Brookings Institution, 1993), pp. 23–5; Sagan *Limits of Safety*, pp. 142–5; Blight and Welch, 'Risking "The Destruction of Nations"'.
6. Gribkov and Smith, *Operation Anadyr*, pp. 4–7, 64–8.
7. For a recent exception, see Nash, *The Other Missiles*, pp. 125–7.
8. B. Tuchman, *The Guns of August* (New York: Macmillan, 1962).
9. Kennedy, *13 Days*, pp. 124–5.
10. Horne, *Macmillan, 1957–1986*, p. 383.
11. For the view that history's lessons were learned in 1962, see R. Neustadt and E. May, *Thinking in Time* (New York: Free Press, 1986), pp. 1–16; see also May and Zelikow, *The Kennedy Tapes*, pp. 1–43; for Kennedy's own view of 1939, see J.F. Kennedy, *Why England Slept* (Hutchinsons, 1940).
12. For discussion of whether this was an appropriate guide, see Lebow and Stein, *We All Lost the Cold War*.
13. May and Zelikow, *The Kennedy Tapes*, p. 87.
14. For discussion, see Sagan, *Limits of Safety*, pp. 66–7. When Kennedy held his only meeting during the crisis with the Joint Chiefs of Staff on 19 October, the issue was not discussed, May and Zelikow, *The Kennedy Tapes*, pp. 173–88.
15. For explanation of the US DEFCON system, see Sagan, *Limits of Safety*, pp. 64–5.
16. Ibid., p. 63.

17. Ibid., p. 62.
18. PRO: FO 371/168421, Air Chief Marshal Sir John Slessor, Speech to the English-Speaking Union, Spring 1963.
19. Ibid.
20. Quoted in Vaisse, *L'Europe et la Crise de Cuba*, p. 69.
21. Ibid.
22. Menaul, *Countdown*, p. 115; each Thor was armed with a 1.45 megaton warhead. A recent estimate of the British nuclear stockpile in 1962 gives a total of 205 nuclear bombs, including 100 thermo-nuclear Yellow Sun Mk. 2s, to which should be added some 72 US bombs for use under Project E, R.S. Norris, A.S. Burrows, and R.W. Fieldhouse, *Nuclear Weapons Databook, Vol. V* (Westview, 1994), pp. 63–5. The RAF had some 140 nuclear armed V-bombers at this time, PRO: AIR 24/2688, Post Exercise Report on Exercise Micky Finn II, September 1962, BC/S.97462. Aside from the squadron equipped with Blue Steel, by November, these were armed with the Yellow Sun II thermo-nuclear bomb, PRO: AIR 24/2689, Commander-in-Chief's Conference of Group, Station and Squadron Commanders held at RAF North Luffenham on 14 and 15 November 1962; see also Appendix.
23. Sagan, *Limits of Safety*, p. 63.
24. *The Communist Bloc and the Western Alliances: Military Balance 1962–1963* (International Institute for Strategic Studies, 1962), p. 10. According to Norris, Burrows and Fieldhouse, however, there were only five naval *Red Beard* atomic bombs in 1962, *Nuclear Weapons Databook*, p. 65.
25. Correspondence, Air Vice-Marshal Arthur Griffiths, 16 July 1993.
26. Sagan, *Limits of Safety*, p. 103.
27. PRO: PREM 11/3689, P. Mason, Tel. 163, 22 October 1962; CIA: Kent, 'The Cuban Missile Crisis', pp. 32–3.
28. PRO: FO 371/166970, Special Report by the Secretary-General of April 17, 1962–C–M(62)48, quoted in Evelyn Shuckburgh, Cuba and Anglo-American Consultation, 6 November 1962; reproduced in J. Baylis (Ed.), *Anglo-American Relations since 1939* (MUP, 1997).
29. PRO: PREM 11/3689, P. Mason, Tel. 163, 22 October 1962.
30. Ibid.
31. PRO: FO 371/162376, Gen. J.E. Moore to Don Guido Colonna di Paliano, Acting Secretary General, NAC, 22 October 1962; these instructions were issued to NATO subordinate commands at 11–23 pm. on 22 October, PRO: FO 371/162377, SACEUR to NATO Commands, 22 October 1962.
32. See Horne, *Macmillan, 1894–1956*, pp. 29–50.
33. Bodleian Library, HMD, 22 October 1962, MS. Macmillan dep.d.47.
34. HMD, 22 October 1962, quoted in Macmillan, *End of the Day*, p. 190.
35. Dwight D. Eisenhower Library: Gen. Norstad to Gen. Moore, LDN 811, 23 October 1962, Box 99.
36. Sections of Norstad's letter to Kennedy have not been declassified.
37. Macmillan, *End of the Day*, p. 195.

38. PRO: PREM 11/3689, FO to Washington, Tel. 7383, 22 October 1962.
39. PRO: PREM 11/3689, Ormsby-Gore, Tel. 2639, 22 October 1962.
40. Garthoff, *Reflections* pp. 60–1 n. This rather belies Horne's claim that Norstad urged Macmillan to place British forces on a higher alert, Horne, *Macmillan, 1957–1986*, p. 366.
41. Sagan, *Limits of Safety*, pp. 104–5.
42. Ibid., p. 105.
43. JFKL: Rusk, Memorandum for the President, Political and Military Considerations Bearing on Turkish and Italian IRBMs, 9 November 1962, covering attachment, Significance to the US of Turkish and Italian IRBM's, NSF: RS: NATO, Weapons, Cables, Turkey, Box 226.
44. S. Twigge, 'Anglo-American Air Force Co-operation and the Cuban Missile Crisis: A British Perspective', in R.G. Miller (Ed.), *Seeing Off the Bear: Anglo-American Air Power Cooperation During the Cold War* (Washington: Royal Air Force Historical Society/Air Force Historical Foundation, 1995), p. 212.
45. Ibid., pp. 210–12; Ian Clark, *Nuclear Diplomacy*, pp. 135–40, 391–4, 430–1; Twigge and Scott, *Fail Deadly?*, pp. 88–92, 156–9, 174–7.
46. For details of 'Project E', see Clark, *Nuclear Diplomacy*, pp. 139, 144–7; H. Wynn, *The RAF's Strategic Deterrent Forces: their origins, roles and deployment 1946–1969* (HMSO, 1994), pp. 262–70; Twigge and Scott, *Fail Deadly?*, pp. 85–8, 202–3.
47. PRO: AIR 24/2689, Commander-in-Chief's Conference of Group, Station and Squadron Commanders held at RAF North Luffenham on 14 and 15 November 1962.
48. Menaul, *Countdown*, p. 114.
49. PRO: FO 371/166970, Evelyn Shuckburgh, Cuba and Anglo-American Consultation, 6 November 1962; reproduced in J. Baylis (Ed.), *Anglo-American Relations since 1939* (MUP, 1997).
50. PRO: PREM 11/3690, Macmillan to Kennedy, Teleprinter Message, T.505/62, 25 October 1962; quoted *in extenso*, Macmillan, *End of the Day*, p. 204.
51. PRO: AIR 19/690, Memo. Attached to President's Letter of 6 February 1961 – Understanding with the British on the Use of British Bases and Nuclear Weapons.
52. PRO: PREM 11/3617, Dean to de Zulueta, 28 May 1960.
53. Ibid.
54. PRO: PREM 11/3167, T.S. Gates to H. Watkinson, 12 July 1960.
55. Menaul, *Countdown*, p. 114. Menaul's dates are, however, misleading – he suggests the crisis had seriously deteriorated by 20th October and then refers to 'the weekend of 25th'.
56. PRO: FO 371/166970, Evelyn Shuckburgh, Cuba and Anglo-American Consultation, 6 November 1962; reproduced in J. Baylis (Ed.), *Anglo-American Relations since 1939* (MUP, 1997).
57. CINCLANT Historical Account of Cuban Crisis, 1963, p. 133 (NSA: CMC), Doc. 03087.
58. Oral History Interview, Vice-Admiral Philip A. Beshany, 8 November 1977, pp. 526–7 (NSA: CMC), Doc. 03275.

59. Ibid, p. 528.
60. The movement of the submarines from the base during the crisis became public knowledge; see, for example, Frank Allaun, *HC Deb.*, Vol. 666, 30 October 1962, col. 95.
61. CINCLANT Historical Account of Cuban Crisis, 1963, p. 133 (NSA: CMC), Doc. 03087.
62. JCS to Sec. of State, JCS 6968, Situation Report as of 0400 October, 25 October 1962 (NSA: CMC), Doc. 01325.
63. Oral History Interview (undated), Peter Thorneycroft (NSA: CMC), Doc. 03338.
64. Sagan, *Limits of Safety*, p. 113.
65. I. Madelin, 'Some Additional Comments on Command and Control of Nuclear Forces During the Cuban Missile Crisis', in Miller, *Seeing off the Bear*, p. 224.
66. Ibid. These remarks reflect the recollections of Air Marshal Cross.
67. JCS to Sec. of State, JCS 6968, Situation Report as of 0400 October, 25 October 1962 (NSA: CMC), Doc. 01325.
68. 'When Britain Went to the Brink', *Daily Mail*, 18 February 1963.
69. Menaul, *Countdown*, pp. 114–17.
70. *Limits of Safety*, pp. 111–13.
71. *HC Deb.*, vol. 672, 28 February 1963, cols. 1439–1444.
72. Macmillan, *End of the Day*, p. 190.
73. *HC Deb.*, vol. 672, 28 February 1963, col. 1441.
74. *Military Balance, 1962–1963*, p. 3.
75. JFKL: Rusk, Memorandum for the President, Political and Military Considerations Bearing on Turkish and Italian IRBMs, 9 November 1962, covering attachment, Significance to the US of Turkish and Italian IRBM's, NSF: RS: NATO, Weapons, Cables, Turkey, Box 226.
76. Garthoff, *Reflections*, p. 208 n.
77. Ibid.
78. Menaul, *Countdown*, pp. 114–15.
79. Ibid., p. 115.
80. PRO: AIR 25/1703, Operations Record Book, HQ. No. 1 Grp., Note 11, October 1962.
81. PRO: AIR 24/2689, Operation Order 38/62 – Measures to Exercise the Readiness of Bomber Command Exercise 'Mick', 2 November 1962.
82. PRO: AIR 25/1703, Operations Record Book, HQ. No. 1 Grp., October 1962, Note 11. RAF Bomber Command comprised two Groups, Nos. 1 and 3.
83. PRO: AIR 25/1703, Operations Record Book, HQ. No. 1 Grp., October 1962. Notes 11 and 13.
84. PRO: AIR 25/1703, Operations Record Book, HQ. No. 1 Grp., October 1962, Note 11.
85. Correspondence, Air Vice-Marshal Arthur Griffiths, 16 July 1993.
86. PRO: AIR 25/1703, Operations Record Book, HQ. No. 1 Grp., October 1962, Note 11.
87. Correspondence, Air Vice-Marshal Ian Campbell, 21 July 1993.

The decision to attack the partridges was taken after consultation with higher authority, and radio contact with base was maintained during the operation.

88. For accounts, see Melissen, *Struggle for Partnership*, pp. 63–92 and I. Clark and D. Angell, 'Britain, the USA and Control of Nuclear Weapons: Diplomacy of the Thor Deployment 1956–58', *Diplomacy and Statecraft*, Vol. 2, No. 3 (November 1991).

89. For accounts of the Jupiter deployments, see B.J. Bernstein, 'Reconsidering the Missile Crisis: Dealing with the Problems of the American Jupiters in Turkey', in Nathan, *The Cuban Missile Crisis Revisited*, pp. 55–129; L. Nuti, 'L'Italie et les missiles *Jupiter*', in Vaisse, *L'Europe et la Crise de Cuba*; Nash, *The Other Missiles of October*; and N.B. Criss, 'Strategic Nuclear Missiles in Turkey: The Jupiter Affair, 1959–1963', *Journal of Strategic Studies*, Vol. 20, No. 3, (September 1997).

90. PRO: DEFE 13/394, MM. 7/59, Meeting of Minister of Defence with the Secretary of State for Air, 24 November 1959. If the warheads were stored at Lakenheath it would take 57 hours to make the Thors operational; it would take 24 hours if they were stored at main bases.

91. PRO: AIR 8/2307, Air Marshal Sir Edmund Hudleston, The Future of Thor, Note by the VCAS, AC(61)44, 2 August 1961.

92. PRO: AIR 20/11371, Cross to the VCAS, Air Marshal Sir Wallace Kyle, 31 October 1962.

93. PRO: AIR 8/2307, Air Marshal Sir Edmund Hudleston, The Future of Thor, Note by the VCAS, AC9(61)44, 2 August 1961.

94. Ibid. Thor could also be kept in the vertical fuelled position, 'about one and a half minutes from launch'; but after two hours certain components become frozen through contact with liquid oxygen, and a six hour recovery period was needed. In these circumstances, 'an absolute maximum of one quarter of the force would be available at any time', ibid.

95. Correspondence, Flt. Lt. G.A. Stalker, 22 November 1992.

96. PRO: AIR 8/2307, Air Marshal Sir Edmund Hudleston, The Future of Thor, Note by the VCAS, AC(61)44, 2 August 1961.

97. For evidence that some missiles were at higher states of readiness during the crisis, see Twigge and Scott, *Fail Deadly?*, pp. 201–2.

98. See Blair, *Accidental Nuclear War*, Sagan, *Limits of Safety* and P. Feaver, *Guarding the Guardians, Civilian Control of Nuclear Weapons in the United States* (New York: Cornell University Press, 1992).

99. Twigge and Scott, *Fail Deadly?*, pp. 183–4.

100. Menaul, *Countdown*, p. 116. For discussion, see *Limits of Safety*, pp. 111–13 and L. Scott, 'La Grande-Bretagne et la crise des missiles', in Vaisse, *'L'Europe et la crise de Cuba*, pp. 69–73; see also Horne, *Macmillan, 1957–1986*, pp. 669–70 n.

101. Sagan, *Limits of Safety*, p. 112.

102. Ibid, p. 112–13.

103. Madelin, 'Some Additional Comments', pp. 223–5.

104. Ibid, p. 224.

105. Ibid.
106. PRO: AIR 20/11371, Cross to the VCAS, Air Marshal Sir Wallace Kyle, 31 October 1962.
107. PRO: DEFE 32/7, Record of a Conversation between the Chief of the Air Staff, First Sea Lord and the Chief of the Imperial General Staff held in the Ministry of Defence at 1430, Sat., 27 October 1962, Annex to COS 1546/29/10/62.
108. Kennedy was not quite so definite about his intention to attack – the President stated that a decision could be necessary within 48 hours; see Chapter Nine.
109. PRO: DEFE 32/7, Record of a Conversation between the Chief of the Air Staff, First Sea Lord and the Chief of the Imperial General Staff held in the Ministry of Defence at 1430, Sat., 27 October 1962, Annex to COS 1546/29/10/62.
110. Ibid. As noted, the bombers were recalled: the order was given at 10.15 am, Sunday 28 October 1962, PRO: AIR 25/1703, Operations Record Book, HQ. No. 1 Grp., October 1962, Note 11.
111. Sagan *Limits of Safety*, p. 112.
112. Gribkov and Smith, *Operation Anadyr*, p. 127.
113. Notes Taken from Transcripts of Meetings of the Joint Chiefs of Staff, October–November, 1962, p. 13. I am grateful to Bart Bernstein for this document.
114. Beschloss, *Kennedy v. Khrushchev*, p. 544.
115. Allison, *Essence of Decision*, p. 198.
116. PRO: DEFE 32/7, Record of a Conversation between the Chief of the Air Staff, First Sea Lord and the Chief of the Imperial General Staff held in the Ministry of Defence at 1430, Sat., 27 October 1962, Annex to COS 1546/29/10/62.
117. PRO: DEFE 13/212, Record of a meeting between the MOD and the COS on 28 October 1962, MM/COS(62)7.
118. PRO: FO 371/162/384, Arthur Hockaday (MOD) to Jeremy Thomas (FO), AK1261/190, 24 October 1962; PREM 11/3690, FO to Havana, Tel. 557, 25 October 1962.
119. PRO: FO 371/162382, Secretary of State for Colonies to Acting Administrator, St Lucia, Tel. 39, AK1261/142, 26 October 1962.
120. Twigge, 'Anglo-American Air Force Collaboration', p. 219.
121. Correspondence, Air Vice-Marshal Ian Campbell, 18 August 1993.
122. Correspondence, Air Vice-Marshal Arhur Griffiths, 16 July 1993.
123. Sagan, *Limits of Safety*, p. 80.
124. Schecter and Deriabin, *Spy Who Saved the World*, p. 138.
125. The Soviet Bloc Armed Forces and the Cuban Missile Crisis – A Chronology July–November 1962, National Indicators Center, 18 June 1963, (NSA: CMC), Doc. 03130.
126. Ivanov, *The Naked Spy*, p. 147.
127. PRO: Post Exercise Report on Exercise Micky Finn II, September 1962, BC/S.97462, AIR 24/2688.
128. PRO: DEFE 4/148, COS (62) 67th Mtg., 25 October 1962.
129. CIA: Khrushchev's Cuban Venture in Retrospective, Ray Cline to McGeorge Bundy, 7 December 1962.

130. PRO: AIR 24/2689, Commander-in-Chief's Conference of Group, Station and Squadron Commanders held at RAF North Luffenham on 14 and 15 November 1962.
131. Ibid.
132. PRO: AIR 20/11371, Cross to the VCAS, Air Marshal Sir Wallace Kyle, 31 October 1962.
133. Ibid.
134. PRO: AIR 8/2307, Fraser to Thorneycroft, 31 October 1962; see also CAB 131/25, Fraser to de Zulueta, 30 October 1962.
135. PRO: AIR 8/2307, Thorneycroft to Fraser, 7 November 1962.
136. See K. Oliver, *Kennedy, Macmillan and the Nuclear Test Ban Debate, 1961–1963* (Macmillan, 1997), pp. 135–43, et seq.

9 'The Frightful Desire to *Do* Something'

1. HMD, 4 November 1962, in Macmillan, *End of the Day*, p. 216.
2. May and Zelikow, *The Kennedy Tapes*, p. 464; three days earlier, the President and his brother had asked Ormsby-Gore how he thought the affair would end. He replied that there could be only two endings: 'either action and counteraction would lead to war, or there would have to be some negotiated settlement', PRO: PREM 11/3690, Ormsby-Gore to Macmillan, Tel. 2662, 24 October 1962, PM's Pers. Tel. T.503/62.
3. PRO: PREM 11/3690, Ormsby-Gore to Home, Tel. 2691, 26 October 1962.
4. Ibid.
5. Ibid.
6. Ibid.
7. Ibid.
8. Memo. from ABC Correspondent John Scali to the Director of the Bureau of Intelligence and Research, *FRUS, 1961–1963, Vol. XI*, p. 227.
9. A. Fursenko and T. Naftali, 'Using KGB Documents: The Scali–Feklisov Channel in the Cuban Missile Crisis', *Cold War International History Project Bulletin*, Issue 5 (Spring, 1995), pp. 58, 60–62; see also Fursenko and Naftali, '*One Hell of a Gamble*', pp. 263–5, 269–71; Lebow and Stein, *We All Lost the Cold War*, pp. 132–3; Garthoff, *Reflections*, pp. 80–1.
10. Khrushchev to Kennedy, 26 October 1962, *FRUS, 1961–1963, Vol. XI*, pp. 235–41; May and Zelikow, *The Kennedy Tapes*, pp. 485–91.
11. May and Zelikow, *The Kennedy Tapes*, p. 585.
12. Macmillan, *End of the Day*, p. 213.
13. Khrushchev to Kennedy, 26 October 1962, p. 239; May and Zelikow, *The Kennedy Tapes*, pp. 489–90.
14. PRO: PREM 11/3690, Ormsby-Gore, Tel. 2697, 26 October 1962.
15. Ibid.
16. Ibid.
17. Ibid. Italics added.
18. PRO: FO 371/162404, Ormsby-Gore to Caccia, AK 1261/586, 7 November 1962.

19. For discussion, see May and Zelikow, *The Kennedy Tapes*, pp. 693, et seq.
20. HMD, 4 November 1962, quoted in Horne, *Macmillan, 1957–1986*, p. 382. Macmillan's published account omits criticism of Eden; *End of the Day*, p. 219.
21. May and Zelikow, *The Kennedy Tapes*, pp. 439, et seq; Lebow and Stein, *We All Lost the Cold War*, pp. 110–45.
22. PRO: FO 371/162394, R.H. Mason, Soviet Reactions to American Moves, AK 1261/398, 27 October 1962. This assessment contributed to a JIC estimate of 27 October not yet declassified.
23. Ibid.
24. Ibid.
25. Macmillan states that there were two 'long' conversations on Friday, HMD, 26 October 1962, quoted in Macmillan, *End of the Day*, p. 209. Records exist of only one conversation, the first part of which was not recorded. Ormsby-Gore was told that nothing was said in this part of the conversation about which he needed to know, PRO: PREM 11/3690, Woodfield to Ormsby-Gore, 27 October 1962. This section of the conversation has been partially reconstructed by May and Zelikow using American sources, May and Zelikow, *The Kennedy Tapes*, pp. 480–4.
26. PRO: PREM 11/3690, Record of a Conversation between the Prime Minister and President Kennedy at 11.15 pm on Friday, 26 October, 1962; May and Zelikow, *The Kennedy Tapes*, p. 481; see also Macmillan, *End of the Day*, p. 210.
27. Record of Conversation, 26 October 1962, ibid.; May and Zelikow, *The Kennedy Tapes*, p. 483; Macmillan, *End of the Day*, p. 211.
28. Ibid.
29. Ibid.
30. PRO: PREM 11/3690, FO to Washington, Tel. 7554, 26 October 1962.
31. Ibid.
32. Ibid.
33. Ibid.
34. PRO: PREM 11/3690, Record of a Conversation between the Prime Minister and President Kennedy at 11.15 on Friday, 26 October, 1962; May and Zelikow, *The Kennedy Tapes*, p. 482; Macmillan, *End of the Day*, p. 210.
35. Ibid.
36. PRO: PREM 11/4052, Macmillan to Kennedy, Teleprinted to Washington, T.513/62, 27 October 1962; May and Zelikow, *The Kennedy Tapes*, pp. 484–5.
37. May and Zelikow, *The Kennedy Tapes*, pp. 492–629.
38. Khrushchev to Kennedy, 27 October 1962, *FRUS, 1961–1963, Vol. XI*, pp. 257–60; May and Zelikow, *The Kennedy Tapes*, pp. 505–8.
39. May and Zelikow, *The Kennedy Tapes*, pp. 520–604.
40. PRO: FO 371/162401, FO Minute, AK 1261/253/G, 30 October 1962.
41. Ibid.

42. PRO: FO 371/162400, Roberts, Tel. 2202, 8 November 1962.
43. Lebow and Stein, *We All Lost the Cold War*, p. 132; Garthoff, *Reflections*, p. 82; Fursenko and Naftali, '*One Hell of a Gamble*', pp. 262–3.
44. PRO: FO 371/162391, I.J.M. Sutherland, The Situation in Florida, AK 1261/325, 26 October 1962.
45. See Lebow and Stein, *We All Lost the Cold War*, pp. 42–50, et seq.
46. See Nash, *The Other Missiles*, pp. 91–116.
47. May and Zelikow, *The Kennedy Tapes*, pp. 213, 222–3; Franklin Sieverts, The Cuban Missile Crisis, 1962, State Department History, August 1963, p. 125, (NSA: CMC), Doc. 03154.
48. Gribkov and Smith., *Operation Anadyr*, pp. 138–9.
49. See Nash, *The Other Missiles*, p. 125; for the Italian Jupiters, see L. Nuti, 'The MRBM Issue and Italy', paper and discussion at Nuclear History Program, Fourth International Study and Review Conference, Sofia–Antipolis, Antibes, France, 24–26 June 1993, Minutes of the Proceedings, pp. 76–82; see also Leopoldo Nuti, 'L'Italie et les missiles Jupiter', in Vaisse, *L'Europe et la Crise de Cuba*, pp. 123–57.
50. Sagan, *Limits of Safety*, p. 109; Nash, *The Other Missiles*, p. 137.
51. JFKL: Rusk, Memorandum for the President, Political and Military Considerations Bearing on Turkish and Italian IRBMs, 9 November 1962, covering attachment, Significance to the US of Turkish and Italian IRBM's, NSF: RS: NATO, Weapons, Cables, Turkey, Box 226. This state of readiness clearly came as a surprise to State Dept. officials, JFKL: William Tyler to Rusk, Turkish and Italian IRBMs, 9 November 1962, NSF: RS: NATO Weapons, Cables, Turkey, Box 226.
52. JCS to Sec. of State, JCS 6968, Situation Report as of 0400 October, 25 October 1962 (NSA: CMC), Doc. 01325.
53. Letter from the Representative to the United Nations (Stevenson) to President Kennedy, 17 October 1962, *FRUS, 1961–1963, Vol. XI*, p. 102. Stevenson, shared Macmillan's reaction that a discrete diplomatic approach to Khrushchev should be considered.
54. PRO: FO 371/162399, Ormsby-Gore, Tel. 2820, 8 November 1962.
55. PRO: FO 371/162401, Ormsby-Gore to Home, Air Bag 185, 9 November 1962. Macmillan's impression, by contrast, was that Stevenson had served Kennedy well, HMD, 4 November 1962, quoted in Macmillan, *End of the Day*, p. 219.
56. For development of US thinking on the Turkish trade, see Nash, *The Other Missiles*, pp. 127–32.
57. PRO: PREM 11/3691, de Zulueta to Bundy, Teleprinter Message, 28 October 1962.
58. PRO: PREM 11/3689, Ormsby-Gore to Macmillan, Tel. 2650, PM's Pers. Tel. T.505/62, 23 October 1962.
59. PRO: PREM 11/3689, P. Mason, Tel. 163, 23 October 1962.
60. Kennedy, *13 Days*, p. 17.
61. Ibid.
62. PRO: FO 371/162380, Burrows, Tel. 1268, 25 October 1962.

63. Nash, *The Other Missiles*, pp. 131–49.
64. Finletter to Rusk, Polto 506, 25 October 1962, *FRUS, 1961–1963, Vol. XI*, p. 213.
65. Ibid.
66. Hare to Rusk, Tel. 587, 26 October 1962, in Chang and Kornbluh, *The Cuban Missile Crisis*, p. 221.
67. Ibid., p. 222.
68. PRO: FO 371/162380, Burrows, Tel. 1268, 25 October 1962.
69. PRO: FO 371/162/390, P. Mason, Tel. 178, 31 October 1962 reporting NAC of same day.
70. PRO: PREM 11/3691, Ormsby-Gore to Home, Tel. 2701, 27 October 1962.
71. Ibid.
72. Ibid.
73. PRO: FO 371/162382, Burrows, Tel. 1284, 28 October 1962. Burrows gave four reasons for Turkish attitudes: they did not believe in compromise with the Soviets; they feared the impact of neutralism on Turkey; they worried that the removal of the missiles would reduce US interest in, and aid for, Turkey; and they felt strongly that NATO as a whole should be involved with the base issue.
74. Ibid.
75. Finletter, Tel. 506, *FRUS, 1961–1963, Vol. XI*, pp. 213–14.
76. JFKL: Henry Owen to McGeorge Bundy, 29 October 1962, NSF: RS: NATO Weapons, Cables, Turkey, Box 226.
77. PRO: PREM 11/3691, T. Bligh to A.C.I. Samuel, 28 October 1962, covering State Dept. brief for Finletter.
78. PRO: FO 371/162382, Burrows, Tel. 1284, 28 October 1962.
79. JFKL: Bohlen to Rusk, Tel. 2082, 11 November 1962, NSF: RS: NATO Weapons, Cables, Turkey, Box 226.
80. David Bruce's Diaries, 23 October 1962, (NSA: CMC), Doc. 01623.
81. JFKL: Bohlen to Rusk, Tel. 2082, 11 November 1962, NSF: RS: NATO Weapons, Cables, Turkey, Box 226.
82. JFKL: Norstad to Kennedy, PRS 2634, 27 October 1962, POF: NATO, Norstad Correspondence, 7/62 to 12/62, Box 103.
83. For example, *The Guardian*, 25 October 1962, p. 10.
84. Lebow and Stein, *We All Lost the Cold War*, pp. 133–4, 441 n, 442 n; Fursenko and Naftali, *'One Hell of a Gamble'*, pp. 275, 393–4 n; Nash, *The Other Missiles*, pp. 133–4.
85. JFKL: Hilsman to Rusk, Trading US Missile Bases in Turkey for Soviet Bases in Cuba, 27 October 1962, NSF: CO: Cuba, General, 10/26/62 to 10/27/62, Box 36.
86. PRO: Roberts, Tel. 2077, 28 October 1962, PREM 11/3691.
87. Ibid.
88. Hare to Rusk, Tel. 587, 26 October 1962, in Chang and Kornbluh, *The Cuban Missile Crisis*, p. 221.
89. PRO: PREM 11/3691, Kennedy to Macmillan, Teleprinter message, CAP 5507–62, PM's Pers. Tel., T.516A/62, 27 October 1962.
90. Ibid.
91. Ibid.

92. PRO: DEFE 32/7, Record of a Conversation between the Chief of the Air Staff, First Sea Lord and the Chief of the Imperial General Staff held in the Ministry of Defence at 1430, Saturday, 27 October 1962, Annex to COS 1546/29/10/62.

93. Macmillan, *End of the Day*, p. 213.

94. PRO: FO 371/162384, Caccia to Home, 27 October 1962.

95. Ibid.

96. PRO: PREM 11/3690, Ormsby-Gore, Tel. 2697, 26 October 1962.

97. PRO: FO 371/162384, Caccia to Home, 27 October 1962.

98. Ibid.

99. Ibid.

100. Ibid.

101. PRO: PREM 11/3691, FO to Washington, Tel. 7574, 27 October 1962.

102. Ibid.

103. PRO: PREM 11/4494, Arran to de Zulueta, 1 November 1962, covering memo. dated 31 October 1962.

104. PRO: FO 371/162387, Home to Dean, Tel. 4020, 27 October 1962.

105. Ibid.

106. Ibid.

107. Ibid.

108. Ibid.

109. Evans, *Downing Street Diary*, pp. 224–6.

110. Ibid., p. 225.

111. Macmillan, *End of the Day*, p. 214.

112. See Chapter Six.

113. Evans, *Downing Street Diary*, p. 225. Kennedy and Macmillan shared a personal antipathy toward the Canadian Prime Minister, whose reservations about US actions were apparent during the crisis.

114. PRO: PREM 11/3691, PM's Pers. Tels. T.517/62 and T.518/62, to Dean and Ormsby-Gore, [27 October 1962].

115. Ibid.

116. Ibid.

117. PRO: PREM 11/3691, Teleprinter message, de Zulueta to Bundy, [27 October 1962], 4.55 pm, London time.

118. PRO: PREM 11/3691, Ormsby-Gore, Tel. No. 2707, 27 October 1962.

119. PRO: FO 371/162383, Dean to FO, Tel. 1800, 27 October 1962.

120. Ibid.

121. PRO: PREM 11/3691, de Zulueta to Bundy, Teleprinter Message, PM's Pers. Tel. T.520/62, 9.52 am, [28 October 1962].

122. Evans, *Downing Street Diary*, p. 225

123. Ibid., pp. 225–6; Thorneycroft joined the group on Sunday morning.

124. PRO: PREM 11/3691, Telephone Conversation between Mr Bundy and Mr de Zulueta at 4 am on Sunday October 28, 1962.

125. Evans, *Downing Street Diary*, p. 226.

126. PRO: PREM 11/3691, de Zulueta to Bundy, Teleprinter Message, PM's Pers. Tel. T.520/62, 9.52 am, [28 October 1962].

127. May and Zelikow, *The Kennedy Tapes*, pp. 520–629.

128. PRO: PREM 11/3691, Ormsby-Gore to Home. Tel. 2710, 28 October 1962.
129. Blight and Welch, *On the Brink*; Fursenko and Naftali, '*One Hell of a Gamble*', May and Zelikow, *The Kennedy Tapes*, pp. 439, et seq; Nash, *The Other Missiles*, pp. 141–71; for a different view of the significance of the secret deal, see Herring, *Danger and Opportunity*, pp. 156–7.
130. Lebow and Stein, *We All Lost the Cold War*, p. 5.
131. Fursenko and Naftali, '*One Hell of a Gamble*', pp. 284–5.
132. Risse-Kappen, nevertheless, suggests that the British, as well as the Turks, were aware of the secret deal, Risse-Kappen, *Cooperation Among Democracies*, pp. 148, 171, 181.
133. Correspondence, McGeorge Bundy, 4 November 1993.
134. Bundy, *Danger and Survival*, pp. 436–7.
135. HMD, 4 November 1962, quoted in Macmillan, *End of the Day*, p. 217.
136. Macmillan, *End of the Day*, pp. 212–13.
137. Correspondence, McGeorge Bundy, 4 November 1993. In contrast Robert McNamara believed that JFK's response was simply a polite way of refusing, Correspondence, Robert McNamara, 4 September 1993.
138. For discussion, see Garthoff, *Reflections*, pp. 94–6; Bundy, *Danger and Survival*, pp. 435–8; May and Zelikow, *The Kennedy Tapes*, pp. 694–6.
139. Letter from Dean Rusk to James Blight, quoted in Blight and Welch, *On the Brink*, pp. 83–4.
140. See Scott and Smith, 'Lessons of October', p. 681.
141. PRO: FO 371/162387, Dean, Tel. 1747, 25 October 1962.
142. Ibid.
143. Ibid.
144. M.J. White, 'Dean Rusk's Revelation: New British Evidence on the Cordier Ploy', *The Society for Historians of American Foreign Relations (SHAFR) Newsletter*, Vol. 25, No. 3 (September 1994), p. 6; see also White, The Cuban Missile Crisis, pp. 202–3.
145. White, 'Dean Rusk's Revelation', ibid., p. 7.
146. See R.L. Garthoff. 'Some Reflections on the History of the Cold War', *SHAFR Newsletter*, Vol. 26, No.3 (September 1995), pp. 1–3; Nash, *The Other Missiles*, p. 206 n. 63.
147. PRO: DEFE 13/212, Record of a meeting between the MOD and the COS on 28 October 1962, MM/COS(62)7; see also Zuckerman, *Monkeys*, p. 303.
148. *HC Deb.*, vol. 666, 30 October 1962, col. 40.
149. PRO: PREM 11/3691, Macmillan to Krushchev, FO to Moscow. Tel. 2758, PM's Pers. Tel. T.521/62, 28 October 1962.
150. Roberts, *Dealing with Dictators*, p. 219.
151. Evans, *Downing Street Diary*, p. 226.
152. Castro to Khrushchev, 26 October 1962 in Blight, Allyn and Welch, *Cuba on the Brink*, pp. 481–2.
153. May and Zelikow, *The Kennedy Tapes*, p. 267.

154. Fursenko and Naftali, '*One Hell of a Gamble*', pp. 210–11, 217; Gribkov and Smith, *Operation Anadyr*, pp. 4–6, 27–8, 46, 62–3.
155. Summary Record of 10th Meeting of ExComm, 28 October 1962, *FRUS, 1961–1963, Vol. XI*, p. 284; May and Zelikow, *The Kennedy Tapes*, p. 636.
156. PRO: AIR 25/1703, Operations Record Book, HQ. No. 1 Grp., Ocrober 1962, Note 11.
157. Schecter and Deriabin, *Spy Who Saved the World*, p. 337.
158. Ibid., pp. 346–7.
159. For discussion, see Sagan, *The Limits of Safety*, pp. 146–50; see also D. Wise, *Molehunt: The Secret Search for Traitors that Shattered the CIA* (New York: Random House, 1992), p. 119.
160. Garthoff, *Reflections*, pp. 64–5.
161. Schecter and Deriabin, *Spy Who Saved the World*, p. 74, et seq.
162. PRO: FO 371/162399, FO Minute, R.M.K. Slater, AK1261/487/G, 12 November 1962.
163. PRO: PREM 11/4695, Telephone Conversation between the Prime Minister and President Kennedy at 11 pm on 14 November 1962; Macmillan *End of the Day*, p. 215.
164. PRO: PREM 11/4695, Record of a Conversation between President Kennedy and the Prime Minister at 10.55 pm, on Thursday, 15 November 1962; Horne, *Macmillan, 1957–1986*, p. 379.
165. PRO: PREM 11/4695, Telephone Conversation between the Prime Minister and President Kennedy at 11 pm on 14 November 1962; Macmillan *End of the Day*, p. 215.
166. PRO: PREM 11/4695, FO to Washington, Tel. 8456, 20 November 1962, Teleprinter Message, Kennedy to Macmillan, PM's Pers. Tel. T. 570/62.
167. Ibid.

Conclusion

1. JFKL: David Ormsby-Gore to Jack Kennedy, 30 October 1962, POF: UK General, Box 127.
2. PRO: PREM 11/3691, Home to Ormsby-Gore, Tel. 7636, 29 October 1962.
3. PRO: PREM 11/3691, Ormsby-Gore to Home, Tel. 2710, 28 October 1962.
4. Memorandum of Conversation, 28 October 1962, *FRUS, 1961–1963, Vol XI*, p. 288.
5. See PRO: PREM 11/3691, Home to Ormsby-Gore, Tel. 7636, 29 October 1962; for Sir Frank Roberts' opposition to the idea, see PRO: PREM 11/3691, Roberts, Tels. 2098, 30 October 1962 and 2117, 31 October 1962; see also PRO: PREM 11/3691, C. Steel [Ambassador to West Germany], Tel. 898, 30 October 1962.
6. PRO: PREM 11/3691, Macmillan to Home, PM's Pers. Minute, M. 298/62, 29 October 1962.
7. 'It was indeed a trial of wills and yours has prevailed,' Macmillan congratulated Kennedy; 'Whatever dangers and difficulties we may

have to face in the future I am proud to feel that I have so resourceful and so firm a comrade', PRO: PREM 11/4052, Bligh to Bundy, PM's Pers. Tel. T.524/62, [28 October 1962], quoted in Horne, *Macmillan, 1957–1986*, p. 378. Kennedy replied in kind: 'I am grateful for your warm generous words. Your heartening support publicly expressed and our daily conversations have been of inestimable value in these past days', ibid. Home cabled Rusk: 'I am filled with admiration for your handling of this very difficult matter. Well done. Alec', PRO: FO 371/162383, FO to Washington, Tel. 7620, 28 October 1962; Rusk told Ormsby-Gore that he 'was much moved' by this message and 'would always treasure it', PRO: PREM 11/3689, Ormsby-Gore to Home, Tel. 2714, 29 October 1962.

8. *HC Deb.*, vol. 666, 30 October 1962, col. 34.
9. PRO: PREM 11/3691, Roberts, Tel. 2081, 29 October 1962.
10. R. Edmonds, *Setting the Mould, The United States and Britain 1945–1950* (OUP, 1986), p. 246.
11. Owen, *Politics of Defence*, p. 35.
12. PRO: PREM 11/3689, Ormsby-Gore to Home, Tel. 2714, 29 October 1962.
13. P.T. Haydon, *The 1962 Cuban Missile Crisis: Canadian Involvement Reconsidered* (Toronto: Canadian Institute of Strategic Studies, 1993), p. 201.
14. HMD, 4 November 1962, quoted in Macmillan, *End of the Day*, p. 216.
15. HMD, 4 November 1962, quoted in Horne, *Macmillan, 1957–1986*, p. 380.
16. PRO: FO 371/162395, Cheetham to Caccia, Cuba, AK1261/412, 30 October 1962.
17. Bundy, *Danger and Survival*, p. 492.
18. A. Horne, 'The Macmillan Years and Afterwards', in W.R. Louis and H. Bull (Eds), *The Special Relationship: Anglo-American Relations since 1945* (OUP, 1986).
19. J. Mander, *Great Britain or Little England* (Secker and Warburg, 1963), p. 21.
20. Nunnerley, *President Kennedy*, p. 39.
21. May and Zelikow, *The Kennedy Tapes*, p. 692; see also Risse-Kappen, *Cooperation Among Democracies*, p. 179; May and Zeikow suspect that by 26 October, 'Kennedy had become sceptical of the quality of Macmillan's advice'.
22. H.G. Nicholas, *The United States and Britain* (University of Chicago Press, 1975), p. 165.
23. Horne, *Macmillan, 1957–1986*, p. 383; Rawnsley, 'How Special is Special', p. 590; Thorne, *Alec Douglas-Home*, p. 249; for discussion, see Horne, pp. 372, 383.
24. Bundy, *Danger and Survival*, p. 434.
25. PRO: FO 371/162384, Caccia to Home, 27 October 1962.
26. Thorne, *Alec Douglas-Home*, p. 249.
27. George Clark, quoted in Taylor, *Against the Bomb*, p. 91.
28. PRO: PREM 11/3689, Ormsby-Gore to Macmillan, Tel. 2650, PM's Pers. Tel. T.505/62, 23 October 1962.

29. PRO: PREM 11/4218, De Zulueta to Macmillan, brief for meeting with Home, 6 November 1962.
30. PRO: PREM 11/3690, Dean, Tel. 1723, 24 October 1962.
31. PRO: FO 371/162408, Marchant to Home, Air Bag No. 62, 10 November 1962.

Bibliography

PRIMARY SOURCES

British

Harold Macmillan Diaries, Bodleian Library, Oxford
Public Record Office
National Museum of Labour History

American

John F. Kennedy Library
Dwight D. Eisenhower Library
Central Intelligence Agency

PUBLISHED PRIMARY SOURCES

Chang, L. and Kornbluh, P. (Eds) *The Cuban Missile Crisis, 1962 – A National Security Archive Documents Reader* (New York: The New Press, 1992).
Foreign Relations of the United States, 1961–1963, Vol. X, Cuba 1961–1962 (Washington: United States Government Printing Office, 1997).
Foreign Relations of the United States, 1961–1963, Vol. XI, Cuban Missile Crisis and Aftermath (Washington: United States Government Printing Office, 1996).
McAuliffe, M.S. (Ed.) *CIA Documents on the Cuban Missile Crisis 1962* (Washington: CIA, 1992).
National Security Archive, *The Cuban Missile Crisis, 1962*, Microfiche Collection (Alexandria, Va.: Chadwyck-Healey, 1990).
National Security Archive, *The Soviet Estimate: US Analysis of the Soviet Union 1947–1991*, Microfiche Collection (Alexandria, Va.: Chadwyck-Healey, 1995).
Ruffner, K.C. (Ed.) *CORONA: America's First Satellite Program* (Washington: CIA, 1995).
Steury, D.P. (Ed.) *Intentions and Capabilities: Estimates on Soviet Strategic Forces, 1950–1983* (Washington: CIA, 1996).

Articles

Bundy, M. (transcriber) and Blight, J.G. (Ed.), 'October 27, 1962: Transcripts of the Meetings of the ExComm', *International Security*, Vol. 12, No. 3 (Winter 1987/1988).
Trachtenberg, T. (Ed.) 'White House Tapes and Minutes of the Cuban

Missile Crisis, ExComm Meetings October 1962', ExComm Meeting, 16 October 1962, *International Security*, Vol. 10, No. 1 (Summer 1985).
Welch, D.A. and Blight, J.G. 'The Eleventh Hour of the Cuban Missile Crisis: An Introduction to the ExComm Transcripts', *International Security*, Vol. 12, No. 3 (Winter 1987/1988).

SECONDARY SOURCES

Place of publication is London unless otherwise stated.

Abbott, J.R. *British Reactions and Attitudes to the Cuban Crisis, 1962* (MScEcon thesis, University of Wales, Aberystwyth, 1969).
Abel, E. *The Missiles of October, The Story of the Cuban Missile Crisis* (MacGibbon and Kee, 1966).
Allison, G.T. *Essence of Decision, Explaining the Cuban Missile Crisis* (Boston: Little, Brown, 1971).
Allyn, B.J., Blight, J.G. and Welch, D.A. *Back to the Brink: Proceedings of the Moscow Conference on the Cuban Missile Conference, January 27–28, 1989*, CSIA Occasional Paper No. 9 (Lanham, Maryland: University of America Press, 1992).
Andrew, C. *For the President's Eyes Only: Secret Intelligence and the American Presidency From Washington to Bush* (HarperCollins, 1995).
Ball, D. *Politics and Force Levels* (University of California Press, 1980).
Baylis, J. *Ambiguity and Deterrence: Bristish Nuclear Strategy 1945–1964* (Oxford University Press, 1995).
—— (Ed.) *Anglo-American Relations since 1939* (Manchester University Press, 1997).
Beschloss, M.R. *Kennedy v. Khrushchev, The Crisis Years 1960–63* (Faber and Faber, 1991).
Bethell, L. *The Cambridge History of Latin America, Volume VII – Latin America since 1930 – Mexico, Central America and the Caribbean* (Cambridge University Press, 1990).
Blair, B.G. *The Logic of Accidental Nuclear War* (Washington: The Brookings Institution, 1993).
Blight, J.G. and Welch, D.A. *On the Brink: Americans and Soviets Reexamine the Cuban Missile Crisis* (New York: Noonday Press, 1990).
Blight, J.G., Allyn, B.J. and Welch, D.A. *Cuba on the Brink: Castro, the Missile Crisis and the Soviet Collapse* (New York: Pantheon Books, 1993).
Blight, J.G. and Kornbluh, P. *Politics of Illusion: The Bay of Pigs Reexamined* (Lynne Rienner, 1998).
Bouchard, J. *Command in Crisis: Four Case Studies* (New York: Columbia University Press, 1991).
Brandon, H. *Special Relationships: A Foreign Correspondent's Memoirs From Roosevelt to Reagan* (Macmillan, 1988).
Brivati, B. *Hugh Gaitskell* (Richard Cohen, 1996).
Brook-Shepherd, G. *The Storm Birds – Soviet Post-war Defectors* (Weidenfeld and Nicolson, 1988).
Brugioni, D.A. (Ed. Robert F. McCort), *Eyeball to Eyeball, The Inside*

Story of the Cuban Missile Crisis (New York: Random House, 1991).

Bundy, M. *Danger and Survival: Choices About the Bomb in the First Fifty Years* (New York: Random House, 1988).

Chayes, A. *The Cuban Missile Crisis* (Oxford University Press, 1974).

Clark, I. *Nuclear Diplomacy and the Special Relationship, Britain's Deterrent and America* (Oxford University Press, 1994).

Clark, R.W. *The Life of Bertrand Russell* (Jonathan Cape, 1975).

Cooper, C.L. *The Lion's Last Roar: Suez, 1956* (Harper and Row, 1978).

Deacon, R. *'C': A Biography of Sir Maurice Oldfield Head of M16* (Futura, 1984).

Dickie, J. *'Special' No More – Anglo-American Relations: Rhetoric and Reality* (Weidenfeld and Nicolson, 1994).

Divine, R.A. (Ed.) *The Cuban Missile Crisis* (New York: Marcus Wiener, 1988).

Dobrynin, A. *In Confidence: Moscow's Ambassador to America's Six Cold War Presidents (1962–1986)* (New York: Times Books, 1995).

Evans, H. *Downing Street Diary: The Macmillan Years 1957–1963* (Hodder and Stoughton, 1981).

Fursenko, A. and Naftali, T. *'One Hell of a Gamble': Khrushchev, Castro, Kennedy and the Cuban Missile Crisis 1958–1964* (John Murray, 1997).

Garthoff, R.L. *Reflections on the Cuban Missile Crisis* (Washington: The Brookings Institution, 1989).

Gribkov, A.I. and Smith, W.Y. *Operation Anadyr: US and Soviet Generals Recount the Cuban Missile Crisis* (Chicago: Edition Q, 1994).

Haydon, P.T. *The 1962 Cuban Missile Crisis: Canadian Involvement Reconsidered* (Toronto: Canadian Institute of Strategic Studies, 1993).

Healey, D.W. *The Time of My Life* (Michael Joseph, 1989).

Hennessy, A. and Lambie, G. (Eds) *The Fractured Blockade, West European–Cuba Relations During the Revolution* (Warwick University Caribbean Studies, Macmillan, 1993).

Herring, E. *Danger and Opportunity* (Manchester University Press, 1995).

Horne, A. *Macmillan 1894–1956, Volume I of The Official Biography* (Macmillan, 1988).

—— *Macmillan 1957–1986, Volume II of The Official Biography* (Macmillan, 1989).

Ivanov, Y. (with Sokolov, G.), *The Naked Spy* (Blake, 1992).

Kaplan, F. *The Wizards of Armageddon* (Stanford: Stanford University Press, 1991).

Kennedy, R.F. *13 Days, The Cuban Missile Crisis 1962* (Pan, 1969).

Khrushchev, N. (edited/translated by Talbott, S.), *Khrushchev Remembers* (Andre Deutsch, 1971).

—— (edited/translated by Schecter, J.L. and Luchkov, V.V.), *Khrushchev Remembers: The Glasnost Tapes* (Little, Brown, 1990).

Knightley, P. and Kennedy, C. *An Affair of State: The Profumo Scandal and the Framing of Stephen Ward* (Jonathan Cape, 1987).

Lebow R.N. and Stein, J.G. *We All Lost the Cold War* (Princeton, New Jersey: Princeton University Press, 1994).

Louis, W.R. and Bull, H. *The Special Relationship: Anglo-American Relations since 1945* (Oxford University Press, 1986).

Macmillan, H. *At the End of the Day, 1961–1963* (Macmillan, 1973).

Marlow, S. *Personality and policy-making: the case of the Cuban missile crisis* (MPhil thesis, University of Keele, 1996).

May, E.R. and Zelikow, P.D. (Eds) *The Kennedy Tapes: Inside the White House During the Cuban Missile Crisis* (Harvard University Press, 1997).

McNamara, R.S. *Blundering into Disaster: Surviving the First Century of the Nuclear Age* (Bloomsbury, 1987).

Menaul, M. *Countdown – Britain's Strategic Nuclear Forces* (Robert Hale, 1980).

Miller, R.G. (Ed.) *Seeing Off the Bear: Anglo-American Air Power Cooperation During the Cold War* (Washington: Royal Air Force Historical Society/ Air Force Historical Foundation, 1995).

Nash, P. *The Other Missiles of October: Eisenhower, Kennedy, and the Jupiters 1957–1963* (Chapel Hill, North Carolina: University of North Carolina Press, 1997).

Nathan, J.A. (Ed.) *The Cuban Missile Crisis Revisited* (New York: St Martin's Press, 1992).

Nitze, P. *From Hiroshima to Glasnost: At the Center of Decision* (New York: Grove Weidenfeld, 1989).

Nunnerley, N. *President Kennedy and Britain* (Bodley Head, 1972).

Oliver, K. *Kennedy, Macmillan and the Nuclear Test Ban Debate, 1961–1963* (Macmillan, 1997).

Owen, D. *The Politics of Defence* (Jonathan Cape, 1972).

Paterson, T.G. (Ed.) *Kennedy's Quest for Victory: American Foreign Policy, 1961–1963* (Oxford University Press, 1989).

——— *Contesting Castro: The United States and the Triumph of the Cuban Revolution* (Oxford University Press, 1994).

Pavlov, Y. *Soviet–Cuban Alliance 1959–1991* (Transaction Publishers, 1994).

Rabe, S.G. *Eisenhower and Latin America: The Foreign Policy of AntiCommunism* (University of North Carolina Press, 1988).

Reynolds, D. *Britannia Overruled: British Power and World Policy in the 20th Century* (Longman, 1991).

Risse-Kappen, T. *Cooperation Among Democracies: The European Influence on U.S. Foreign Policy* (Princeton, New Jersey: Princeton University Press, 1995).

Roberts, F. *Dealing with Dictators: The Destruction and Revival of Europe 1930–1970* (Weidenfeld and Nicolson, 1991).

Roosevelt, A. *For Lust of Knowing, Memoirs of an Intelligence Officer* (Weidenfeld and Nicolson, 1988).

Russell, B. *Unarmed Victory* (Penguin, 1963).

Sagan, S.D. *The Limits of Safety – Organisations, Accidents, and Nuclear Weapons* (Princeton, New Jersey: Princeton University Press, 1993).

Schecter, J.L. and Deriabin, P.S. *The Spy Who Saved the World* (New York: Charles Scribner's Sons, 1992).

Schlesinger, A. *A Thousand Days – John F. Kennedy in the White House* (Andre Deutsch, 1965).

Schwartz, D.N. *NATO's Nuclear Dilemmas* (Washington: The Brookings Institution, 1983).

Smith, G. *Britain and the Cuban Missile Crisis* (BA dissertation, University of London, 1994).

Sorenson, T.C. *Kennedy* (Hodder and Stoughton, 1965).
—— *Robert Kennedy and His Times* (Andre Deutsch, 1978).
Stromseth, J.E. *The Origins of Flexible Response: NATO's Debate over Strategy in the 1960s* (Macmillan, 1988).
Strong, K. *Intelligence at the Top – The Recollections of an Intelligence Officer* (Cassell, 1968).
Summers, A. and Dorril, S. *Honeytrap: The Secret Worlds of Stephen Ward* (Weidenfeld and Nicolson, 1987).
Taylor, R. *Against the Bomb: The British Peace Movement, 1958–1965* (Oxford University Press, 1988).
Thomas, H. *Cuba or the Pursuit of Freedom* (Eyre and Spottiswoode, 1971).
Thompson, R.S. *The Missiles of October – The Declassified Story of John F. Kennedy and the Cuban Missile Crisis* (New York: Simon and Schuster, 1992).
Thorne, D.R. *Alec Douglas–Home* (Sinclair–Stevenson, 1996).
Trachtenberg, M. *History and Strategy* (Princeton, New Jersey: Princeton University Press, 1991).
Twigge, S. and Scott, L. *Fail Deadly? Britain and the Control of Nuclear Weapons 1945–64* (Nuclear History Program Report, Aberystwyth, 1997).
Vaisse, M. (Ed.) *L'Europe et la Crise de Cuba* (Paris: Armand Colin, 1993).
Verrier, A. *Through the Looking Glass – British Foreign Policy in an Age Illusions* (Jonathan Cape, 1983).
White, M.J. *The Cuban Missile Crisis* (Macmillan, 1996).
Williams, P.M. *Hugh Gaitskell: A Political Biography* (Jonathan Cape, 1979).
Wright, P. (with Greengrass, P.), *Spycatcher* (Richmond, Victoria, Australia: Heinemann, 1987).
Wynn, H. *The RAF's Strategic Deterrent Forces: their origins, roles and deployment 1946–1969* (HMSO, 1994).
Zubok, V. and Pleshakov, C. *Inside the Kremlin's Cold War* (Harvard University Press, 1996).

Articles

Aldrich, R. 'British Intelligence and the Anglo-American "Special Relationship" during the Cold War', *Review of International Studies*, Vol. 24, No. 3 (Autumn 1998).
Allyn, B.J., Blight, J.G. and Welch, D.A. 'Essence of Revision: Moscow, Havana and the Cuban Missile Crisis', *International Security*, Vol. 14, No. 3 (Winter 1989/90).
Blight, J.G. and Welch, D.A. 'Risking "The Destruction of Nations": Lessons of the Cuban Missile Crisis for New and Aspiring Nuclear States', *Security Studies*, Vol. 4, No. 4 (Summer 1995).
Boyle, P.G. 'The British Government's View of the Cuban Missile Crisis', *Contemporary Record*, Vol. 10, No. 3 (Autumn 1996).
Caldwell, D. 'A Research Note on the Quarantine of Cuba, October, 1962', *International Studies Quarterly*, Vol. 22, No. 4 (December 1978).
Costigliola, F. 'Kennedy, the European Allies, and the Failure to Consult', *Political Science Quarterly*, Vol. 110, No. 1 (1995).
Criss, N.B. 'Strategic Nuclear Missiles in Turkey: The Jupiter Affair,

1959–1963', *Journal of Strategic Studies*, Vol. 20, No. 3 (September 1997).

Fursenko, A. and Naftali, T. 'Using KGB Documents: The Scali–Feklisov Channel in the Cuban Missile Crisis', *Cold War International History Project Bulletin*, Issue 5 (Spring 1995).

Garthoff, R.L. 'Some Reflections on the History of the Cold War', *The Society for Historians of American Foreign Relations Newsletter*, Vol. 26, No. 3 (September 1995).

Gleijeses, Piero, 'Ships in the Night: The CIA, the White House and the Bay of Pigs', *Journal of Latin American Studies*, Vol. 27 (1995).

Kent, S. 'The Cuban Missile Crisis of 1962: Presenting the Photographic Evidence Abroad', *Studies in Intelligence*, Vol. 10, No. 2 (Spring 1972).

Rawnsley, G.D. 'How Special is Special? The Anglo-American Alliance During the Cuban Missile Crisis', *Contemporary Record*, Vol. 9, No. 3 (Winter 1995).

Scott, L. and Smith, S. 'Lessons of October: historians, political scientists, policy-makers and the Cuban missile crisis', *International Affairs*, Vol. 70, No. 4 (October 1994).

Scott, L. 'On the Brink: Britain and the Cuban Missile Crisis', *Contemporary Record*, Vol. 5, No. 3 (Winter, 1991).

Trachtenberg, M. 'The Influence of Nuclear Weapons in the Cuban Missile Crisis', *International Security*, Vol. 10, No. 1 (Summer 1985).

Twigge, S. and Scott, L. 'Fail Deadly? Britain and The Command and Control of Nuclear Forces, 1945–1964 (Aberystwyth: Nuclear Program Report, 1997).

Welch, D. 'Intelligence Assessment in the Cuban Missile Crisis', *Queen's Quarterly*, Vol. 100, No. 2 (Summer 1993).

White, M.J. 'Belligerent Beginnings: John F. Kennedy on the Opening Day of the Cuba Missile Crisis', *Journal of Strategic Studies*, Vol. 15, No. 1 (March 1992).

———— 'Dean Rusk's Revelation: New British Evidence on the Cordier Ploy', *The Society for Historians of American Foreign Relations Newsletter*, Vol. 25, No. 3 (September 1994).

Other publications

Hansard, House of Commons Debates: Vol. 638, 11–21 April 1961; Vol. 664, 30 July–25 October 1962; Vol. 666, 30 October–9 November 1962; Vol. 672, 18 February–1 March 1963; Vol. 679, 17–28 June 1963.

Labour Party Conference Report 1962 (Labour Party, 1963).

Lord Denning's Report, Cmnd 2512 (September 1963).

Index

Abel, Elie, 40
Abraham Lincoln USS, 135, 141
Acheson, Dean, 8, 19, 48, 60, 65, 72, 75, 136–7, 162, 204
Adenauer, Konrad, 48
Air Ministry, 143, 147, 151
Albania, 123
Alliance for Progress, 22
Allison, Graham, 113
Alpha 66, 27–8, 197
Alphand, Herve, 110, 155
Angleton, James, 121
American foreign policy, 13–14, 15–16, 22, 23, 27, 30, 44, 46, 94–5, 126, 165, 170, 174
    State Department, 28, 30, 41, 66, 72, 74, 79, 90, 107, 120, 138, 141, 159, 164, 165, 207, 208, 229
arms control, 152, 168, 187
Arran, Lord, 107, 108, 109, 168
Arrowsmith, Pat, 3
Attlee, Clement, 82

B47 bombers, 134, 135
B52 bombers, 2, 134
Ball, George, 6, 74–5
Ballistic Missile Early Warning System (BMEWS), 64–5, 83
Batista, General Fulgencio, 15, 16, 17, 194
Bay of Pigs, 21–3, 39, 79, 194, 199
    British reaction to, 21–3
Berlin, 8, 23, 39, 40, 43, 53, 56, 59–61, 63, 66–7, 85, 86, 114, 139, 152, 153, 180, 183
    British concern over, 39, 44, 56, 59, 60, 62–3, 65–8, 96, 104, 132, 138, 148, 152, 179
    and Kennedy, 8, 30, 39, 44, 46, 48, 56, 60, 95–6, 98–9, 132, 162

    and Khrushchev, 8, 23, 39, 46, 50–1, 59, 60–1, 63, 65–8, 180
    and Macmillan, 50–1, 52–3, 60, 132, 157
Berlin crisis, 4, 23, 104, 120
Beshany, Vice Admiral, 141,
blockade, *see* quarantine
Bolshakov, Georgi, 33, 103, 108–9, 198
Bomber Command, 6, 12, 113, 134, 135–6, 139–51, 176, 187
    Alert conditions, 7, 113, 142, 143, 147, 149–50, 176–7, 186
    see also Thor missiles
'bomber gap', 124
Boothroyd, Basil, 3–4
Brandon, Henry, 34, 194, 199
Brimelow, Thomas, 40
British–American relations, 8–9, 28, 29, 31, 35, 39, 42, 59, 60, 69, 73, 76, 78, 85, 90, 91, 92, 105, 107, 112, 135, 140, 141, 151, 152, 167, 180–5
    consultation with US over crisis, 4, 9, 35–6, 37–40, 42, 54, 56–7, 58, 59, 60–1, 76, 79, 80, 82, 86, 91, 92, 98–9, 140, 151, 153–6, 166, 180–5, 212
    and special relationship, 8–9, 11, 35–9, 56, 58–9, 76, 78, 133, 166, 178, 180–5, 186
British Broadcasting Corporation (BBC), 118–19, 217
British foreign policy, 5, 11, 12, 13, 24–5, 32–3, 52, 59, 60–1, 68, 69, 77–8, 122, 133, 150, 152, 161–2, 179, 185, 187
British–Cuban relations, 13, 17–18, 31, 32, 195

242

British embassy, Havana, 28,
34, 87, 148, 197
see also Home, Ormsby-Gore,
Macmillan, Foreign Office
Brodie, Bernard, 59
Brown, George, 54, 81–5, 208–9
Bruce, David, 27, 48–51, 54, 73,
82–5, 87–8, 94, 107, 117–19,
191, 202, 217
Brugioni, Dino, 49, 50, 118,
208–9, 210
Burrows, Sir Bernard 162, 163–4,
230
Buccaneer aircraft, 135
Bundy, McGeorge, 8, 64–5, 96–7,
120, 129, 161, 170–1, 172–3,
181, 184
Butler, Rab, 5, 171
Butlin, Wendy, 3

Cabinet, 1, 5, 11, 35, 52, 63, 70,
73, 75, 78, 80, 90–1, 102,
107, 147, 201, 210
Caccia, Sir Harold, 18, 33, 41,
104, 106, 166–7, 171, 185,
186, 198
Caldwell, Dan, 113
Campaign for Nuclear
Disarmament (CND), 4, 10,
77, 79, 84, 88, 92, 187
Campbell, Ian, 144
Canada, 181
see also Diefenbaker
Canberra bombers, 139, 142
Carter, General Marshall, 127
Castro, Fidel, 13, 19, 20–2, 24,
31, 32, 35, 61, 66, 95, 154,
166, 168, 175–6, 178, 179,
194
beard, possible loss of, 15, 194
and Britain, 17–19
character and ideology of,
14–16, 17, 195
Castro, Raul, 16
Central Intelligence Agency
(CIA), 18, 23, 33, 40, 119,
120–30, 136, 177, 217, 218
Cuban operations, 20–1, 24,
27–8, 194, 197

and Britain, 40, 82–3, 119, 181
and missile crisis, 23, 33–4,
41, 66, 80, 109, 150, 215
and Penkovsky, 12, 120–30, 149,
177, 181, 217–18, 220
see also Operation Mongoose
CHICKADEE, 125, 128, 218
Chiefs of Staff, 132, 146–8, 150,
152, 166
Chinese–Soviet relations, 66, 156
Chinese–Indian conflict, 68, 84, 91
Churchill, Winston, 13, 17
Commander in Chief US Forces
in Europe (CINCEUR), 136
Cline, Ray, 40, 118
Cordier, Andrew, 173–4
Commander in Chief, Atlantic
(CINCLANT), 27
Commander in Chief United
States Air Force Europe
(CINCUSAFE), 139
Committee of 100, 4, 79, 87–8
Commonwealth, 19, 169, 181
communism, 15–16, 18, 21, 31,
32, 44
British view of, 19–20
Congress (US), 15, 32, 55, 67,
70, 176
Conservative Party, 11, 35, 78–9,
81, 92
Cooper, Chet, 48–9, 50, 54,
82–3, 116, 118–19, 202
Coordinating Committee on
Export Controls (COCOM),
24–6, 29–30
Macmillan view of, 24, 26, 30
CORONA, satellite
reconnaissance programme,
124, 126
covert operations, *see* CIA,
Operation Mongoose
Crewe, Wilhelm, 155
cricket, 2, 13, 189
Cross, Sir Kenneth, 135, 139,
142, 143, 145–7, 150–1
Crossman Richard, 58
Cuba
arms sales, 17–18, 26, 29, 30,
32, 73, 81, 101

Cuba – *continued*
  and Britain, 13, 17, 18, 31, 32, 195
  economic sanctions, 13, 15–36, 38, 69, 181–2
  and emigres, 16, 21, 27, 34, 194; *see also* Alpha 66
  and Spanish colonialism, 13
  and USSR, 8, 16, 18–20, 28–9, 31, 32, 61–9, 123–4, 175–8
  see also Cuban missile crisis
Cuban missile crisis
  British public response, 2–4, 51, 53–4, 79, 80, 84, 87–8, 90, 96, 100, 117–19, 165, 208
  consequences of, 3, 10, 12, 180
  historiography, 6, 7, 114, 130, 132, 145, 171–2, 186, 193
  and Kennedy, 2, 9, 31, 42, 43–4, 46, 47, 66, 128, 133–4, 156, 157, 159, 161, 166, 176, 177, 184, 226
  resolution of, 7, 144, 151, 152, 153–178
  Soviet Union, defence of Cuba, 7, 16, 19–20, 28, 31–2, 61, 63–4, 97, 109, 110, 122–3
  see also Kennedy, Khrushchev, Macmillan, nuclear weapons

Daily Express, 53, 79
Daily Herald, 100
Daily Mail, 53–4, 80, 142
Daily Telegraph, 100
Dean, Patrick Sir, 72, 101, 167–8, 170, 173–4
DEFCON-2, 1, 97, 134, 140, 143, 150, 176
DEFCON-3, 134, 136, 139, 141
de Gaulle, Charles, 48, 53, 181
Denmark, 25, 30, 164
Denning, Lord, 102, 103, 105
Deriabin, Peter, 120, 125, 128, 130
detente, 92, 179, 188
de Zulueta, Philip, 49, 57, 116, 118, 161, 170, 171, 188

Diefenbaker, John, 168, 181, 231
Dilhorne Lord, 52, 70–1, 74, 86
DISTANT early warning procedure, 177
Dobrynin, Anatoli, 33, 109
Dowling, Walter, 48
Dulles Allen, 18, 195

East Germany, 5, 66, 123
  see also Berlin
Eden, Sir Anthony, 156
Edmonds, Robin, 180
Egypt, 176
European Economic Community (EEC), 11, 78, 96
Eisenhower, Dwight, 15, 17, 18, 20–1, 25, 28, 78, 124, 140, 199
Erkin, Feridun, 163
Erroll, Frederick, 24–5
Evans, Sir, Harold, 117, 168–9, 171, 175
Evening Standard, 80
Esso, 18
ExComm, 37, 76, 97, 115, 145, 153, 155, 159, 161, 171, 176, 184, 216

F 100s, 102s, 103s, 104s, 105s, 135
FALLEX exercise, 147
Feklisov, Aleksandr 103, 108, 154–5
Financial Times, The, 21
Finletter, Thomas, 162–4
Fleming, Ian, 194
Fomin Aleksandr, *see* Feklisov, Aleksandr
Fordham, Alfred, 17
Foreign Office, 5, 27, 28, 29, 31, 32, 33–4, 52, 59, 62, 64, 66–7, 70, 72–5, 76, 81, 89, 94–7, 102, 104, 105, 107, 110, 138, 139, 157–8, 159, 166, 168, 173, 177, 180, 185, 189, 198
  Northern Department, 36–7, 63–6, 156–7, 205
Forrestal, Michael, 119

France, 38, 39, 48, 59, 61, 66, 70, 97, 135, 153, 159, 163–4, 166, 181, 184
see also de Gaulle, Alphand
Fraser, Sir Hugh, 146, 151
Fylingdales, 65

Gagarin, 216
Gaitskell, Hugh, 10, 11, 22–3, 78, 79, 119
  on Castro, 17, 22
  and missile crisis, 4, 37, 54, 58, 77–86, 88, 90–2, 119, 164, 208, 210
Garthoff, Raymond, 120–1, 123, 138, 143, 177, 215
General Council of British Shipping, 71
German Air Force (Luftwaffe) 5
Gilpatrick, Roswell, 127
Godber, Joseph, 32
Golitsyn, Anatoly, 121
Graham, Billy, 2
Greece, 29, 30, 158
Greenhill, Denis, 211
Gromyko, Andrei, 33, 198–9
Ground Launched Cruise Missiles (GLCMs), 189
GRU (Soviet Military Intelligence), 33, 103, 105, 111, 120, 149, 213
Guatemala, 18
Guantanamo Bay naval base, 14, 27, 47, 154, 156, 176
Guardian, The, 16, 21, 53, 58
Guevara, Che, 16, 122

Hailsham, Quintin, 1, 51, 71, 78
Hare, Raymond, 163–5
Hawk missiles, 35
Healey, Denis, 22–3, 77, 79, 83–4, 91
Heath, Edward, 5, 171
Helms, Richard, 128–9
Henderson, Sir Nicholas, 121, 205
Hennessy, Alistair, 35
Herter, Christian, 17–18
Hitler, Adolf, 21, 88, 195

Hilsman, Roger, 110, 118–19, 155, 165
Hobson, Sir John, 70
Holy Loch, 135, 140–1
Home, Alec Douglas, 5, 19, 29, 41, 50–1, 107, 211
  and economic sanctions against Cuba, 24–7, 30
  and Macmillan, 30, 35, 46, 50, 76, 81, 168–9, 186
  and missile crisis, 39, 46–7, 50–1, 63, 68–9, 72–3, 76, 81–2, 96, 101, 110, 167–9, 170–1, 179, 181, 185, 186, 191, 234
  and Soviet approaches, 90, 92, 97, 107, 108, 110, 111–12, 180
Hood, Lord, 74
Horne, Alistair, 99, 117, 120, 121, 133, 182, 210, 212, 216, 223
Hotspur, Tottenham, 2
Howard, Anthony, 58, 79, 81
Hungary, 39
Hunter jets, 18

Il-28 bombers, 41, 76, 115, 176–7, 190, 200, 216
Independent Television (ITV), 119
Indonesia, 110, 176
intelligence
  back channels, 33, 102, 103, 154–5
  British–American relations, 9, 12, 27–8, 39–41, 49, 54–5, 62–3, 78, 120–30, 181, 182, 217
  Cuban, 159
  Dutch, 33
  French, 33
  photographic intelligence, 33, 38, 42, 45–6, 50, 62, 101, 116–20, 124, 126, 127, 176, 197, 204–5, 219
  publication of photographs, 101, 116–20, 183, 217
  Soviet, 121, 150, 159
  see also CIA, SIS, Penkovsky

Inter-American Treaty of
Reciprocal Assistance (Rio
Treaty), 45, 69–70
Inter-Continental Ballistic Missiles
(ICBMs), 2, 64, 122, 124–7,
134, 190
Minuteman, 64
SS-6, 125
Intermediate Range Ballistic
Missiles (IRBMs), 128, 133,
139, 143, 151, 161, 162,
190
Soviet (SS5s) in Cuba, 42, 62,
69, 109, 122, 205, 216
see also Thor, Jupiter missiles
international law, 51–2, 69–74,
206, 207
see also quarantine/blockade
International Longshoremen's
Association, 30
Iran, 52
Ireland, 91
IRONBARK, 218
Israel, 35
Italy, 57, 96, 110, 144, 151, 158,
160, 162, 165, 181, 190
see also Jupiter missiles
Ivanov, Captain, Yevgeny, 93,
102–12, 149, 158, 167, 168,
213
and disinformation, 108–10,
111–12

Japan, 215
Jodrell Bank, 65
Joint Intelligence Bureau (JIB),
40, 124, 197
Joint Intelligence Committee
(JIC), 40, 62–3, 106, 121,
123, 150, 177, 204–5, 228
Joint Chiefs of Staff, 27, 39,
64, 136, 141, 147–8, 160,
221
Jupiter missiles, 7, 47–8, 53, 61,
82–3, 85, 95, 139, 142, 144,
145, 151, 157–8, 181, 184,
190
operational state of, 160,
161–2, 163, 229

trade with Cuban missiles, 53,
82, 91, 96–7, 159, 160–5,
171–4, 181, 184, 232
see also Turkey, Italy

Katzenbach, Nicholas, 72
Kennedy, John F., 1, 4, 7, 21,
22, 23, 32, 33, 34, 60, 65,
78, 79, 86, 88–9, 101, 105,
106, 107, 110, 122, 125–30,
131, 133, 134, 137, 148,
161, 180, 199, 201, 218, 231
and Berlin, 30, 39, 44, 46, 48,
60, 62, 63, 95–6, 98–9,
132, 162
domestic pressure, 29–30, 31,
44, 51, 54, 55, 96
and Jupiter missiles, 47–8, 53,
95, 160, 162, 163, 172–5
and Khrushchev, 8, 33, 43–4,
46, 50, 92, 103, 132, 146,
155, 162, 172, 175
and Macmillan, 7, 8, 9, 11, 21,
35–6, 37–9, 45–57, 58–9,
68, 76, 78, 85, 90, 92, 94,
98, 99, 100, 101, 112,
117, 138, 139, 140, 146,
151–2, 153, 157–9, 162,
165–73, 177–8, 183–4,
187, 228, 233, 234
and nuclear disarmament, 48,
188
and Ormsby-Gore, 7, 41–8, 51,
58, 60, 69, 75, 94–5,
113–16, 151, 153, 162,
167, 168, 172, 183–4, 187,
188, 227, 228
and possible attack on Cuba,
2, 9, 31, 42–4, 47, 57, 88,
98, 99, 128, 132, 146,
153–7, 159, 160, 166–8,
169, 173, 176, 184, 201,
226
and quarantine/blockade, 4,
11, 37, 42–5, 54, 69–70,
71–2, 75–6, 97–9, 100,
113–16, 204
Kennedy, Robert, 47, 69, 89, 97,
103, 109, 119, 161, 162, 206

Kent, Sherman, 48, 49, 59, 82–3, 120, 136, 208–9
KGB (Soviet Committee of State Security), 1, 103, 121, 126, 130, 149, 154, 177
Khrushchev, Nikita, 1, 2, 4–5, 12, 23, 36, 43–4, 50, 52, 54, 57, 59, 60–1, 68, 76, 88–9, 97, 101, 103, 105–6, 107, 116, 121, 122–3, 126, 144, 146, 148, 159, 175, 177, 179
  and Berlin, 8, 23, 39, 46, 50–1, 59, 60–1, 63, 65–8, 180
  deployment of missiles in Cuba, 7, 32–3, 43–4, 61–9, 87, 110, 122–3, 124, 160
  and Jupiters in Turkey, 7, 8, 157–9, 160, 161, 163, 165, 172
  and Kennedy, 8, 33, 43–4, 46, 50, 92, 103, 132, 146, 155, 162, 172, 176
  and withdrawal of missiles, 144, 148, 155, 157–8, 160, 161, 163, 171–2, 175, 189
Kimovsk, 116, 216
Knox, William, 97, 110, 116
Kyle, Sir Wallace, 150–1

Laos, 35
Labour Party, 77, 78–9, 188
  and Bay of Pigs, 21–2, 79
  internal debate over nuclear weapons, 10–11, 22, 77, 87, 90–2, 187
  and missile crisis 4, 54, 78–93, 100, 165, 209
  National Executive Committee (NEC), 83–7, 100, 119, 209
  see also Gaitskell
Lambie, George, 35
Landon, General Truman, 139
Le May, General Curtis, 148
Lebow, Ned. R, 61, 129, 172
Liberal Party, 77
Lippman, Walter, 165
Lloyd, Selwyn, 17–18, 90

Loginov, V.A., 105–8, 110–11, 167, 180, 181, 215
Lundahl, Art, 117, 127, 129

Macmillan, Harold, 5, 29, 41, 54, 78, 80, 81, 86, 88, 93, 101, 116, 121, 133, 144, 147, 152, 174–5, 188, 191, 201, 229, 231
  and Berlin, 50–1, 52–3, 62, 132, 148, 157, 179
  and Conservative Party, 11, 35, 78–9, 81
  and economic sanctions against Cuba, 17–18, 20–1, 24, 25–6, 30, 35, 38, 182
  and Kennedy, 7, 8, 9, 11, 21, 35–6, 37–9, 45–57, 58–9, 68, 72, 76, 78, 80–1, 82, 85, 92, 93, 94, 98, 99, 100, 101, 112, 117, 138, 139, 146, 151–2, 153, 157–9, 162, 165–73, 177–8, 183–4, 187, 228, 233, 234
  and Khrushchev, 42–3, 50, 52, 169–171, 229
  and military preparations, 10, 57, 99, 133, 134, 137–8, 140, 142, 145, 146–7, 148, 152, 156, 186, 223
  and Ormsby Gore, 41–3, 46–8, 50–1, 54, 57, 95–7, 102, 117, 168, 183, 201, 203, 211
  and Parliament, 4, 72, 89–90, 100, 102, 104, 106, 107–8, 112, 142, 175
  and phone conversations with Kennedy, 5, 7, 51, 57, 58–9, 68, 85, 90–1, 94, 96, 98–9, 118, 140, 153, 157–9, 165, 166, 177–8, 183–4, 201, 203, 206, 217, 228
  and quarantine/blockade, 49–58, 72–6, 81
  and Soviet approaches, 91, 102, 104, 106–8, 112, 168, 175, 185, 229

Macmillan – *continued*
and summit/conference, 47–8,
50–1, 53, 57, 76, 91, 96–7,
100, 102, 106–8, 112, 158,
166–7, 168, 175, 183,
185–6
and test ban treaty, 92, 175,
188
and Thors, 158, 165, 169–71,
172–3, 184
and Turkish Jupiters, 53, 57,
161–2, 165, 171, 172, 184
view of crisis, 8–9, 10, 12, 52,
90, 137, 162, 180–1, 185,
188
Madelin, Ian, 145
Mafia, 14, 24
Maine, USS, 13
Marchant, Herbert (Bill), 12, 14,
15, 31, 34, 189
Marucla, 75
Martin, Kingsley, 3
Mason, R.H., 205
Maudling, Reginald, 3
May, Ernest, 183
Mayaguana Island, 27, 148
McCone, John, 41, 80, 128, 129
McNamara, Robert, 1, 5, 64,
113, 115–16, 119, 124–5,
127, 128, 134, 155, 161,
173, 232
Medium Range Ballistic Missiles
(MRBMs), 37, 42, 46, 62,
64, 69, 109, 111, 122,
127–9, 133, 139, 143, 157,
161, 190, 199, 215
SS-3, 62, 109, 127, 203, 220
SS-4, 33, 62, 109, 122, 127–8,
203, 220
military importance of, in Cuba,
43, 64–5, 101–2, 186
operational state of, 42, 46,
62, 70, 90, 98–9, 127–9,
133, 153–8, 167, 170, 174
Menaul, Air Vice-Marshal,
Stewart, 135, 139, 140, 142,
143, 145, 223
MI5 (British Security Service),
105, 121, 213

Middleton, Drew, 85
Midhurst Grammar School, 4, 191
MIG 17 aircraft, 216
'missile gap', 124–7, 220
see also nuclear weapons
Ministry of Defence (MOD), 145,
147, 157
Ministry of Defence Air
Historical Branch, 145
Monroe doctrine, 13–15, 29, 198
Moore, General, 137
Mossadeq, Mohammed, 26
Mountbatten, Lord Louis, 131,
164

Nasser, Gamal Abdul, 21, 26
National Intelligence Estimates
(NIEs), 28, 125–6
NIE 11-8-61, 125, 220
NIE 11-8/1-61, 126
National Photographic
Interpretation Centre
(NPIC), 117, 127
National Security Council (NSC),
37, 55, 69, 80, 119, 216
New Statesman, 3–4, 58, 81
New York Times, 28, 85
Nicholson, Sir Godfrey, 104,
106, 168, 213
Nicholson, Sir Harold, 198–9
Nicholas, H.G, 184
Nitze, Paul, 70, 110, 114, 155
Nixon, Richard, 16, 21
Norstad, General Lauris, 80,
136–40, 148, 164, 191, 223
North Atlantic Council (NAC),
26, 29, 48, 60, 65, 76,
136–8, 153, 162–4, 204
North Atlantic Treaty Organisation
(NATO), 4, 5, 7, 10, 79, 94,
96, 101, 104, 112, 123, 132,
147, 184, 187, 189, 230
and Cuba, 24–30, 35, 161–5
and missile crisis, 37, 38, 39,
48, 54, 58–60, 65, 109,
110, 134, 136–9, 142, 152,
169, 178, 181, 182, 183,
222
see also NAC

Norway, 29, 30, 111, 164
Novosti Press Agency, 103
nuclear weapons, 5–6, 10, 60,
  British, 6, 7, 9, 10, 11, 58, 77,
    92, 142, 149, 152, 187,
    193, 222, 223; *see also*
    Bomber Command, Thor,
    V-bombers
  cruise missiles, 189, 190, 216
  disarmament, 48, 51, 152, 154,
    162, 167, 168, 188
  risk of nuclear war, 8, 10, 12,
    36, 88, 89, 131, 137,
    145–6, 150, 156–7, 159,
    160, 177, 178, 185–9
  role in crisis, 7, 9, 12, 124–30,
    131, 149–52, 220
  Soviet threat to Europe, 8, 49,
    51–3, 90, 112, 132–3, 161,
    186
  SS-2 missile, 109
  strategic balance, 61, 64–5, 83,
    85, 124–7, 131; *see also*
    missile gap
  strategy, 38, 42, 60, 77–9, 128,
    131, 132, 133, 142, 149,
    152, 183, 186–7
  tactical, 33, 109, 122–3, 132,
    135, 137, 176, 190, 201
  warheads in Cuba, 42, 62, 70,
    109, 110, 119, 123, 129,
    144, 154, 155, 160, 163
  see also MRBMs, IRBMs,
    ICBMs, SLBMs, Bomber
    Command, SAC
Nunnerley, David, 8

Oldfield, Maurice, 121, 218
Operation Mongoose, 23–4
oil, refineries, 18
  British tankers, 17, 20–1,
    30–1, 74–5, 198
  see also POL
Organisation of American States
  (OAS), 24, 45, 69–70, 100, 206
Orient, Leyton, 2
Ormsby-Gore, Sir David, 12, 29,
  31, 33, 54, 60, 102, 120,
  130, 138, 157, 161

  and Kennedy, 7, 41–8, 51, 58,
    60, 69, 75, 94–5, 113–16,
    151, 153, 162, 167, 168,
    172, 183–4, 187, 188, 227,
    228
  and Macmillan, 41–3, 46–8,
    50–1, 54, 57, 76, 95–7,
    102, 117, 168, 170, 183,
    185, 201, 203, 211
  and publication of photographs,
    116–18, 120, 183
  and quarantine/blockade,
    113–16, 120, 183, 204,
    211
  role in crisis, 7, 9, 38, 40–8,
    56, 64, 69, 73, 75–6, 81,
    90, 94–7, 107, 130, 138,
    151, 153–8, 161–3, 170,
    180, 181, 182, 183, 188,
    200, 216, 217, 227, 228,
    234
  views on crisis, 8–9, 161, 171,
    179, 211–12, 227
Owen, David, 100, 180

Partial Test Ban Treaty, 179
  nuclear tests, 152, 175, 188
Pavlov, General, 103
Peace News, 88
Pentagon (Department of
  Defense), 1, 27, 28, 41, 115,
  118, 119, 123, 125
Penkovsky, Oleg, 12, 105, 113,
  120–30, 149, 177, 181,
  213–14, 217, 218, 220
Permissive Action Links (PALs),
  145
Pershing-2 missiles, 189
Petroleum, Oil, Lubricants
  (POL), 45, 72, 75–6, 90, 178
Phibriglex-62 exercise, 32
Pike, Sir Thomas, 146–7, 166
Pincher, Chapman, 122
Platt Amendment, 14
Plesetsk, 126
Poland, 107
Polaris, 2, 11, 38, 77, 134–5,
  141, 164, 181–2, 224
Popular Socialist Party (PSP), 16

Power, General Tommy, 142
Presidium, 1, 116, 159
Profumo, John, 102–4
Proteus USS, 135, 141
Punch, 3

quarantine/blockade, 4, 11, 37,
    39, 42–57, 58–61, 68, 69–76,
    85–6, 88, 89, 94, 97–101,
    106, 111, 113–16, 137, 148,
    153–4, 169, 176, 177–8, 183,
    190, 201, 204, 209, 216
  and British shipping, 69, 71,
    73–5, 79, 81, 86
  legality of, 44–5, 51–2, 69–76,
    81–2, 86, 102, 112, 185,
    206, 209
  line of, 113–15, 116
  see also Macmillan
Queen Elizabeth, 3, 191
Quick Reaction Alert (QRA),
    136, 139, 142, 144

R-11 missile, 123, 219
Rawlinson, Sir Peter, 70
Red Beard atomic bomb, 222
Redmayne, Martin, 104
Risse-Kappen, Thomas, 232
Roberts, Sir Frank, 67–8, 104–6,
    121, 126, 159, 165, 175,
    177, 180, 198–9, 233
Roosevelt, Archie, 82, 83, 218
Roosevelt, Franklin, 14, 72
Roosevelt, Theodore, 14
Royal Air Force (RAF), 2, 6, 113,
    135, 142, 144, 145, 146,
    149, 186, 222
  RAF Driffield, 144
  RAF Waddington, 136, 144
  see also Bomber Command, Thor
royal family, 3
Royal Navy, 28, 135, 141, 148
Rusk, Dean, 6, 24, 26–7, 37, 39,
    55, 61, 66, 69, 72, 87, 95,
    107, 128, 129, 138, 153–4,
    155–6, 160, 165–6, 173–4,
    180, 182, 184, 234
Russell, Bertrand, 1, 87–9, 97,
    105, 157, 210

Sagan, Scott, 132, 134, 139, 142,
    145
Salinger, Pierre, 117
San Cristobal, 33
Sandys, Duncan, 148
Scali, John, 154
Schecter, Jerrold, 120, 125, 128, 130
Schlesinger, Arthur, 22–3, 43,
    115, 161, 173
Schroeder, Gerhard, 95–6
Sea Fury fighter aircraft, 17, 194
Serov, General Ivan, 120
Shackleton aircraft, 148
Shell, 18, 197
Shuckburgh, Sir Evelyn, 56, 159,
    203
Secret Intelligence Service (SIS),
    12, 121–3, 126, 149, 177,
    181, 197, 217, 218
Skybolt missile, 11, 92, 150, 181
Slessor, Sir John, 23, 37, 39,
    134–5
Smith, General William, 147
Sokolov, Gennady, 103
Sorenson, Ted, 173
Soskice, Sir Frank, 86
Soviet–Cuban relations, 7, 16,
    19–20, 28, 31–2, 61, 63–4,
    122–3, 175–8
  see also Khrushchev, Cuban
    missile crisis
Soviet Long Range Air Force, 150
Spain, 135
Stalin, Josef, 5, 21
Stein, Janice, G, 61, 129, 172
Stephenson, Sir Hugh, 40–1,
    106, 150, 200
Stevenson, Adlai, 101, 119, 154,
    161, 165, 174, 229
Strategic Air Command (SAC),
    1–2, 38, 97, 127, 134–5,
    139–40, 141–3, 150, 151,
    176, 186
Streatham Hill SS, 28
Strong, Sir Kenneth, 40–1, 124
Submarine Launched Ballistic
    Missiles (SLBMs), 2, 134,
    141, 143
  see also Polaris

Suez, 11, 22–3, 38, 39, 57, 78–9
Suiaca SS, 75
Sunday Times, The, 34
Supreme Allied Commander
    Europe (SACEUR), 80, 136,
    150
Surface to Air Missiles (SAMs)
    33, 34, 82, 166
Sutherland, Iain, 123
Sweden, 30
Sweeney, General Walter, 201

tankers, *see* oil
TASS news agency, 33, 108
Texaco, 18
Taylor, General Maxwell, 147
Taylor, Richard 10, 88, 92
Thor missiles, 2, 6, 77, 111,
    133, 135, 139, 142, 144–5,
    150–1, 161, 172, 184, 190,
    222
  diplomacy and, 151, 157–9,
    165, 167, 168–71, 232
  dual key, 6, 139, 144–5, 160,
    190
  operational state of, 133, 142,
    144–5, 150–1, 160, 225
Thorne, D.R., 186
Thorneycroft, Peter, 1, 5, 8, 131,
    151, 231
Times, The, 3
Titmus, Fred, 2
Trades Union Congress (TUC),
    84–5, 88
Trend, Sir Burke, 40, 124
Trollope ploy, 171, 173, 185
Tuchman, Barbara, 133, 137, 152
Turkey, 7, 47, 48, 50, 52, 53,
    57, 59, 61, 82–3, 84–5, 91,
    95, 110, 111, 132, 144, 151,
    157–65, 170–4, 181, 184,
    190, 230, 232
  see also Jupiter missiles

U Thant, 88, 96, 101, 106,
    153–4, 155, 158–9, 163, 165,
    167, 168, 170, 173
U-2 aircraft, 33, 37, 42, 124,
    127, 140, 159, 199, 219

United Nations, 43, 50, 53, 61,
    63, 83–6, 89, 91, 96, 155,
    170, 209, 212
  Charter, 71–2, 100, 106–7, 207
  Security Council, 51, 69, 70,
    72, 81, 86, 100–2, 109,
    119, 161, 189, 209
  verification, 153–4, 157–8,
    167–8, 169, 173–6
  see also U Thant
United States Air Force (USAF),
    6, 27, 33, 37, 125–6, 135,
    140, 144, 148, 149, 152,
    190
United States Navy, 75, 140

V-bombers, 135, 139, 142,
    149–50, 152, 175, 222
  Valiants, 142
  Vulcans, 143
Vallat, Sir Francis, 70, 74
Varentsov, Marshal Sergei, 120,
    125
Vienna Summit, 23

Washington Post, 164
Ward, Stephen, 103, 104, 106–7,
    109, 110, 213
West Germany, 29, 30, 48, 59,
    66, 70, 86, 95–6, 139, 153,
    166, 181, 184
  see also Adenauer
Wheeler, General Earle, 148
White, Mark, 174
Woodcock, George, 85
Wigg, George, 104
Wilson, Harold, 81–3, 100, 104,
    213
Wright, Peter, 121, 122, 219
Wynne, Greville, 121

Yellow Sun, thermo nuclear
    bomb, 222

Zelikow, Philip, 183–4
Zilliacus, Konni, 86
Zorin, Valerian, 101, 109–10,
    215
Zuckerman, Sir Solly 145